Lecture Notes in Computer Science 8828

Commenced Publication in 1973
Founding and Former Series Editors:
Gerhard Goos, Juris Hartmanis, and Jan van Leeuwen

More information about this series at http://www.springer.com/series/7407

Walfredo Cirne · Narayan Desai (Eds.)

Job Scheduling Strategies for Parallel Processing

18th International Workshop, JSSPP 2014
Phoenix, AZ, USA, May 23, 2014
Revised Selected Papers

 Springer

Editors
Walfredo Cirne
Google
Mountain View, CA
USA

Narayan Desai
Ericsson
San Jose, CA
USA

ISSN 0302-9743 ISSN 1611-3349 (electronic)
Lecture Notes in Computer Science
ISBN 978-3-319-15788-7 ISBN 978-3-319-15789-4 (eBook)
DOI 10.1007/978-3-319-15789-4

Library of Congress Control Number: 2015931917

LNCS Sublibrary: SL1 – Theoretical Computer Science and General Issues

Springer Cham Heidelberg New York Dordrecht London

Printed on acid-free paper

Springer International Publishing AG Switzerland is part of Springer Science+Business Media
(www.springer.com)

Preface

This volume contains the papers presented at the 18th Workshop on Job Scheduling Strategies for Parallel Processing (JSSPP 2014), which was held in Phoenix, USA, on May 23, 2014 in conjunction with the IEEE International Parallel Processing Symposium 2014 (IPDPS 2014).

The proceedings of the previous workshops are also available from Springer-Verlag as LNCS volumes 949, 1162, 1291, 1459, 1659, 1911, 2221, 2537, 2862, 3277, 3834, 4376, 4942, 5798, 6253, 7698, and 8429. These volumes are available as printed books and online.

This year, we had 24 papers submitted to the workshop, of which we accepted nine. All submitted papers went through a complete review process, with the full version being read and evaluated by an average of four reviewers. We would like to especially thank the Program Committee members and the additional referees for their willingness to participate in this effort and their detailed, constructive reviews.

As a primary venue of the parallel scheduling community, the Job Scheduling Strategies for Parallel Processors workshop offers a good vantage point to witness its evolution. During these two decades, we have seen parallel scheduling grow in scope and importance, following the popularization of parallel systems. Fundamental issues in the area remain relevant today (e.g., scheduling goal and evaluation, workload modeling, and performance prediction). Meanwhile, a new set of issues have emerged, due to new workloads, increased scale, and the differing priorities of cloud systems. Together, the traditional and new issues make for a lively and discussion-rich workshop, where academic researchers and participants from industry meet and exchange ideas and experiences.

The workshop began with a keynote talk by Liana Fong, from IBM. She discussed how cognitive computing places new challenges for parallel job scheduling. These computations must not merely achieve performance levels that were unthinkable a decade ago, but do so in a very flexible manner, interactively steering the computation to support human cognitive processes.

At the paper presentations, the blend of old and new challenges in parallel job scheduling set the tone of the discussions. Even the most classical scenario of single node parallelism remained a very active area. This trend is no surprise, both as the number of cores sharing the same memory increases and special purpose parallel processors like GPUs have become prevalent.

We had three papers tackling single-core parallelism. Seo et al. introduced Bubble Task, which scheduled memory access among tasks running in a multi-core machine by throttling the tasks. Looking beyond memory contention, Herz and Pinkau addressed the problem of scheduling of task graphs on shared memory machine, with special focus on task graphs generated automatically. Finally, for the second time in the workshop history, we visited the intersection of parallel job scheduling and real-time systems. Qamhieh and Midonnet investigated the effects of parallelism in real-time systems, showing that some reservations of the real-time community regarding parallelism were not fully justified.

Moving to distributed-memory, larger scale systems, scheduling fairness was a particularly hot topic this year. Klusáček and Rudová presented a new approach that supported multiresource aware user prioritization mechanism to ensure fairness. Importantly, this approach is capable of dealing with the heterogeneity of both jobs and resources. Rodrigo et al. investigated which basic prioritization primitives would make it easier to achieve fair scheduling in large, decentralized distributed. Tóth and Klusáček had a new take on the basic question of how to evaluate different scheduling algorithms. They proposed a user-centric approach that tries to measure the deviation of job end time from what the user would expect. The expectation of the user is based on fairness, which in itself generated a very interesting discussion on whether this model favors schedulers that strive for fairness.

The last three works presented this year touched different areas of parallel job scheduling. Kumar and Vadhiyar revisited the traditional question for batch systems of wait time prediction. They pushed the state of the art in prediction accuracy by using more sophisticated statistical models. They also evaluated how much meta-schedulers can improve performance by using such predictions.

Kuzmanovska et al. addressed how to schedule parallel jobs when these jobs are written using frameworks to deal with parallelism (e.g., MapReduce, Dryad, Pregel). They proposed a two-level approach in which each framework asks for the resources needed, and then distributes them to the jobs written in the framework.

Schwiegelshohn explored his long-time experience to distill lessons for scheduler algorithm designers. Starting with the provocative observation that most research papers in the area have had negligible impact on the state-of-practice, he identified constraints, objectives, and evaluation as the key reasons for this mismatch, and prescribed solutions based on his observations. The paper concluded by applying its own advice on designing a scheduling solution for an Infrastructure as a Service provider.

Enjoy the reading!

We hope you can join us in the next JSSPP workshop, in Hyderabad, India, in May 2015.

November 2014   Walfredo Cirne
                                                                Narayan Desai

Organization

Program Committee

Henri Casanova	University of Hawaii at Manoa, USA
Julita Corbalan	Technical University of Catalonia, Spain
Dick Epema	Delft University of Technology, The Netherlands
Gilles Fedak	Inria, France
Dror Feitelson	The Hebrew University, Israel
Liana Fong	IBM T.J. Watson Research Center, USA
Eitan Frachtenberg	Facebook, USA
Ali Ghodsi	University of California, Berkeley, USA
Alfredo Goldman	University of São Paulo, Brazil
Allan Gottlieb	New York University, USA
Alexandru Iosup	Delft University of Technology, The Netherlands
Morris Jette	SchedMD LLC, USA
Rajkumar Kettimuthu	Argonne National Laboratory, USA
Dalibor Klusáček	Masaryk University, Czech Republic
Zhiling Lan	Illinois Institute of Technology, USA
Bill Nitzberg	Altair Engineering, USA
Larry Rudolph	MIT, USA
Uwe Schwiegelshohn	Technical University of Dortmund, Germany
Mark Squillante	IBM T.J. Watson Research Center, USA
Murray Stokely	Google, USA
Wei Tang	Argonne National Laboratory, USA
Dan Tsafrir	Technion – Israel Institute of Technology, Israel
Ramin Yahyapour	GWDG – University of Göttingen, Germany

Contents

Bubble Task: A Dynamic Execution Throttling Method for Multi-core Resource Management

Dongyou Seo[1], Myungsun Kim[2], Hyeonsang Eom[1]([✉]), and Heon Y. Yeom[1]

[1] School of Computer Science and Engineering,
Seoul National University, Seoul, Korea
{dyseo,hseom,yeom}@dcslab.snu.ac.kr
[2] DMC R&D Samsung Electronics, Suwon, Korea
kmsjames.kim@samsung.com

Abstract. Memory bandwidth is a major resource which is shared among all CPU cores. The development speed of memory bandwidth cannot catch up with the increasing number of CPU cores. Thus, the contention for occupying more memory bandwidth among concurrently executing tasks occurs. In this paper, we have presented Bubble Task method which mitigates memory contention via throttling technique. We made a memory contention modeling for dynamically deciding throttling ratio and implemented both software and hardware versions to present trade-off between fine-grained adjustment and stable fairness. Bubble Task can lead to performance improvement in STREAM benchmark suite which is one of the most memory hungry benchmark by 21 % and fairness in memory bandwidth sharing among SPEC CPU 2006 applications which have different memory access patterns.

Keywords: Multicore processor · SMP platform · CPU execution throttling · Resource contention · Bandwidth fairness

1 Introduction

The number of CPU cores on a chip has been increasing rapidly. Intel plans to have an architecture that can scale up to 1,000 cores on a single processor [1]. However, the improvement speed of memory bandwidth, an important shared resource, cannot keep up with the increasing number of cores. For example, 8 cores on Xeon E5-2690 in 2012 share 51.2 GB/sec memory bandwidth, where 12 cores on Xeon E5-2695v2 introduced in 2013 share 59.7 GB/sec memory bandwidth [2]. Although the number of CPU cores increased by 50 %, the memory bandwidth only increases by about 16 %. Considering this trend, Patterson anticipated that off-chip memory bandwidth will often be the constraining resource in system performance [3].

In this environment, numerous tasks can be concurrently executed on increasing number of cores. The tasks share memory subsystems such as Last Level Cache (LLC) and memory bandwidth while the sharing can lead to memory contention which makes system performance unpredictable and degraded [4–7].

© Springer International Publishing Switzerland 2015
W. Cirne and N. Desai (Eds.): JSSPP 2014, LNCS 8828, pp. 1–16, 2015.
DOI: 10.1007/978-3-319-15789-4_1

Several methods have been presented for mitigating the contention. Among these methods, task classification is the most well known example. This method decides which tasks share same LLC and memory bandwidth and avoids the worst cases by minimizing performance interference [4, 6, 8, 9]. However, task classification cannot mitigate the contention when most of running tasks are memory intensive tasks on a physical node as Ahn et al. [10] pointed out. In this paper, we present Bubble Task which can dynamically recognize and mitigate unavoidable memory contention via throttling approach. It can reduce concurrent memory access and thus improve resource efficiency. Also, memory bandwidth can be more fairly distributed by our throttling policy.

The primary contributions of this paper are the following:

- We presented a simple model, memory contention model, to show the level of contention. Bubble Task Scheduler can efficiently decide per-core throttling ratio with respect to current contention level.
- We evaluated Bubble Task by using STREAM and lmbench benchmark suites which are the most well known of memory stressors. Bubble Task can lead to performance improvement in both stress tests.
- We implemented both software and hardware versions Bubble Task. We compared the versions in terms of trade-off between fine-grained adjustment and stable fairness.

The focus of our method lies on long-running, compute-bound and independent tasks. Also, we assume that the tasks hardly perform I/O operations and never communicate with one another while a task is the sole owner of a CPU core. The rest of the paper is organized as follows: Sect. 2 discusses the related work. Section 3 presents our contention model and describes our Bubble Task Scheduler. Section 4 shows the experimental results. Section 5 concludes this paper.

2   Related Work

Various solutions have been developed to mitigate the contention for shared resources via scheduling. Jiang et al. [8] presented the methodology regarded as a perfect scheduling policy. Their method constructs a graph where tasks are depicted as nodes connected by edges, the weights of which are the sums of the levels in performance degradation due to their resource contention between the two tasks. The methodology analyzes which tasks should share the same resource to minimize performance degradation caused by resource contention. However, it is feasible only for offline evaluation in contrast to ours. The overhead in graph construction is $O(n^2)$ (n is the number of tasks). It is not a practical method if the number of tasks is considerably large. Xie et al. [9] introduced the animalistic classification, where each application can belong to one of the four different classes (turtle, sheep, rabbit and devil). Basically, it is hard to classify each application which has various usage patterns for sharing resources with only four classes. Moreover, some applications may belong to multiple classes such as both devil and rabbit classes. Also, the application is sensitive to the usage patterns of co-located tasks by polluting cache lines seriously. Thus, Xie's methodology may lack accuracy.

Zhuravlev et al. [4] proposed pain classification and Distributed Intensity (DI) which remedies the shortcomings of above mentioned methodologies in terms of practicality and accuracy. In their method, task has two scores, sensitivity and intensity. In their method, task has two scores, sensitivity and intensity. The higher locality the task has, the higher sensitivity score does the task get. The locality of shared cache is measured by using the stack distance profile [11] and miss rate heuristic. Intensity is defined by the number of LLC references per one million instructions. Their method avoids co-locating the high sensitive task with the high intensive task. Also, they presented a detailed analysis to identify which shared resource in a CPU platform is an major factor causing performance degradation.

The methodology proposed by Kim et al. [6] is similar to Zhuravlev's classification. But, their classification and scheduling algorithm are much simpler to classify many tasks and stronger to deal with them. However, this classification methods cannot make effect in cases where there are so many memory intensive tasks. Bubble Task can throttle specific cores and can lead to the mitigation of memory subsystems.

Ahn et al. [10] presented a migration method among physical nodes in virtualized environments to deal with the unavoidable cases and their method also avoids remote accesses on Non-Uniform Memory Access architecture via VM live migration. However, Bubble Tasks is an intra-node method which does not consider virtualization and migration method among physical nodes.

Throttling method was presented by Zhang et al. [12] to control the execution speed or resource usage efficiency before us. They proposed hardware execution throttling method using Intel's duty-cycle modulation mechanism [13]. Their hardware approach can lead to more stable fairness due to its fine-grained execution speed regulation than previous software approach presented by Fedorova et al. [14]. However, they did not present dynamic throttling policy. Bubble Task method adapts per-core throttling by using our memory contention model which can dynamically decide how much a CPU core should be throttled. We refered to their approach and implemented both software and hardware versions of Bubble Task.

3   Bubble Task

Bubble Task dynamically recognizes memory contention and decides the degree of per-core throttling ratio with respect to current contention level. In this section, we will introduce a new memory contention model and also show the correlation between our model and the performance to demonstrate the usefulness of the model. Lastly, we present our dynamic Bubble Task policy.

3.1   Memory Contention Modeling

The contention for memory subsystems degrades performance. Figure 1(a) presents the runtime results with respect to the number of concurrently executing STREAM applications on 8cores Xeon E5-2690. STREAM benchmark is the most of the memory hungry application and the memory access patterns is invariable from start to end as seen in Fig. 1(b). This means that the memory subsystems can be steadily stressed during the execution time of STREAM application and the stress degree can be adjusted with respect to the number of running STREAM applications concurrently accessing memory subsystems.

The more the number of STREAMs, the more exponentially the performance of STREAM applications degrades due to the high memory contention. In this section, we will propose a new memory contention model which efficiently indicates the degree of the contention for memory subsystems and evaluate the correlation between our contention model and performance.

Figure 2 shows the average memory bandwidth and memory request buffer full rate with respect to the number of STREAM applications [16] on 8cores Xeon E5-2690. The memory bandwidth is the amount of retired memory traffic multiplied by 64 bytes (size of a cacheline) [18], and Intel provides off-core response events which can permit measuring retired memory traffics [19]. Retired memory traffic is the number of LLC miss events and prefetcher requests, and the traffic eventually flows into integrated memory controller. There is no single dominant component contributing to the contention for memory subsystems and several components play an important role [5]. Retired memory traffic is thus a good metric to monitor the overall utilization of memory subsystems including LLC, prefetcher and memory controller.

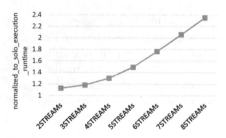 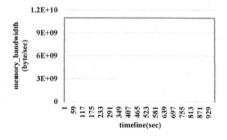

(a) **The runtime results with respect to the number of co-executing applications**

(b) **Memory bandwidth of solo execution**

Fig. 1. Runtime comparision and memory bandwidth of STREAM benchmark

Memory bandwidth does not increase linearly even though the number of STREAM applications increases. The bandwidth is saturated at a constant level, which is near the maximum memory bandwidth of E5-2690 (about 50 GB/sec).

In contrast to the saturated memory bandwidth, memory request buffer full rate increases exponentially as the number of STREAM applications grows. A memory request buffer full event indicates a wasted cycle due to the failure in enqueuing a memory request when the memory request buffer is full. To measure it, we monitored SQ_FULL event [19]. As the number of STREAM applications increases, more memory requests are simultaneously generated while the number of failures increases because the capacity of memory request buffer is limited. The memory bandwidth and memory request buffer full rate shown in Fig. 2 are symmetric with respect to the $y = a \times x$ line. The more gentle the inclination of memory bandwidth curve gets, the more exponential does the inclination of memory request buffer full rate become.

We constructed our memory contention model based on the correlation between memory bandwidth and memory request buffer full rate as seen in Fig. 2. Equation (1) shows our model. Memory contention level is the number of retries to make a memory request retire. High memory contention level indicates a lot of retries because many tasks compete in enqueuing their memory requests into the buffer and hence the memory request buffer is often full. Also, many retries imply the high contention for overall memory subsystems because the retired memory traffic is closely connected to LLC, prefetcher and integrated memory controller.

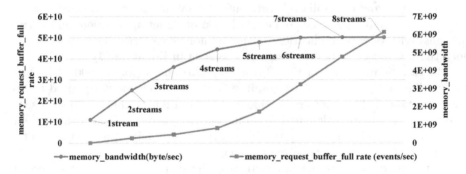

Fig. 2. The correlation between memory request buffer full rate and memory bandwidth with respect to the number of STREAM applications on 8core Xeon E5-2690

To evaluate the correlation between our memory contention model and performance, we did the stress tests for memory subsystems similar to [15] on 2 different CPU platforms. The specifications of our CPU platforms are organized in Table 1. We designated a STREAM application as a stressor because a stream application has high memory intensity and the memory intensity of a STREAM application is invariable from start to end. We used SPEC CPU applications. The memory bandwidth for each target application is different (see the value in the x-axis of the point labeled solo in Figs. 3 and 4). We do the stress tests on both an i7-2600 (with four cores) and a Xeon E5-2690 (with eight cores). To stress

Table 1. The specifications of our SMP CPU platforms

Descriptions	Xeon E5-2690	i7-2600
# of cores	8	4
Clock speed	2.9 GHz (Turbo boost: 3.8 GHz)	3.4 GHz (Turbo boost: 3.8 GHz)
LLC capacity	20 MB	8 MB
Max memory bandwidth	51.2 GB/sec	21 GB/sec
CPU category	Server level CPU	Desktop level CPU
Microacrcitecture	Sandy-bridge	Sandy-bridge

memory subsystems during the entire execution time of each target application, the stressors continued to run until the target application terminated.

Memory contention level is a system-wide metric. It indicates the level of overall contention in the CPU platform. We need to precisely figure out the correlation between the level and performance of target application because the sensitivity of each application to the contention for memory subsystems is different. We thus use the sensitivity model presented in [6]. This sensitivity model is a very simple model, but the model is effective and powerful. Equation (2) shows the sensitivity model. The sensitivity model considers the reuse ratio of LLC (LLC_{hit} $ratio$) and the stall cycle ratio affected by the usage of memory subsystems. We calculated the predicted degradation of target application multiplying the sensitivity of each application by the memory contention level increased by both the target application and stressors as seen in Equation (3).

The results are shown in Figs. 3 (for E5-2690) and 4 (for i7-2600). The blue vertical line (left y-axis) of each graph indicates the runtime normalized to the sole execution of the target application and the red line (right y-axis) shows the predicted degradation calculated by Equation (3). X-axis indicates the system-wide memory bandwidth. The predicted degradation is fairly proportional to the measured degradation (normalized runtime).

As the predicted degradation increases, the measured degradation accordingly increases on all CPU platforms. The memory bandwidth of Xeon E5-2690 increases as the number of stressors grows. The highest memory bandwidth reaches the maximum memory bandwidth (about 50 GB/sec) when the number of stressors is 5 or 6. In contrast, the highest memory bandwidth of i7-2600 reaches the maximum memory bandwidth (about 21 GB/s) when the number of stressors is 1 or 2. In the cases of executing lbm, soplex and GemsFDTD, the memory bandwidth decreases when each target application is executed with 3 stressors. The memory contention levels of the applications with 3 stressors are much higher than that of the non-memory intensive application which is tonto (lbm:11.6; soplex:10.88; GemsFDTD:9.55; tonto:7.68).

The results imply that the system-wide memory bandwidth can be decreased by too many retries in enqueuing memory requests into the buffer. The results demonstrate that memory contention level effectively indicates the contention degree closely correlated with the performance of target application.

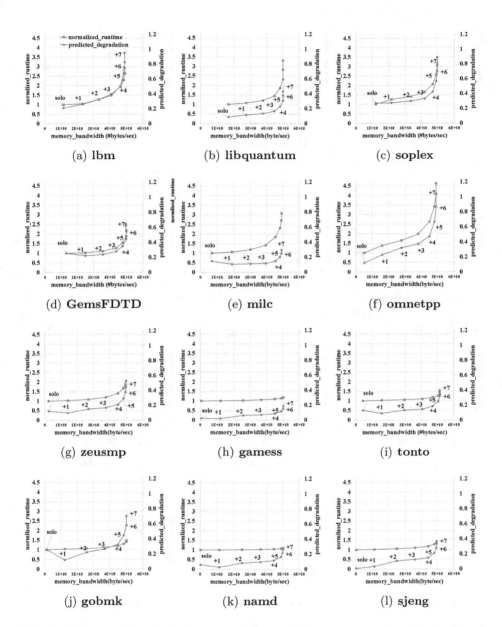

Fig. 3. The correlation between memory bandwidth, memory contention level and performance. Figures (a)–(l) show the results for Xeon E5-2690

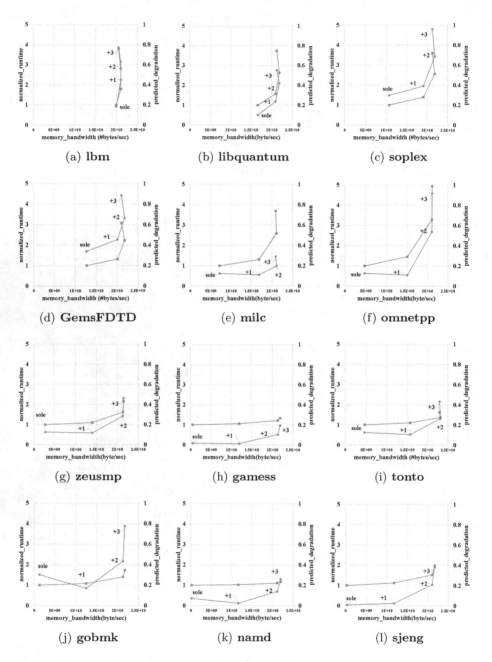

Fig. 4. The correlation between memory bandwidth, memory contention level and performance. Figures (a)–(l) show the results for i7-2600

$$Memory\ Contention\ Level_{current}$$
$$= \frac{Memory\ Request\ Buffer\ full\ rate}{Retired\ memory\ traffic\ rate} \tag{1}$$

$$Sensitivity = (1 - \frac{LLC_{miss}}{LLC_{reference}}) \times \frac{Cycle_{stall}}{Cycle_{retired}} \tag{2}$$

$$Predicted\ Degradation_{target\_application}$$
$$= Memory\ Contention\ Level_{system\_wide} \tag{3}$$
$$\times\ Sensitivity_{target\_application}$$

3.2 Dynamic Bubble Task Policy

In Bubble Task policy, current throttling load is determined with respect to current contention level and the load is distributed between CPU cores in proportional to the per-core intensity ratio during the interval (1 s). Dynamic Bubble Task policy is organized in Algorithm 1 and Bubble Task architecture is described in Fig. 5.

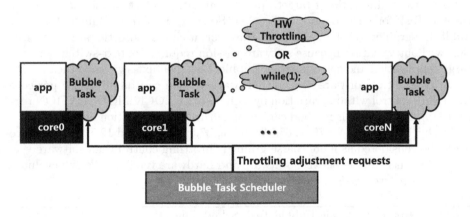

Fig. 5. Bubble Task architecture

Current contention load is dynamically calculated with respect to current contention level (Line 3 and 4). We adapted 21 and 200 for E5-2690 CPU in maximum contention level and maximum throttling load, respectively. Average intensity is the average traffic among CPU cores during the interval (Line 5) and the CPU cores generating more memory traffics than average intensity are selected as antogonists which should be throttled in next step. Current throttling load is distributed between the cores in proportional to per-core memory traffic ratio (From Line 6 to Line 15).

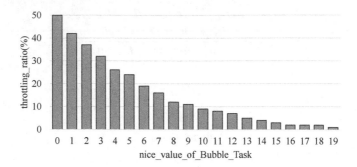

Fig. 6. Per core throttling ratio with respect to nice value of software version Bubble Task

We implemented both software and hardware versions of Bubble Task. In software version, Bubble Task Scheduler forks artificial Bubble Tasks which execute infinite while loop and dynamically adjusts the nice value of Bubble Task to throttle target application on the same core. Bubble Task Scheduler sends new nice value with respect to per-core throttling ratio to corresponding Bubble Task and it adapts the nice value by using set priority system call. Figure 6 presents throttling ratio of target application with respect to the nice value of Bubble Task for CPU-bound application. Software version of Bubble Task can fulfill fine-grained throttling control. However, it cannot throttle target application without variation because software version requires context-switch between target application and corresponding Bubble Task (context-switch overhead) [12].

In contrast to software version, hardware version can fulfill precise per-core throttling control without variation by using IA32_CLOCK_MODULATION register [19]. However, this method can throttle the CPU utilization of target application by 12.5 % (87.5 %, 75 %, 63.5 %, 50 %, 37.5 %, 25 % and 12.5 %) and hence it can be considered as more coarse-grained throttling control than software version. There is trade-off between software and hardware versions. We will evaluate and compare two versions in Sect. 4.2.

Algorithm 1. Dynamic Bubble Task Scheduling

---

1. **Dynamic_Bubble_Task_Scheduling() begin**
2. current_contention_level = get_contention_level()
3. current_throttling_ratio = current_contention_level / max_contention_level
4. current_throttling_load =
   $current\_throttling\_ratio \times max\_throttling\_load$
5. avg_intensity = get_avg_intensity()
6. **for each** c in all CPU cores **do**
7.   **if** $avg\_intensity \leq c.mem\_traffic$ **then**
8.   intensity_sum += c.mem_traffic
9.   throttling_list.insert(c)
10.   **end if**
11. **end for**
12. **for each** c in throttling_list **do**
13.   per_core_throttling_ratio = c.mem_traffic / intensity_sum
14.   c.throttle($per\_core\_throttling\_ratio \times current\_throttling\_load$)
15. **end for**

---

4   Evaluation

First, we did stress tests by executing STREAM [16] and lmbench [17] applications on 8cores Xeon E5-2690. Identical eight stressors, STREAM or lmbench, are pinned on each core and Bubble Task Scheduler dynamically throttle the CPU utilization of the stressors during the runtime. We monitored five performance metrics, retired_memory_traffic rate, LLC_miss rate, LLC_reference rate, memory_request _buffer_full rate and runtime and next compared Bubble Task method with naive Linux scheduler. We also executed four pairs of SPEC CPU 2006 applications, 2lbms, 2libquantums, 2GemsFDTDs and 2soplexs and compared the bandwidth fairness between software version, naive and hardware version.

4.1   Stress Test

We executed STREAM and lmbench sets which are known as the best of memory stressor to identify how Bubble Task method can mitigate the contention for memory subsystem and hence improve system performance. We used software version Bubble Task method in this section because software version can fulfill fine-grained throttling control. The major difference between software and hardware versions will be handled in Sect. 4.2. We monitored 5 performance metrics on E5-2690 and the results are presented in Fig. 7. We normalized the results of Bubble Task method to naive.

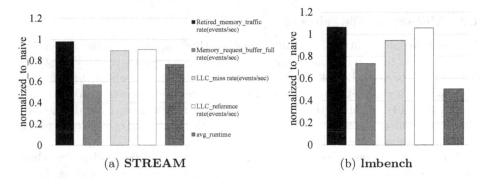

(a) **STREAM**   (b) **lmbench**

Fig. 7. Performance metric results of STREAM and lmbench applications

In case of STREAM, LLC reference rate and LLC miss rate decrease by about 10 % (memory bandwidth also decreases by about 1 %). In particular, memory request buffer full rate decreases by 43 %. Memory request buffer full is a metric which can indicate the contention level for memory controller. The mitigation for memory controller leads to performance improvement (about 21 %) in STREAM case because the contention for memory controller is more fatal in performance than other resources [4,5].

However, the reduction ratio of memory request buffer full rate is higher in STREAM than lmbench but, performance improves more in lmbench case (about 50 %). To establish the cause, we compared the absolute results between STREAM and lmbench cases in Fig. 8, not normalized results. Fundamentally, average memory contention level presented in Equation 1 is higher in lmbench and absolute mitigation degree of memory contention is higher in lmbench although relative mitigation degree is lower in lmbench. Also, LLC miss ratio is higher in lmbench and absolute reduction ratio of LLC miss is more noticeable. As a result, we conclude that Bubble Task can take effect more in high memory contention case.

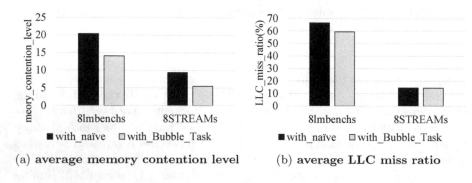

(a) **average memory contention level**   (b) **average LLC miss ratio**

Fig. 8. Performance analysis between lmbench and STREAM

4.2   Memory Traffic Fairness

Although we can identify that Bubble Task method can mitigate the contention through stress tests, it can also improve the fairness of memory traffic among executing tasks because Bubble Task Scheduler uses the policy which throttles the tasks generating more memory traffics than average traffic as seen in Algorithm 1 (Line 13 and 14). In this section, we evaluated how Bubble Task method can guarantee the fairness of memory traffic among executing tasks and compared between software and hardware versions.

To evaluate fairness, we executed 4 pairs of SPEC CPU 2006 applications which have different memory access patterns with software version, naive and hardware version and pinned an application on a core to prevent the contention for CPU usage. We monitored per-task memory traffic from start to 1000 s. Fairness results are presented in Fig. 9.

With hardware version, standard deviation of memory traffic between executing tasks is lower than naive by about 17 % as seen in Fig. 9(b) and (c). The victim tasks, soplex_0 and soplex_1, can occupy more memory traffic because Bubble Tasks Scheduler throttles other tasks unfairly occupying memory traffic. Memory traffic can be distributed more fairly between executing tasks with hardware version.

However, memory traffic of executing tasks is very changeable with software version as seen in Fig. 9(a) although victim tasks can occupy more memory traffic.

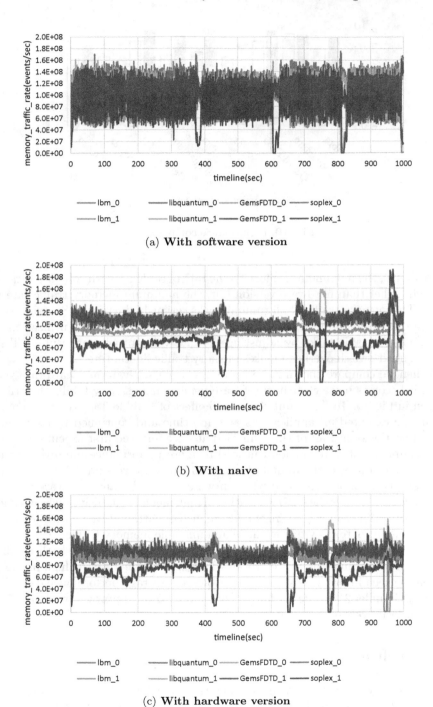

(a) **With software version**

(b) **With naive**

(c) **With hardware version**

Fig. 9. Bandwidth fairness

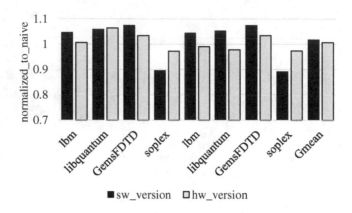

Fig. 10. Performance comparision

For example, the maximum memory traffic rate of soplex_1 with software version is much higher than hardware version but, the minimum memory traffic rate is lower. The memory traffic of all running tasks seriously fluctuates. Software version can fulfill fine-grained throttling and precisely decrease CPU utilization of high memory traffic tasks by adjusting the nice value of per-core Bubble Task while context-switch overhead makes memory traffic fluctuating.

When we compare the runtime results between software and hardware versions, it becomes more clear how software version aggressively fulfills throttling as seen in Fig. 10. To figure out the overall effect of Bubble Task to every application, we executed all applications at same time and continued to re-execute the applications until all of them finished at once and the first execution times were sampled. Software version can lead to more performance improvement in soplex_0 and soplex_1, the most victims, than hardware version. However, other applications are more degraded with software version because software version aggressively decreases the CPU utilization of high memory intensive tasks via fine-grained throttling control. Average performance is a little bit worse with software version due to context switch overhead and unstable memory traffic.

The improvement in system performance did not happen with both Bubble Task versions because the SPEC workload set cannot generate the high memory contention seen in previous stress tests. However, average performance degradation ratio is under 2 % while the fairness of memory traffic improves by about 17 % with hardware version.

5   Conclusion

In this paper, we presented memory contention model and dynamic Bubble Task policy. Bubble Task method dynamically decides current throttling load with respect to current contention level and calculates per-core throttling load in proportional to the memory intensity ratio among CPU cores during the interval.

We implemented and evaluated both software and hardware versions of Bubble Task. Software version forks Bubble Tasks executing infinite while loop and co-locate them with the tasks unfairly occupying memory bandwidth. Bubble Task shares timeslice of the target task via context-switch mechanism. In contrast, hardware version uses IA32_CLOCK_MODULATION, Intel's model specific register, and can throttle target task without context switch overhead.

The two versions have pros and cons each other. Software version provides fine-grained throttling through the nice value control of Bubble Task and can throttle the CPU utilization of target application more precisely while it cannot guarantee stable fairness of memory traffic due to context switch overhead and unstable memory traffic. In contrast, hardware version can guarantee stable bandwidth fairness through low-overhead hardware throttling control although hardware version provides coarse-grained throttling control.

Through stress test, we can conclude that the more serious the contention for memory subsystems, the more Bubble Task method can take effect as seen in Figs. 7 and 8. Future multi-core CPU will be developed with the increasing number of CPU cores but, memory bandwidth cannot catch up with the CPU development speed. Thus, the contention for memory subsystems will occur more and more and then Bubble Task method will contribute to mitigate the contention.

Acknowledgment. This work was supported by Basic Science Research Program through the National Research Foundation of Korea (NRF) funded by the Ministry of Education (NRF-2013R1A1A2064629), Next-Generation Information Computing Development Program through the National Research Foundation of Korea (NRF) funded by the Ministry of Science, ICT &Future Planning (No. 2010-0020731), and Educational-Industrial Cooperation Project sponsored by Samsung Electronics DMC R&D Center.

References

1. http://www.neoseeker.com/news/15313-1000-core-processor-possible-says-intel/
2. http://ark.intel.com/products/
3. Patterson, D.: Latency lags bandwidth. In: Communication of the ACM (2004)
4. Zhuravlev, S., Blagodurov, S., Fedorova, A.: Addressing shared resource contention in multicore processors via Scheduling. In: ASPLOS (2010)
5. Zhuravlev, S., Saez, J.C., Blagodurov, S., Fedorova, A.: Survey of scheduling techniques for addressing shared resources in multicore processors. In: ACM Computing Surveys, September 2011
6. Kim, S., Eom, H., Yeom, H.Y.: Virtual machine consilidation based on interference modeling. J. Supercomput. **64**, 28–37 (2013)
7. Merkel, A., Stoess, H., Bellosa, F.: Resource-conscious scheduling for energy efficiency on multicore processors. In: EuroSys (2010)
8. Jiang, Y., Shen, X., Chen, J., Tripathi, R.: Analysis and approximation of optimal co-scheduling on chip multiprocessors. In: PACT (2008)
9. Xie, Y., Loh, G.: Dynamic classification of program memory behaviors in CMPs. In: Proceedings of CMP-MSI, held in conjunction with ISCA (2008)
10. Ahn, J., Kim, C., Han, J.: Dynamic virtual machine scheduling in clouds for architectural shared resources. In: HotCloud (2012)

11. Chandra, D., Guo, F., Kim, S., Solihin, Y.: Predicting interthread cache contention on a chip multi-processor architecture. In: HPCA (2005)
12. Zhang, X., Dwarkadas, S., Shen, K.: Hardware execution throttling for multi-core resource management. In: ATC (2009)
13. Naveh, A., Rotem, E., Mendelson, A., Gochman, S., Chabukswar, R., Krishnan, K., Kumar, A.: Power and thermal management in the Intel Core Duo processor. Intel Technol. J. **10**(2), 109–122 (2006)
14. Fedorova, A., Seltzer, M., Smith, M.: Improving performance isolation on chip multiprocessors via an operating system scheduler. In: 16th International Conference on Parallel Architecture and Compilation Techniques, pp. 25–36. Brasov, Romania, September 2007
15. Mars, J., Tang, L., Hundt, R., Skdron, K., Soffa, M.L.: Bubble-up: increasing utilization in modern warehouse scale computers via sensible co-locations. In: MICRO (2011)
16. http://www.cs.virginia.edu/stream/
17. http://www.bitmover.com/lmbench/
18. http://software.intel.com/en-us/articles/detecting-memory-bandwidth-saturation-in-threaded-applications
19. Intel(R) 64 and IA-32 Arhcitectures Software Develper's Manual, Volume 3B. System Programming Guide, Part 2
20. http://www.spec.org/cpu2006/

Real-World Clustering for Task Graphs
on Shared Memory Systems

Alexander Herz[✉] and Chris Pinkau

Lehrstuhl Für Informatik II/XIV, Technische Universität München,
Boltzmannstraße 3, 85748 Garching b. München, Germany
{herz,pinkau}@in.tum.de

Abstract. Due to the increasing desire for safe and (semi-)automated parallelization of software, the scheduling of automatically generated task graphs becomes increasingly important. Previous *static* scheduling algorithms assume negligible run-time overhead of spawning and joining tasks. We show that this overhead is significant for small- to medium-sized tasks which can often be found in automatically generated task graphs and in existing parallel applications.

By comparing real-world execution times of a schedule to the predicted static schedule lengths we show that the static schedule lengths are uncorrelated to the measured execution times and underestimate the execution times of task graphs by factors up to a thousand if the task graph contains small tasks. The static schedules are realistic only in the limiting case when all tasks are vastly larger than the scheduling overhead. Thus, for non-large tasks the real-world speedup achieved with these algorithms may be arbitrarily bad, maybe using many cores to realize a speedup even smaller than one, irrespective of any theoretical guarantees given for these algorithms. This is especially harmful on battery driven devices that would shut down unused cores.

We derive a model to predict parallel task execution times on symmetric schedulers, i.e. where the run-time scheduling overhead is homogeneous. The soundness of the model is verified by comparing static and real-world overhead of different run-time schedulers. Finally, we present the first clustering algorithm which guarantees a real-world speedup by clustering all parallel tasks in the task graph that cannot be efficiently executed in parallel. Our algorithm considers both, the specific target hardware and scheduler implementation and is cubic in the size of the task graph.

Our results are confirmed by applying our algorithm to a large set of randomly generated benchmark task graphs.

Keywords: Static scheduling · Run-time overhead · Execution time prediction

Introduction

The diminishing clock speed gains realized in new processor designs and fabrication processes have produced a rise of multi- and many-core CPUs for servers,

© Springer International Publishing Switzerland 2015
W. Cirne and N. Desai (Eds.): JSSPP 2014, LNCS 8828, pp. 17–35, 2015.
DOI: 10.1007/978-3-319-15789-4_2

desktops and even embedded devices. This development increases the pressure to produce parallel software and schedules for this software which are efficient in terms of overall execution time and power consumption, especially for battery driven devices. Due to the NP-completeness of many instances of the scheduling problem, a set of heuristics trying to approximate the best solution have been proposed. Kwok [14] and McCreary [13] have compared the quality of a range of well-known heuristics in terms of the static schedule length predicted by the different scheduling heuristics for a versatile set of input task graphs. For some heuristics (e.g. linear clustering [8]) it has been proven that the produced schedule length (the makespan as predicted by the heuristic) is no longer than the fully sequential schedule. For large-grain task graphs it has been shown that the schedule lengths from greedy algorithms are within a factor of two of the optimal schedule [11].

To the best of our knowledge, no comparison of static schedule lengths to the real-world execution time of the schedule has been undertaken. If the real execution time of a schedule on a specific target platform does not at least roughly correlate to the static schedule length, then any guarantees or schedule length advantages of one heuristic compared to another are purely theoretical as the static schedule does not model reality.

Developments in the research community show that automatic parallelization is an important part of the future of computer science. Implicitly parallel compilers automatically extract task graphs from user programs. Typically, the extracted task sizes are small [9] because all computations are considered for parallel execution. Therefore, the proper scheduling of small-grain task graphs is fundamental for automatic parallelization.

In contrast to a Gantt-chart's implication that tasks are started at a predefined time, most parallel systems (e.g. [12,21]) implement a dynamic signaling mechanism to spawn and join tasks as soon as all preconditions are satisfied. This removes the burden of providing hard real-time guarantees for the soft- and hardware which may produce unnecessary long schedules as worst case estimates must be used everywhere.

Our measurements show that on some platforms the overhead is in the order of $2 \cdot 10^4$ [clocks] so that it can be ignored only in the limiting case when all tasks are in the order of 10^6 [clocks] and larger. The maximum possible task size for a game or numerical simulation running at 60 frames per second on 2 GHz CPUs is in the order of 10^7 [clocks] and typically much smaller for non-trivially parallelizable problems. This shows that the overhead is relevant for typical parallel applications. For task graphs that contain tasks with sizes in the order of the overhead, traditional scheduling algorithms may produce schedules with arbitrarily bad speedup (e.g. a speedup smaller than one on more than one core compared to the fully sequential schedule) as they ignore the run-time overhead (cost of spawning and joining tasks). This includes algorithms that in theory guarantee a schedule length shorter than the fully sequential schedule. The insufficient speedup produced by these algorithms is especially harmful on battery driven devices that could shut down cores that are used inefficiently.

Furthermore, the neglected overhead may shift data ready times used to perform scheduling in most algorithms asymmetrically, so that tasks which appear to run in parallel for the algorithm will not run in parallel in reality.

Our main contributions to solve these problems are:

- We derive a generic model to predict run-time scheduler overhead for symmetric schedulers, i.e. the scheduling overhead is homogeneous.
- We show that our model accurately predicts scheduling overhead for stealing [4] and non-stealing schedulers on different hardware.
- We define a task granularity for communication-free task graphs related to the parallel task execution times on a specific platform.
- We present the first clustering algorithm that guarantees a minimum real-world speedup per core for communication-free task graphs.

The rest of the paper is structured as follows. In Sect. 1 we show that the measured execution times of a simple task graph have a non-linear relationship to the static schedule length from traditional scheduling algorithms that ignore the scheduling overhead. Afterwards, in Sect. 2, we derive a statistical model to predict scheduling overhead for symmetric schedulers where the run-time scheduling overhead is homogeneous. This is followed by Sect. 3, where we show that our overhead model accurately predicts the scheduling overhead on several platforms and scheduler implementations. The model is used in Sect. 4, to construct a clustering algorithm which guarantees a user defined minimum speedup per core in $O(n^3)$. Section 5 presents benchmarks showing how our algorithm improves the average speedup of a large set of randomly generated task graphs with small and large task sizes. Finally, we discuss related work and our results in Sect. 6, as well as possible future work in Sect. 7.

1 Example

We will examine the task graph in Fig. 1.

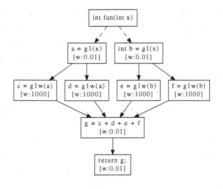

Fig. 1. Example task graph containing small tasks.

Scheduling the program depicted in Fig. 1 on multi-core hardware appears trivial. Given a machine with more than four cores, perfect scheduling [6] can be applied to produce the best possible schedule, according to the scheduler's model of program execution, in $O(n + m)$. This may produce the Gantt-chart shown in Fig. 2.

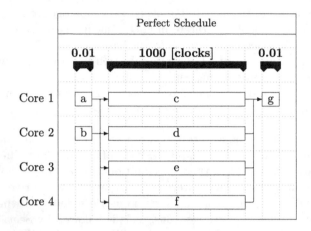

Fig. 2. Gantt-chart for task graph in Fig. 1 produced using perfect scheduling [6]. Arrows show dependencies but do not require any time according to the scheduling algorithm. The predicted sequential execution time of 4000 clocks compared to the predicted parallel execution time of 1000 clocks suggests a speedup of about 4. Actually executing the task graph yields a measured execution time of ca. 4000 clocks on a 4 Core Nehalem for the fully sequential program and a measured ececution time of 6000 clocks for the fully parallel program. In contrast to the prediction shown in the Gantt-chart, sequential execution is about 1.5 times faster than parallel execution, not 4 times slower.

Although the Gantt-chart implies that tasks may start execution at a specified time this is rarely implemented. In order to start tasks based on the times from the chart, hard real-time constraints need to be placed on the executing hard- and software and sound worst case execution times for all tasks must be calculated. In addition, the executed schedule might be less than optimal as some tasks may be able to execute before the worst case finish time of their predecessors because the predecessors finished earlier than the conservative estimate.

Most scheduler implementations (e.g. [12,21]) signal waiting tasks as soon as all their preconditions have been fulfilled so that they can start executing as soon as possible. Usually, spawning tasks without preconditions also requires to signal to another thread.

The Gantt-chart in Fig. 2 suggests a parallel execution time of about $0.01 + 1000 + 0.01 = 1000.01$ clocks, so a speedup of about 4 compared to the sequential execution of ca. $2 \cdot 0.01 + 4 \cdot 1000 + 0.01 = 4000.03$ clocks is predicted. Actually running the program in its fully parallel version using TBB's [12] stealing scheduler takes about 6000 clocks per task graph execution on a 4 Core Nehalem.

In contrast, executing the sequential version of the program on the same hardware yields an execution time of ca. 4000 clocks which is about 1.5 times faster than the parallel version.

Apparently, the existing scheduling algorithms do not model the real-world scheduling process, but an artificial scheduler that has no run-time overhead and always yields linear speedup. This leads to unrealistically small execution time predictions from these scheduling algorithms. The existing literature does not define a grain size for task graphs without communication costs (and an unrealistic one for small tasks with small communication costs). In Sect. 2 we define such a grain size in direct connection to the parallel execution time of a task on a specific platform.

In Sects. 3 and 5, it will be shown that the scheduling overhead is not negligible on real-world systems even for bigger task sizes up to 10^5 clocks and more (depending on the specific hardware and scheduler implementation). This emphasizes that the effect is relevant for normal task graphs that do not contain minuscule tasks.

2 Model

In this section, a model for the prediction of task execution times that accounts for the scheduling overhead is derived, improving the execution time prediction accuracy by up to 1000 % (compared to previous scheduling algorithms which neglect the scheduling overhead for smaller tasks).

Since the actual execution times on real hardware fluctuate heavily depending on the overall system state, a stochastic model is developed. Adve and Vernon [1] have found that random fluctuations have little impact on the parallel execution time, so that the expectation values we derive should be a good model of the real execution time. First, we derive the model for a stealing scheduler as implemented in Thread Building Blocks 4.1 (TBB [12]). Then we generalize the model to schedulers with symmetric scheduling overhead, i.e. the overhead is homogeneous.

2.1 Two Node Fork/Join Graphs

In the following, the execution of fork/join task graphs with two tasks are modeled. After deriving a model for two tasks, we will extend the model for more tasks.

The work weight associated with each task represents the average execution time of the task on the target platform including all costs (i.e. resource contention, cache effects, etc.) except for the dynamic scheduling costs. Without loss of generality, we assume that the task calculating a (from Fig. 3 with $n = 2$) is executed locally after the second task calculating b has been spawned at time t_0. For stealing schedulers, spawning means that the task is enqueued in a list on the thread where the task is spawned. If no other idle core steals the task from this list for parallel execution, the task will eventually be executed

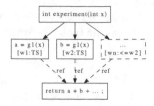

Fig. 3. Generic fork/join task graph with n nodes. Here $g1$ performs a trivial loop that takes TS clocks and does not interfere with the other tasks. The tasks are spawned by the root node and the last task is notified as soon as all predecessor tasks have finished.

locally on the thread that originally spawned the task. The spawned task can be stolen (and hence be executed in parallel) from the time it was spawned up until the first task finished execution at $t_0 + TS$ (where $TS = \max\{w_1, w_2, .., w_n\}$ is the maximum size of all tasks because the largest task determines the overall execution time) and starts to execute the spawned task itself. For convenience, we set $t_0 = 0$.

First, the time to spawn a task on another core is calculated.

Since the stealing process is independent from the spawn (other idle cores check regularly if there is something to steal), the normalized probability that a steal attempt is made at time t is

$$p_{\text{attempt}} = \frac{\sigma}{TS}, \tag{1}$$

where $0 < \sigma < 1$ determines the steal attempt frequency which depends on the actual scheduler and hardware. The frequency is smaller than one because less than one attempt per clock can be made on real systems. A steal attempt need not succeed, e.g. if there is nothing to steal. The probability that the available task was not stolen until time t is given by the inverse of the probability that it was stolen:

$$p_{\text{not-stolen}}(t) = 1 - \int_0^t p_{\text{attempt}}\, dt = 1 - \frac{\sigma}{TS} \cdot t. \tag{2}$$

So the probability that a steal attempt is successful at time t is given by the probability that it was not yet stolen times the steal attempt probability (when within the time frame where the task can be stolen at all):

$$p_{\text{stolen}}(t) = \begin{cases} p_{\text{not-stolen}}(t) \cdot p_{\text{attempt}} & 0 \le t \le TS \\ 0 & \text{else.} \end{cases} \tag{3}$$

Finally, the expected time T_{steal} for the second task being stolen is

$$T_{\text{steal}} = \int_0^{TS} p_{\text{stolen}}(t) \cdot t\, dt = \frac{(3\sigma - 2\sigma^2)}{6} \cdot TS =: \beta \cdot TS. \tag{4}$$

The overall parallel execution time (PET) of the potentially stolen task is given by

$$pet(TS) = \beta \cdot TS + \alpha' + TS. \tag{5}$$

Here, α' is the expectation value of the fixed overhead required to execute the steal (which is initiated at time T_{steal}) and the join to wait for both tasks. After all overhead is accounted for, the time TS needed to execute the task must be added. Like σ, α' depends on the hard- and software and must be obtained by running an experiment on the specific target platform.

The speedup achieved when running all tasks in parallel is obtained via

$$su(w_1, ..., w_n) = \frac{\sum_i^n w_i}{pet(\max\{w_i\})}, \tag{6}$$

where $\sum_i^n w_i$ is the sequential execution time (SET).

For non-stealing schedulers (e.g. MPI [21] based code), the derivation is essentially identical. The tasks are signaled rather than stolen. The signaling is implemented via MPI_send and MPI_receive or MPI_barrier so that only negligible data sizes are communicated, transmission of larger amounts of data is not modeled as the article's scope is limited to cost-free communication. Hence, p_{attempt} becomes the probability that the signal starting the second task arrives at time t. In addition, the second task can be signaled long after the first finished executing when a non-stealing scheduler is used. Assuming there exists a maximum time $T_{\max} > TS$, after which the second task is guaranteed to have been signaled, we substitute $T_{\max}$ for all TS in Eqs. 1 to 4 to obtain the expectation time that the signal arrives $T_{\text{signal}} = \beta \cdot T_{\max}$. Rewriting this with $T_{\max} = TS + \delta T$ we get

$$T_{\text{signal}} = \beta \cdot TS + \beta \cdot \delta T. \tag{7}$$

As $\beta \cdot \delta T$ is a hardware dependent constant we can subsume it into $\alpha = \alpha' + \beta \cdot \delta T$ and add it to the final parallel execution time prediction by substituting α' by α in Eq. 5:

$$pet_{\text{general}}(TS) = \beta \cdot TS + \alpha + TS. \tag{8}$$

The form of the final expression to evaluate the parallel execution time pet_{general} of the tasks is independent of the underlying scheduler.

The break even point (BEP) on a specific target platform is defined as the task size BEP that gives a speedup of 1:

$$su(BEP, BEP) = 1. \tag{9}$$

Finally, granularity for communication-free task graphs is defined as follows. A task is said to be small-grain if its associated work is smaller than the BEP. Conversely, it is considered large-grain if its work exceeds the BEP. A task graph is said to be small-grain if it contains any small-grain tasks.

2.2 Many Node Fork/Join Graphs

Fork/Join graphs with more than two spawned nodes as shown in Fig. 3 are handled as follows. The base overhead γ of parallel execution (as determined by the measured execution time of two empty tasks) is subtracted from the predicted two node execution time pet_{general} and divided by the sequential execution time to get the speedup of both tasks compared to the sequential execution. The square root of the combined speedup gives the speedup per task.

$$su_{\text{task}}(TS) = \sqrt{\frac{pet_{\text{general}}(TS) - \gamma}{TS}} \qquad (10)$$

The final execution time for a fork/join graph with n tasks is given in Eq. 11 by applying the speedup per task for every task and adding the base overhead:

$$pet^n(TS) = su_{\text{task}}(TS)^n \cdot TS + \gamma \qquad (11)$$

The algorithm presented in Sect. 4 will decompose more complex task graphs into simple fork/join task graphs compatible to Eq. 11 to predict their speedup. In order to apply this model, the target (scheduler and hardware) specific constants α and β as well as the base overhead γ must be measured.

In the next section, the quality of the model for two task predictions for several different target platforms is evaluated. In Sect. 5, the model for many tasks is applied on a large range of randomly generated task graphs showing that Eq. 11 can accurately predict parallel execution times.

3   Verification of the Two Task Model

In order to verify that the model derived in Eq. 5 is sound, the execution time of fork/join task graphs as shown in Fig. 3 executed on several different hardware platforms with different scheduler implementations are measured and compared to the model predictions.

Figure 4 shows that the execution times of tasks of different lengths depend only on the longest task (assuming there are enough hardware resources to execute all tasks in parallel).

Figure 5 shows that the model predictions are in very good agreement with the real behavior of the analyzed hardware and schedulers.

As to be expected, TBB's stealing-based scheduler performs better than the MPI based scheduler for smaller tasks. The BEP is about half the size for the stealing scheduler (2242 vs. 4636 clocks) on the Nehalem[1] platform. The difference is more pronounced on the mobile Sandy[2] platform (6812 vs. 22918 clocks). For the experiments, all MPI processes were placed on the same node, so that no actual network communication was executed.

The final values for α and β for each target platform (hardware and scheduler combination) are obtained by fitting the model from Eq. 6 to the measurements.

TBB's stealing scheduler and MPI's non-stealing task execution differ completely from a conceptual and implementation point of view. As shown in this section, they are both well represented by the model.

---

[1] Intel(R) Core(TM) i7 CPU 860 @ 2.80GHz SMP x86_64 GNU/Linux 3.5.0-37-generic.

[2] Intel(R) Core(TM) i7-3667U CPU @ 2.00GHz SMP x86_64 GNU/Linux 3.5.0-17-generic.

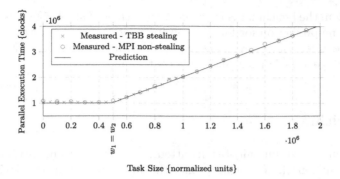

Fig. 4. Comparison of the execution times of two parallel tasks of different size to the prediction that the overall run-time is dominated by the longer task. The first task's size is increased from 0 to $2 \cdot 10^6$ while the size of the second task is fixed to $0.5 \cdot 10^6$ (and vice versa). Error bars have been omitted for readability, all measured data points lie within one standard deviation from the model prediction.

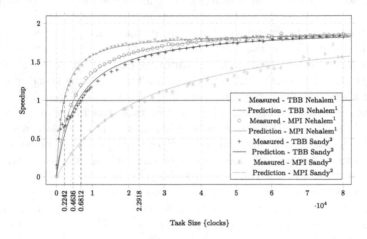

Fig. 5. Comparison of the speedup of two parallel tasks with the predicted speedup from Eq. 6. Here, α and β are determined by fitting the model to the measured data. β is related to the signal probability per time and α quantifies the delay after the second thread has received the signal until it can start processing the second task. The experiment measures the average time it takes the scheduler to spawn, execute and join two completely independent tasks with equal task size. Error bars have been omitted for readability, all measured data points lie within one standard deviation from the model prediction and are in the order of 10 % of the measured value. TBB denotes Thread Building Blocks 4.1 and MPI denotes open MPI 1.4.5. Speedstep was disabled on all systems during measurement to avoid large fluctuations due to the processors power management. The minimum task size required to realize 98 % of the possible speedup for the these platforms reaches from 10^5 to 10^6 [clocks]. For larger tasks, the overhead may be neglected.

In addition, the benchmarks from Sect. 5 will show that Eq. 11 gives a realistic execution time prediction for fork/join graphs with more than two tasks.

In the next section, a preconditioning algorithm is presented that uses the model to merge tasks in a task graph that cannot be efficiently executed in parallel.

4 Algorithm

Some previous scheduling algorithms attempt to give guarantees that the produced schedule length is no longer than the fully sequentialized version of the task graph [8] or that the schedule length is within a factor of two from the optimal schedule for task graphs where the computation to communication ratio is high [11]. As will be shown in Sect. 5, scheduling small-grain (w.r.t. task size) task graphs with scheduling algorithms that ignore scheduling overhead (even with perfect scheduling) can lead to surprisingly bad results where the real execution time of the task graph is orders of magnitude worse than the sequential execution.

This shows that the guarantee of the traditional scheduling algorithms is of theoretical nature. The actual execution times and speedups predicted by the traditional algorithms hold only in the limiting case when all tasks sizes are much larger than the BEP. Still, our algorithm improves the speedup even for such large tasks on average by 16 % as shown in Sect. 5. Figure 5 shows that close to linear speedup can be expected only for task sizes in the order of tens to hundreds of thousands of clocks or more. This means that the data ready times used to schedule tasks in many traditional algorithms [8] will be underestimated for many tasks and may shift tasks that appear to be parallel by different time offsets so that they will not run in parallel in practice.

In this section we present our clustering and execution time prediction algorithm which preconditions the task graph by collapsing parallel tasks that do not yield a minimum real-world speedup of ρ per core. The algorithm guarantees that the real-world execution time of the preconditioned task graph (on sufficiently many cores and if it actually contains any parallelism) is strictly smaller than the sequential execution time.

In principle, the algorithm decomposes input task graphs into instances of our modeled fork/join task graph from Fig. 3, applies our model via Eq. 11 and composes the results. This is achieved by the following steps. Due to the Hasse property enforced on the graph, all predecessors of join nodes are parallel nodes. For parallel nodes, the algorithm finds the lowest common ancestor and the highest common descendant, which form a fork/join graph. The model is applied to these fork/join graphs to predict the speedup and merges parallel nodes if the speedup is insufficient. After merging the nodes, the Hasse property is restored. This last step is intuitively done in $O(n^4)$, but we present a more elaborate approach to get an upper bound of $O(n^3)$.

In the following, the algorithm is presented in several parts. The first part, as seen in Algorithm 1, is the preprocessing part. Here we build several data structures to make sure that the overall upper bound of $O(n^3)$ is met. In the second part, see Algorithm 2, the real work is done by calculating the estimated processing times of all tasks and merging appropriate tasks together.

The preprocessing shown in Algorithm 1 computes for all predecessor pairs of join nodes the lowest common ancestor (LCA) with the minimal speedup, as well as the shortest paths from the LCA to the respective pair nodes in the unmerged graph. Later on, the corresponding paths inside the merged graph will be constructed from the paths from the LCA. Transitive edges are removed from the input graph by applying the Hasse reduction, as the algorithm assumes that tasks preceding a join node may execute in parallel which is not true for transitive edges. In addition, all linear task chains are removed from the graph. Both operations reduce the signaling overhead of the graph, as every edge in the graph can be interpreted as a signaling operation for the run-time scheduler.

Algorithm 1. preprocessing

Require: graph G
  $H \leftarrow$ HasseReduction(G)
  $H' \leftarrow H$
  calculate APSP
  preprocessing for common ancestors
  create hashmap um from unmerged to merged nodes $um : \{\text{nodes}\} \rightarrow \mathcal{P}(\{\text{nodes}\})$
  initialize um: node $\mapsto \{\text{node}\}$
  create hashmap pp^A from pairs of nodes to (lca, path1, path2) $pp^A : (\text{node}, \text{node}) \rightarrow$
  $(LCA, \text{path}, \text{path})$
  initialize pp^A:
  for all join nodes j' **do**
    for all predecessor pairs (i', k') of j' **do**
      get the LCA with minimal speedup: $lca' \leftarrow$ getLCA(i', k')
      $p_{i'} \leftarrow$ shortestPath(lca', i')
      $p_{k'} \leftarrow$ shortestPath(lca', k')
      $pp^A \leftarrow pp^A + \{(i', k') \mapsto (lca', p_{i'}, p_{k'})\}$
    end for
  end for

Next, the outer loop of the actual algorithm is shown in Algorithm 2. The nodes are visited in a topological order and data ready times are computed from the predecessors unless the current node is a join node which needs the special treatment shown in the **merge** procedure in Algorithm 5.

In the following, the merge operation $ik \leftarrow i \cup k$ means that a new node ik is created in the merged graph $\hat{H}$ that inherits all edges from i and k before these nodes are deleted from the graph.

mergeLinear is used in order to remove the overhead generated by the communication between consecutive tasks.

mergeParallel is used to merge the parallel predecessors of join nodes. If the indegree of the merged node is greater than one then the **merge** procedure is recursively applied to the merged node as it may be a newly created join node.

Algorithm 2. outer loop

while traverse nodes j in topological order **do**
    mergeLinear (predecessor of j, j)
    if node j is a join node **then**
        merge j
        mergeLinear (predecessor of j, j)
    end if
    store estimated starting time est and estimated finishing time drt for current node
end while

Algorithm 3. mergeLinear

Require: task sets i, k to be merged and k has exactly 1 predecessor
  $ik \leftarrow i \cup k$
  for all tasks t in ik **do**
    $um \leftarrow um + \{t \mapsto ik\}$
  end for
  remove Hasse violating edges
  update nsp distances and paths and drt

Algorithm 4. mergeParallel

Require: task sets i and k to be merged
  $ik \leftarrow i \cup k$
  for all tasks t in ik **do**
    $um \leftarrow um + \{t \mapsto ik\}$
  end for
  remove Hasse violating edges
  update nsp distances and paths and drt transitively
  if indegree $ik > 1$ **then**
    merge ik
  end if

The general **merge** procedure applied to the join nodes is shown in Algorithm 5.

Here, variables with hat, like $\hat{H}$, denote information from the merged graph in its current state, whereas variables with prime, like i', denote unmerged information. Variables without hat or prime refer to information from the unmerged graph available from preprocessing. The information from the unmerged graph is translated into the domain of the merged graph using the um mapping.

In order to obtain realistic task execution times, the available parallel work (fork/join tasks preceding the join node) must be calculated. The algorithm performs this by considering the paths from the lowest common ancestor [3] for each pair of nodes preceding a join node. These paths may be considerably larger than the pair nodes alone. So, for each predecessor of a join node, the longest path from common ancestor to the predecessor node along with the path's start time is stored in the *tasklist*. The *tasklist* is passed to the multifit algorithm from Coffman, Garey and Johnson [5] to find a schedule for the parallel tasks preceding the current join node. The multifit algorithm uses a k-step binary

---

Algorithm 5. merge

Require: join node j
  create list *tasklist*
  $drt_{min} = Infinity$
  for all predecessors i of j in $\hat{H}$ **do**
    for all predecessors $k \neq i$ of j in $\hat{H}$ **do**
      unmerged nodes inside merged nodes
      for all $i' \in i, k' \in k$ **and** $um(i') \neq um(k')$ **and** $pp^A(i', k')$ exists **do**
        get the LCA and the corresponding paths from the unmerged graph H' :
        $(lca', p_{i'}, p_{k'}) \leftarrow pp^A(i', k')$
        get the corresponding merged nodes and paths : $(est_i^p, est_k^p, \hat{p}_i, \hat{p}_k) \leftarrow$
        $um(lca', p_{i'}, p_{k'})$
        $\hat{lca} \leftarrow$ update$(lca', est_i^p, est_k^p, \hat{p}_i, \hat{p}_k)$: $\hat{lca}$ is last common node in $\hat{p}_i, \hat{p}_k$ and all
        arguments of update are modified accordingly
        if $work(\hat{p}_i) > maxwork_i$ **then**
          get path's run time (includes delays from nodes the path depends on) :
          $maxwork_i \leftarrow work(\hat{p}_i)$
          $est_i \leftarrow est_i^p$
        end if
        calculate drt_{min} for common ancestors :
        $drt_{min} \leftarrow \min\{drt_{min}, drt_{\hat{lca}}\}$
      end for
    end for
    $tasklist \leftarrow tasklist + (i, maxwork_i, est_i)$
  end for
  start with maximal parallelism : cores = size of *tasklist*
  $C \leftarrow$ **multifit**$(tasklist, \text{cores})$
  while cores > 1 **and**
    $(\sum_i maxwork_i)/(\text{cores} > 1 \,?\, pet^{cores}(C) : C) <$
    $\max(1, \rho \cdot \text{cores})$ **do**
  decrement cores
  $C \leftarrow$ **multifit**$(tasklist, \text{cores})$
  end while
  put the unmerged tasks into bins according to **multifit**
  update hashmap with all pairs of nodes that are in different bins
  for all bins b **do**
    mergeParallel (tasks in b)
  end for
  recalc drt_{min} for merged predecessors
  handle overhead : $est \leftarrow drt_{min} + \text{cores} > 1 \,?\, pet^{cores}(C) : C$
  finish time of join node : $drt = est + work(j)$

---

search to find a schedule for n independent tasks in $k \cdot O(n \cdot log(n))$ with w.c. error bound $1.22 \cdot opt + \frac{1}{2^k}$. Experimental results for multifit indicate that the average error is in the order of 1.01 for $k = 7$, so slightly above optimal execution times are expected. If better heuristics than multifit are found to solve this specific scheduling problem then these can be plugged in instead. The schedule length returned by multifit must be corrected using the model from Eq. 11 if more than one core is used to obtain realistic data ready times.

Multifit is modified to not merge pairs of nodes where it has been already established that merging them is not effective. This information is stored in a hashmap.

The final while loop searches for the biggest number of cores which yields a speedup of at least ρ per core rather than minimizing the (parallel) execution time of the tasks in question. This avoids that a large number of cores is utilized to achieve small speedups (e.g. 100 cores for speedup 1.01). Obviously, the algorithm could be modified here to minimize the execution times. This might be desirable if the given task graph describes the complete program. Often, hierarchical task graphs are used [10] to represent complex programs so that one individual subgraph describes only part of a larger program that may run in parallel to the subgraph under consideration. In this situation or when energy efficiency is considered, optimizing for speedup per core yields better results as cores are used only if a minimum speedup can be achieved.

Eventually, all tasks scheduled to the same core by multifit are merged using **mergeParallel** while maintaining that the graph is a Hasse diagram.

Both merge operations update the mapping um from unmerged to merged nodes and the DRTs of the merged node (and all nodes reachable from it) by adding the work from all nodes that were merged to the previous DRT. Moreover, both operations update the distances of the nearly shortest paths (NSP), as well as the paths themselves, which represent approximations of the shortest paths inside the merged graph after merging the nodes. They do so by iterating over all ancestors of the merged node, calculating their distances to it, and checking whether there is now a shorter path to a descendant of the merged node over a path that traverses the merged node. In order to retain the Hasse property, transitive edges are removed inside **mergeParallel**. Therefore, the NSPs are correct paths, but might not be the actual shortest paths in general.

As a side effect, the algorithm calculates an execution time prediction for the complete task graph in $O(n^3)$. If only this prediction is desired the last while loop of **merge** in Algorithm 5 and everything beyond that can be omitted.

Our algorithm correctly predicts that the task graph from Fig. 1 will be executed about 1.5 times faster on the specific target platform if all nodes are collapsed into a sequential program compared to the fully parallel program. Of course, the quality of the prediction is highly dependent on the quality of the (target specific) task size estimates. So far, the preconditioning algorithm assumes infinitely many cores. If the maximum parallelism in the result graph does not exceed the available cores of the target hardware then the result graph can be executed without further modifications. This may often be the case, as the preconditioning algorithm removes all inefficient parallelism and the number of available cores in modern hardware increases. If the graph contains too much parallelism after preconditioning, any traditional algorithm may be used to produce a schedule. If this algorithm uses data ready times then it must be modified to incorporate the realistic execution time prediction from Eq. 5 in order to produce realistic schedules.

Running a scheduling overhead corrected version of a traditional scheduling algorithm without the preconditioning algorithm is not sufficient to avoid bad schedules as these algorithms are not aware of the overhead and would treat it like useful computation.

As an alternative, when dealing with finitely many cores, the preconditioning algorithm may be turned into a complete scheduling algorithm. The algorithm is executed k times in order to find the ρ-speedup value which produces a task graph with as many or less tasks as the hardware supports. ρ is obtained by performing a k-step binary search with $\rho \in [0 \leq \rho_{min} .. 1]$. This increases the execution time of the algorithm to $k \cdot O(n^3)$ and finds the optimal ρ value with an error of $\frac{1-\rho_{min}}{2^k}$.

5   Experimental Results

We have generated 1000 random task graphs of varying complexity and a wide range of task sizes using the TGFF library from Dick, Rhodes and Wolf [7] to evaluate the preconditioning algorithm. All task graphs are preconditioned and their execution times averaged 250000 times on the Intel(R) Core(TM) i7 CPU 860 @ 2.80GHz SMP x86_64 GNU/Linux 3.5.0-37-generic (hyper-threading and speedstep disabled) system. Eight task graphs were removed from the data set because they contained more than 4 parallel tasks after preconditioning and a precise measurement of their execution times was not possible on the 4 core system. The results are presented in Fig. 6.

The relative uncorrected error depicted in Fig. 6(a) shows how much the measured run time of a given task graph deviated from the prediction generated using perfect scheduling (which neglects scheduling overhead). This error is relatively large with an average of $16\% \pm 14\%$ for average task sizes bigger 5000 clocks (logarithmic scale). For smaller tasks the execution times are mispredicted by up to $10^7\%$ showing that it is essential to take the overhead into account.

The relative corrected error depicted in Fig. 6(b) shows how much the measured run time of a given task graph deviated from the prediction generated using our algorithm (which incorporates scheduling overhead). The average deviation is 4.6% with a standard deviation of 3.1% (for average task sizes bigger 1000 clocks). For extremely small tasks with an average task size near zero the error increases up to 40% (but is still many orders of magnitude smaller compared to perfect scheduling) for some graphs because the timer resolution on the test system is not good enough to create such small tasks more precisely.

Figure 6(c) shows that the speedup per core achieved by our algorithm relative to perfect scheduling is $\geq$ one, so that our algorithm never creates a schedule with a speedup per core that is worse than the original schedule. For bigger tasks, the speedup per core is improved on average by 117%. For smaller tasks the improvement is much stronger because the dynamic scheduling overhead dominates the execution time.

Our algorithms optimizes for speedup per core rather than overall speedup. Nevertheless, Fig. 6(d) shows that on average the overall speedup of the task

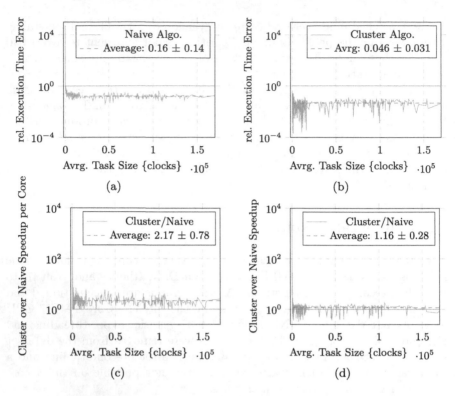

Fig. 6. Experimental results comparing our clustering algorithm to naive scheduling algorithms that neglect run-time scheduling overhead (perfect scheduling). Averages were calculated for average task sizes bigger 1000 clocks so that they are not biased from the values for on average small task sizes where our algorithm outperforms the classical algorithm by several orders of magnitude.

graphs is improved by 16 % by our algorithm compared to perfect scheduling. Again, for smaller tasks the effect is much more pronounced. Therefore, it can be seen that speedup per core is a measure that does not generally lead to decreased overall speedup. In some specific instances, optimizing for speedup may yield slightly shorter execution times at the expense of utilizing many more cores (and highly reducing energy efficiency).

Our algorithm merges all parallel tasks of local fork/join sub-graphs until the desired speedup per core (and a local speedup > 1) is achieved. Globally, a task graph's critical path consists of sequences of fork/join sub-graphs. Inductively it follows that the task graph's sink node finishes before or at the same time as in the fully sequentialized version of the task graph so that the global speedup ≥ 1. Also, the speedup per core $\geq \rho$ as all parallelism that would violate this invariant is removed. This holds if α, β and γ from Eq. 11 are chosen so that all task execution times prediction $\leq$ real execution times. Otherwise, since there is an average error of 4.6 % $\pm$ 3.1 % associated with the predicted task execution times, slight violations of these constraints are possible.

6   Related Work

Adve and Vernon [2] predict task graph execution times for a given scheduler model and complete program input data in $O(n + m)$. They present a system model where the scheduler and most other parts are modeled using queuing theory. For large task sizes their predictions are fairly good, results for small task sizes are not shown but would suffer from the lack of detailed scheduling overhead modeling. Their results are not applied to scheduling.

McCreary, Khan and Thompson [19] and Kwok [14] compare the makespan and Liu [17] compares worst case bounds of various scheduling heuristics but neglect the real-world execution times and overheads.

Most of the known scheduling heuristics have a complexity of $O(n^2)$ to $O(n^3)$ while operating on local information inside the task graph like edge weights and data ready times. Our algorithm is within the usual complexity of $O(n^3)$ while preprocessing allows us to examine a wider view of the parallelism inside the graph by considering the paths leading from lowest common ancestors via parallel nodes to the next join node (local fork/join sub-graphs).

Liou [16] suggests that clustering before scheduling is beneficial for the final result and McCreary and Gill [18] present a grain packing algorithm. This algorithm is limited to linear and pure fork/join parallelism, more complex graphs are not accounted for in detail and scheduling overhead is neglected. Many other clustering algorithms that do not take scheduling overhead into account have been proposed [15, 22].

Power efficient scheduling has been investigated by [20] and others, taking into account special hardware features to run specific tasks slower and with lower power consumption or better thermal footprint with minimal impact on the makespan. Our algorithm guarantees a minimum core utilization efficiency, so that additional cores are used only if a user defined speedup per core can be achieved. This allows otherwise inefficiently used cores to be turned off completely and can be combined with other power saving techniques.

To the best of our knowledge, none of the previous scheduling algorithms consider scheduling overhead, so in contrast to our algorithm no guarantees on real-world speedup and core utilization efficiency can be given.

7   Conclusion and Outlook

We have shown that task graphs which contain tasks with sizes in the order of 10^5 clocks and higher are not realistically scheduled by traditional scheduling algorithms as the scheduling overhead is neglected. We derived a sound model for the scheduling overhead of symmetric schedulers and presented a task graph clustering algorithm which unlike previous scheduling algorithms guarantees a real-world speedup and core utilization efficiency. Generally, our algorithm provides a vastly more accurate execution time model compared to existing algorithms and improves the speedup per core in most cases while never making it worse. The effect is viable for large task sizes with improved speedup by 16 %

and improved speedup per core by 117 %. For smaller tasks we improve existing methods by several orders of magnitude. Furthermore, we have shown that the scheduling overhead predictions should be incorporated into the existing scheduling algorithms to obtain realistic data ready times.

By extending the scheduler model and preconditioning algorithm to incorporate communication overhead, fully automatic and efficient schedules for cloud and HPC systems may become possible.

References

1. Adve, V.S., Vernon, M.K.: The influence of random delays on parallel execution times. SIGMETRICS Perfom. Eval. Rev. **21**(1), 61–73 (1993)
2. Adve, V.S., Vernon, M.K.: Parallel program performance prediction using deterministic task graph analysis. ACM Trans. Comput. Syst. **22**(1), 94–136 (2004)
3. Bender, M.A., Farach-Colton, M., Pemmasani, G., Skiena, S., Sumazin, P.: Lowest common ancestors in trees and directed acyclic graphs. J. Algorithms **57**(2), 75–94 (2005)
4. Blumofe, R.D., Leiserson, C.E.: Scheduling multithreaded computations by work stealing. J. ACM **46**(5), 720–748 (1999)
5. Coffman Jr., E.G., Garey, M.R., Johnson, D.S.: An application of bin-packing to multiprocessor scheduling. SIAM J. Comput. **7**(1), 1–17 (1978)
6. Darte, A., Robert, Y.P., Vivien, F.: Scheduling and Automatic Parallelization. Birkhäuser Boston (2000)
7. Dick, R.P., Rhodes, D.L., Wolf, W.: Tgff: Task graphs for free. In Proceedings of the 6th International Workshop on Hardware/Software Codesign, pp. 97–101. IEEE Computer Society (1998)
8. Gerasoulis, A., Yang, T.: On the granularity and clustering of directed acyclic task graphs. IEEE Trans. Parallel Distrib. Syst. **4**(6), 686–701 (1993)
9. Girkar, M., Polychronopoulos, C.D.: Automatic extraction of functional parallelism from ordinary programs. IEEE Trans. Parallel Distrib. Syst. **3**(2), 166–178 (1992)
10. Girkar, M., Polychronopoulos, C.D.: The hierarchical task graph as a universal intermediate representation. Int. J. Parallel Prog. **22**(5), 519–551 (1994)
11. Graham, R.L.: Bounds on multiprocessing timing anomalies. SIAM J. Appl. Math. **17**(2), 416–429 (1969)
12. Intel. Thread building blocks 4.1 (2013). http://www.threadingbuildingblocks.org/
13. Khan, A.A., McCreary, C.L., Gong, Y.: A Numerical Comparative Analysis of Partitioning Heuristics for Scheduling Tak Graphs on Multiprocessors. Auburn University, Auburn (1993)
14. Kwok, Y.-K., Ahmad, I.: Benchmarking the Task Graph Scheduling Algorithms, pp. 531–537 (1998)
15. Liou, J.-C., Palis, M.A.: An efficient task clustering heuristic for scheduling dags on multiprocessors. In: Workshop on Resource Management, Symposium on Parallel and Distributed Processing, pp. 152–156. Citeseer (1996)
16. Liou, J.-C., Palis, M.A.: A Comparison of General Approaches to Multiprocessor Scheduling, pp. 152–156. IEEE Computer Society, Washington, DC (1997)
17. Liu, Z.: Worst-case analysis of scheduling heuristics of parallel systems. Parallel Comput. **24**(5–6), 863–891 (1998)
18. McCreary, C., Gill, H.: Automatic determination of grain size for efficient parallel processing. Commun. ACM **32**(9), 1073–1078 (1989)

19. McCreary, C.L., Khan, A., Thompson, J., McArdle, M.: A comparison of heuristics for scheduling dags on multiprocessors. In: Proceedings on the Eighth International Parallel Processing Symposium, pp. 446–451. IEEE Computer Society (1994)
20. Shin, D., Kim, J.: Power-aware Scheduling of Conditional Task Graphs in Real-time Multiprocessor Systems, pp. 408–413. ACM, New York (2003)
21. Indiana University. Open mpi 1(4), 5 (2013). http://www.open-mpi.org/
22. Yang, T., Gerasoulis, A.: Dsc: Scheduling parallel tasks on an unbounded number of processors. IEEE Trans. Parallel Distrib. Syst. 5(9), 951–967 (1994)

Experimental Analysis of the Tardiness of Parallel Tasks in Soft Real-Time Systems

Manar Qamhieh$^{(\boxtimes)}$ and Serge Midonnet

Université Paris-Est, Champs-sur-Marne, France
{manar.qamhieh,serge.midonnet}@univ-paris-est.fr

Abstract. A parallel application is defined as the application that can be executed on multiple processors simultaneously. In software, parallelism is a useful programming technique to take advantage of the hardware advancement in processors manufacturing nowadays. In real-time systems, where tasks have to respect certain timing constraints during execution, a single task has a shorter response time when executed in parallel than the sequential execution. However, the same cannot be trivially applied to a set of parallel tasks (taskset) sharing the same processing platform, and there is a negative intuition regarding parallelism in real-time systems. In this work, we are interested in analyzing this statement and providing an experimental analysis regarding the effect of parallelism soft on real-time systems. By performing an extensive simulation of the scheduling process of parallel taskset on multiprocessor systems using a known scheduling algorithm called the global Earliest-Deadline First (gEDF), we aim at providing an indication about the effects (positive or negative) of parallelism in real-time scheduling.

Keywords: Parallelism · Stretching techniques · Real-time systems · Soft real-time systems · Scheduling simulation · Global earliest deadline first

1 Introduction

Uniprocessor platforms have been widely used in computer systems and applications for a long time. However, making processors smaller and faster has become more challenging for manufacturers recently due to the physical constraints such as heating and power problems. As a result, manufacturers are moving toward building multicore and multiprocessor systems so as to overcome these physical constrains. In the last few years, we have witnessed a dramatic increase in the number of cores in computational systems, such as the 72-core processor of the TILE-Gx family from Tilera, and the 192-core processor released by ClearSpeed in 2008.

Unfortunately, there is a gap between the advancement in software and hardware, and most of the currently used applications are still designed to target uniprocessor systems as execution platforms [1]. In order to get full advantage of multicore and multiprocessor systems, parallel programming has been

© Springer International Publishing Switzerland 2015
W. Cirne and N. Desai (Eds.): JSSPP 2014, LNCS 8828, pp. 36–52, 2015.
DOI: 10.1007/978-3-319-15789-4_3

employed so as to perform computations and calculations simultaneously on multiple processors. Lately, it has gained a higher importance although it has been used for many years.

The concept of parallel programming is to write a code that can be executed simultaneously on different processors. Usually, these programs are harder to be written than the sequential ones, and they consist of dependent parts. However, global scheduling, in which the scheduler can execute any job on any available processor at any time instant, is more suitable for parallel programs than partitioned scheduling (in which jobs are assigned first to individual processors and are forced to execute without processor migration).

From practical implementation's point of view, there exist certain libraries, APIs and models created specially for parallel programming like POSIX threads [2] and OpenMP [3]. Except these are not designed normally for real-time systems. In embedded systems, software usually is subjected to certain timing constraints, such as operational deadlines and the frequency of job arrivals. These constraints affect the correctness of its results along with the correctness of the calculations, and these systems are referred to as real-time systems.

Based on the criticality of the timing constraints, real-time systems are classified as either hard or soft. In hard real-time systems, the consequences of deadline misses can cause catastrophic effects, while soft real-time systems can tolerate delays in the execution of tasks, and a deadline miss only degrades the quality of service provided by the application. Avionic and transportation systems are examples of hard real-time systems, while communication and media systems (such as in video surveillance) are considered as soft real-time systems.

In real-time systems, many researches focused on the sequential task model in the case of multiprocessor systems [4]. In comparison, Few studies are conducted on the different models of parallel tasks, such as the multi-threaded segment and the Directed Acyclic Graph (DAG) model [5,6]. Mainly, a parallel task model is divided into three categories:

- rigid if the number of processors is assigned externally to the scheduler and can't be changed during execution,
- moldable if the number of processors is assigned by the scheduler and can't be changed during execution (this is the model we consider in this paper),
- malleable if the number of processors can be changed by the scheduler during execution.

In real-time systems, it has been believed that parallelism has negative effect on the schedulability of tasksets, as it has been stated in [7]. In that paper, the authors proposed to stretch the parallel tasks of the Fork-join model[1] as a way to avoid parallelism, and their results encourage the execution of parallel tasks as sequentially as possible. The reason why this was possible is that *fork-join tasks*

---

[1] A fork-join model is parallel task model in which the incoming jobs are split on arrival for service by numerous processors and joined before departure. It is the base of the OpenMP parallel programming API.

have schedulable utilization bounds slightly greater than and arbitrarily close to uniprocessors[2].

In this work, we aim at providing a basic intuition regarding the validity of this assumption, and we will study the effect of parallelism on the scheduling of tasksets on multiprocessor soft real-time systems. We use experimental analyses through extensive simulations as an indication tool towards our purpose. By choosing soft real-time systems, we can measure the performance of parallel tasks by calculating the tardiness of their jobs (how many time units a job needs after its deadline to complete its execution) in such systems when executed in parallel and sequentially, without worrying about the catastrophic effects of not respecting the timing constraints. To the best of our knowledge, we are not aware of similar researches or studies done regarding this assumption.

The structure of this paper is denoted as follows: Sect. 2 describes our parallel task model which is used in this paper, and it also includes two stretching transformations we propose in order to execute parallel tasks as sequentially as possible. These transformations are necessary as comparison references to the parallel execution. Then Sect. 3 contains a description about soft real-time systems and some details and discussion about an upper bound of tardiness found in literature. The contributions of this paper are included in Sect. 4, which provides a description about the simulation process used in this work, and the analysis of the conducted results. Finally, we conclude this paper by Sect. 5 which includes future work as well.

2   System Model and Its Transformations

2.1   Parallel Task Model

In this work, we consider a taskset τ that consists of n parallel sporadic implicit-deadline real-time tasks on a platform of m identical processors. Each task τ_i, where $1 \leq i \leq n$, is a parallel task that consists of a number of identical sequential threads, and it is characterized by (n_i, C_i, T_i), where n_i is the count of the threads belong to τ_i that can execute in parallel, C_i is the worst-case execution time (WCET) of τ_i which equals to the total WCET of its threads, and T_i is the minimum inter-arrival time (or simply the period) between successive jobs of the task, which defines the sporadic task. As in an implicit-deadline task, the deadline D_i of task τ_i, which is defined as the time interval in which τ_i has to complete its execution, is equal to the period of the task.

Let $\tau_{i,j}$ denote the jth thread of τ_i, where $1 \leq j \leq n_i$. All the threads of the same task share the same period and deadline of their task. Let $C_{i,j}$ be the WCET of thread $\tau_{i,j}$, where $C_i = \sum_{j=1}^{n_i} C_{i,j}$. In this paper, we consider ide ntical threads, however, the model can be generalized more by allowing non-identical threads.

---

[2] The remark regarding the utilization of Fork-join tasks is quoted from [7].

The utilization of thread $\tau_{i,j}$ is defined as $U_{i,j} = \frac{C_{i,j}}{T_i}$, and the utilization of the parallel task τ_i is defined as $U_i = \frac{C_i}{T_i} = \sum_{j=1}^{n_i} U_{i,j}$.

An example of our considered parallel task is shown in Fig. 1(a), in which task τ_i consists of 8 threads and has a deadline and a period equal to 11.

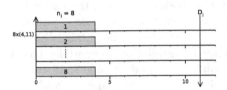

(a) All the threads of task τ_i execute in parallel.

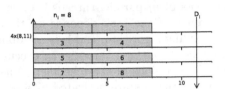

(b) The threads of task τ_i execute as sequentially as possible without any migrations or preemptions due to transformation.

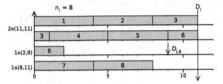

(c) All the threads of task τ_i execute as sequentially as possible. At most one constrained-deadline thread results.

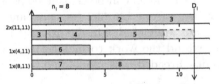

(d) The transformation in Subfigure 1(c) is modified so as to get rid of the constrained-deadline thread.

Fig. 1. An example of a parallel task τ_i that consists of 8 threads and it has a deadline and period equal to 11. The rectangles represent the threads of the task, and the numbers within them indicate their indexes.

In real-time systems, a scheduling algorithm is defined as the algorithm that assigns priorities to the active jobs in the system, and it chooses which jobs can execute on the available processors at time t. If active jobs are authorized to migrate between processors, which means that a job can start its execution on one processor and then continue on another, then the scheduling algorithm is called global. In multiprocessor systems, few optimal algorithms[3] exist for global scheduling of tasksets. These algorithms suffer usually from high overhead costs consist of large number of jobs migrations and preemptions. However, there exist non-optimal algorithms that have good performance with lower costs such as the global earliest deadline first (gEDF), which we will use in this paper. The gEDF algorithm assigns the highest priority to the job with the earliest absolute

---

[3] An optimal algorithm is the one that can schedule successfully any feasible taskset. If the optimal algorithm fails in scheduling a taskset, then no other algorithm can schedule it.

deadline. It belongs to the fixed job priority family, in which the priority of the job is fixed during its execution but jobs of the same task have different priorities. Also we consider a preemptive scheduling, in which a higher priority job can interrupt the execution of a lower priority job, and the interrupted job can start its execution on a different processor.

Based on the categories of the parallel tasks in real-time systems, our considered parallel task model rigid w.r.t. the number of threads. A given task τ_i consists of n_i parallel threads is defined by the model. However, the execution behavior of the task depends on the number of available processors and the scheduling algorithm, and it is not obligatory to execute all the parallel threads together. So, these threads can execute either in parallel or sequentially based on the decisions of the scheduler. When a job is activated at time t, all the n_i parallel threads are activated as well. But if there exist less than n_i available processors at time t, then the scheduler executes partial set of the threads in parallel while the rest are executed later.

In this paper, we considered a simplified task model of parallelism, in order to better show the effect of parallelism on the scheduling of soft real-time systems. Our task model can be considered as a Fork-join task model, in which each task consists of one parallel segment, and the costs of fork and join events of the threads are included in the execution time of each thread. In the future, we aim to extend the work to include more realistic parallel task models such as the multi-threaded task model and the Directed Acyclic Graphs (DAGs).

2.2 Stretching Parallel Tasks

In order to provide an analysis of the effect of parallelism on the scheduling of soft real-time systems, we will study the scheduling of a parallel taskset τ when executing on m identical processors using gEDF scheduling algorithm while considering some execution scenarios, that vary from parallel execution to sequential execution. As we described earlier in Sect. 2.1, the threads of a parallel task can execute either in parallel or sequentially based on the availability of processors and on the decisions of the chosen scheduling algorithm.

Hence, each parallel task τ_i in taskset τ can execute based on the following execution scenarios:

- the Parallel Scenario: all the threads τ_i execute in parallel, and they are activated at the same activation time of their parallel task τ_i (please refer to Fig. 1(a)),
- the Fully-Stretched Scenario: all the threads of τ_i execute as sequentially as possible, and τ_i is transformed into a set of fully stretched threads and a thread is broken into at most two pieces which execute in parallel, while the stretched threads can be assigned dedicated processors (please refer to Fig. 1(c)). A straight-froward transformation is provided in the following section in order to fully stretch the parallel threads.
- the Partially-Stretched Scenario: all the threads of τ_i execute as sequentially as possible, without causing interruptions and migrations due to transformation

(please refer to Fig. 1(b)). This transformation will be explained in more details in the following section.

The example of the proposed execution scenarios in Fig. 1 might seem unclear now. We invite the reader to consult the following detailed sections regarding the execution scenarios while referring to the example in Fig. 1.

The Parallel Scenario. The Parallel scenario represents the default execution behavior of our parallel task model. According to this scenario, the threads of each parallel task are activated by the activation event of the original task, and they have its deadline and minimum arrival time between the jobs. Hence, all the threads have the same priority according to gEDF, and they have the same utilization. So, the scheduling of the parallel tasks on m identical processors can be treated as the scheduling problem of a taskset of $(n_i, \forall \tau_i \in \tau)$ sequential sporadic implicit-deadline threads. An example of the parallel scenario is shown in Inset 1(a), in which each thread of task τ_i has a worst-case execution time of 4 and a deadline equal to 11.

However, the maximum tardiness of a parallel task is determined by the maximum tardiness of all of its threads among all possible scenarios of jobs' activation.

Fully-Stretched Scenario. The purpose of the Fully-Stretched transformation is to avoid the parallelism within the tasks when possible, by executing them as sequentially as possible. So, instead of activating all the parallel threads of a certain task at the same time (as in the Parallel scenario), this transformation determines which threads are activated in parallel and which are delayed to be executed sequentially. The objective is to transform the majority of the parallel threads of each task into fully-stretched threads which have a WCET equals to the period (utilization equals to 1). As a result, we can dedicate an entire processor for each transformed thread, which will guarantee their scheduling by the use of partitioned scheduling (tasks are assigned to a processor have to execute on this processor without authorizing migrations). Hence, the rest of the threads (not fully stretched) are the ones to be scheduled using gEDF, which will reduce their tardiness.

The Fully-Stretched Transformation is straight forward due to the simplicity of the considered parallel model. Let us consider a parallel task τ_i which consists of n_i threads and each thread $\tau_{i,j}$ has a WCET of $C_{i,j}$. The Fully-Stretched transformation will generate the following sets of modified threads $\tau'_{i,j}$:

- A set of fully-stretched threads $\tau'_{stretch}$: which consists of $\lfloor U_i \rfloor$ threads each has a total WCET equals to the original period, and utilization $U'_{i,j} = 1$, where $\tau'_{i,j} \in \tau'_{stretched}$. If the capacity of the processor cannot contain entire threads (i.e. $\frac{T_i}{C_{i,j}}$ is not an integer), then a thread will be forced to execute on 2 processors in order to fill the first one. As a result, the transformation will cause at most $\lfloor U_i \rfloor$ threads to migrate between processors.

- When the utilization of the parallel task is not integer, then there exist a set of threads that cannot fill an entire processor. Let the total remaining execution time be denoted as $C_{rem} = (U_i - \lfloor U_i \rfloor) * T_i$. The remaining threads are divided into the following two types:
  - At most, one implicit-deadline thread τ'_{imp} from each transformed parallel task is generated. This thread is created by merging the remaining threads that did not fit into the stretched tasks without the thread that is used to partially fill the last processor. The WCET of τ'_{imp} is calculated as $C_{imp} = (\lfloor \frac{C_{rem}}{C_{i,j}} \rfloor * C_{i,j})$, and it has a deadline and period equal to the original parallel task τ_i.
  - At most one constrained deadline[4] thread τ'_{cd} is generated, which has a WCET calculated as $C_{cd} = C_{rem} - C_{imp}$. Its period is the same as the original task τ_i, and it has a deadline calculated as $D_{cd} = (D_i - (C_{i,j} - C_{cd}))$. This thread contains the remaining execution time of the thread that had to fill the last stretched processor. The conversion from an implicit-deadline thread into a constrained deadline one is necessary to prevent the sequential thread from executing in parallel since its execution is divided between two processors.

Back to the example in Fig. 1, Inset 1(c) shows an example of the Fully-Stretched transformation when applied on task τ_i shown in Inset 1(a). As shown in the figure, the original task consists of 8 threads each has a WCET equals to 4 and a deadline equals to 11. After transformation, the fully-stretched tasks $\tau'_{stretch}$ contains two threads. The first consists of threads $\tau_{i,1}$, $\tau_{i,2}$ and the ending part of $\tau_{i,3}$. While the second task consists of the beginning part of the $\tau_{i,3}$ (complementary to the part in the previous task), threads $\tau_{i,4}$, $\tau_{i,5}$ and the ending part of thread $\tau_{i,6}$. The remaining execution time of thread $\tau_{i,6}$ forms the constrained deadline independent thread τ'_{cd}, with a deadline $D_{i,6} = 9$ as shown in the figure. Threads $\tau_{i,7}$ and $\tau_{i,8}$ are merged together, in order to form a single implicit-deadline task with a WCET equals to 8 and a deadline equals to 11.

The advantage of the Fully-Stretched Transformation is that, at most, two threads (τ'_{imp} and τ'_{cd}) are scheduled using gEDF, and they are the ones that may cause a tardiness during the scheduling process. While the rest of the generated threads ($\{\tau'_{stretch}\}$) are scheduled using partitioned scheduling algorithms, and they are guaranteed to respect their deadline each on a single processor independently.

Partially-Stretched Scenario. A modification to the Fully-Stretched transformation can be proposed so as to avoid the thread migrations between processors. In this transformation, we authorize the parallel threads to be stretched up to the maximum possible thread-capacity of a processor, which can be at most the deadline of the parallel task. Let x denote the thread-capacity of a particular processor (all identical processors have the same value), which is calculated as $x = \lfloor \frac{D_i}{C_{i,j}} \rfloor$. This means that each processor can contain at most x complete

---

[4] A constrained deadline real-time task has a deadline no more than its period.

threads executing sequentially. The result of the transformation is a set of $\lfloor \frac{C_i}{x} \rfloor$ implicit-deadline threads each has a WCET equals to $(x * C_{i,j})$. Also, at most on implicit-deadline thread which has a WCET equals to $(C_i - ((x * C_{i,j}) * \lfloor \frac{C_i}{x} \rfloor))$. The resulted threads are scheduled using gEDF on m identical multiprocessors.

As shown in the example in Fig. 1, parallel task τ_i from Inset 1(a) is transformed using the Partially-Stretched Transformation, and the result is shown in Inset 1(b). The processor capacity of task τ_i is equal to 2, and the result of transformation is 4 sequential implicit-deadline threads characterized by $(8, 11, 11)$. It is clear that the Partially-Stretched transformation does not force any threads to migrate prior to the scheduling process, and this is the advantage of this transformation over the Fully-Stretched Transformation.

The worst-case execution time of a task is a pessimist value, and usually the jobs do not execute up to this value. In the case of a global work-conserving scheduling algorithm, when a job finishes its execution earlier than expected by the WCET, then the scheduler will not allow to leave a processor idle while there are active jobs ready to execute, and it will allow an active job to be released earlier. In the case of partitioned scheduling, the scheduling algorithm assigns tasks to processors, and then migration between processors is not allowed. Hence, if a job finishes its execution earlier than expected and there are no active jobs waiting on this processor, the processor will stay idle even of there are active jobs waiting on the other processors.

Also, it had been proved in [8] that fixed job priority algorithms (which include gEDF) are predictable, *i.e.* a schedulable taskset is guaranteed to stay schedulable when one or more of its tasks execute for less than its worst-case execution time. This property is another advantage of global scheduling over partitioned scheduling. We can conclude that the Parallel and Partially-Stretched scenarios, which use gEDF to schedule all the threads of the taskset, behave better than the Fully-Stretched scenario (which uses partitioned scheduling for most of the executed tasks) in the case of lower execution time of jobs. Hence, the processors will be efficiently used.

Advantage of Stretching over Parallelism in Real-Time Systems. The scheduling of real-time tasksets on multiprocessor systems is more complicated than the uniprocessor systems. A famous problem had been shown in [9] called the *Dhall effect*, in which a low utilization taskset can be non-schedulable regardless of the number of processors in the platform. Later, it had been proved in [10] that this problem happens when a low utilization taskset contains a high utilization task. We will show using an example, that this problem happens in the case of the Parallel Scenario, while the stretching scenarios solves it. The used example is inspired from [10].

Let us consider a taskset τ that consists of 2 tasks that executes on 3 unit-speed processors $(m = 3)$. The first task τ_1 has a deadline equal to 1, and it consists of 3 threads each has a WCET equals to 2ϵ, where ϵ is slightly greater than zero. The second task τ_2 has a deadline equals to $1 + \epsilon$, and it has a single thread with WCET equals to 1. The utilization of each task is calculated as

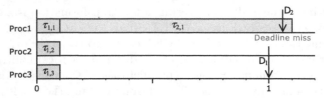

(a) Parallel Scenario: All the threads of the task τ_1, which have the highest priority according to gEDF, execute on all 3 processors. While the highest utilization task τ_2 is delayed and hence it misses its deadline.

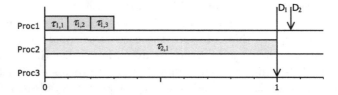

Fig. 2. An example shows how stretching a parallel task helps in solving the Dhall effect problem.

$U_1 = 2m\epsilon$ and $U_2 = \frac{1}{1+\epsilon}$. Hence, the total system's utilization approaches to 1 since $\epsilon \to 0$. The taskset is shown in Fig. 2.

When gEDF is used, at time $t = 0$, the first job of task τ_1 has a higher priority than the job of task τ_2, because it has an earlier absolute deadline. All the threads of τ_1 have the same priority of τ_1, and according to the Parallel Scenario, they will execute in parallel and they will occupy all the available processors in the systems. At time $t = 2\epsilon$, the threads finish their execution, and then task τ_2 can start its own. Unfortunately, task τ_2 misses its deadline. The scenario is shown in Inset 2(a).

However, when a stretching scenario is used (either fully-stretched or partially-stretched transformation has the same result), the parallel threads of the low utilization task will be forced to execute sequentially and hence they will occupy lower number of processors. As a result, the higher utilization task (τ_2 in the example) will start its execution earlier and it will respect its deadline. Inset 2(b) shows the effect of stretching on the Dhall effect problem, and how it solved it.

3   The Effect of Parallelism on the Tardiness of Soft Real-Time Systems

In soft real-time systems, a deadline miss during the scheduling process of a taskset does not have catastrophic effects on the correctness of the system as in hard real-time systems. However, a deadline miss of a task will reduce the quality of service (QoS) provided by the application. So, in order to keep the QoS at an acceptable rate and better analyze it, it is necessary to determine an upper bound of tardiness for each task in a system regarding a specific scheduling algorithm.

A tardiness of a job in real-time systems is defined as its delay time, *i.e.* the time difference between the deadline and the actual finish time of this job. For a real-time task that generates a number of jobs, the tardiness of one job has a cascaded effect on the successor jobs, since the next jobs have to wait for the delayed one to finish its execution before they can start their own execution, which means that they will be delayed as well. The tardiness of a task is defined as the maximum tardiness among its generated jobs (Fig. 3).

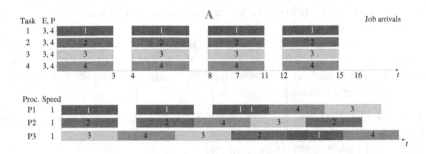

Fig. 3. An example (from [11]) shows the tardiness of tasks during the scheduling of a taskset consists of 4 tasks on 3 identical processors using gEDF.

Few researches have been done regarding the problem of identifying an upper bound to the tardiness of sporadic sequential implicit-deadline tasks on multiprocessors when global EDF is used, such as in [11][5]. In [13], an upper bound of tardiness under preemptive and non-preemptive global EDF is proved. In this work, we intend to present the latter tardiness bound in the case of preemptive gEDF and discuss its usefulness in the calculations of tardiness in the case of parallel tasks. In the future, we aim at calculating an adapted upper bound for parallel tasks.

For the sake of explaining the upper bound of tardiness from [13], Consider that τ is a sporadic taskset that is scheduled using gEDF on m identical processors. Each task $\tau_k \in \tau$ is a sequential implicit-deadline task that has a WCET C_k and a deadline D_k(equal to minimum arrival time or period). The upper bound of tardiness of each task in τ is given in the following theorem:

Theorem 1 (from [13]). *Global EDF (gEDF) ensures a tardiness bound of*

$$\frac{\sum_{i=1}^{\Lambda} \varepsilon_i - C_{min}}{m - \sum_{i=1}^{\Lambda-1} \mu_i} + C_k \tag{1}$$

---

[5] In [12], the authors mentioned that a proof published in [11] contains an error. Until now, we are not aware of the availability of a correction for this error.

to every sequential task τ_k of a sporadic implicit-deadline task system τ with $U_{sum} \leq m$, where:
ε_i *(resp. μ_i) denotes the ith execution cost (resp. task utilization) in non-increasing order of the execution costs (resp. utilization) of all the tasks.*

$$\Lambda = \begin{cases} U_{sum} - 1, & U_{sum} \text{ is integral} \\ \lfloor U_{sum} \rfloor, & \text{otherwise} \end{cases} \tag{2}$$

The detailed proof of Theorem 1 can be found in [13]. The used approach is based on comparing the processors allocations using gEDF with a concrete task system in a processor sharing[6].

As we can notice from Eq. 1, the tardiness is calculated as the worst-case execution time of each task plus a fixed value w.r.t. the global parameters of the taskset. By analyzing this bound, we conclude that the tardiness of a taskset is reduced if, at least, one of the following is applied:

– a decrease in the value of the highest WCET and utilization of the tasks in the set (ε and μ),
– an increase in the WCET of tasks in τ (C_{min}),
– an increase in the number of processors,
– a decrease in the total utilization of the taskset (U_{sum}) which affects the value of Λ from Eq. 2.

In our parallelism model described in Sect. 2, a thread in a parallel task is considered as a sequential task. Hence, we can apply Theorem 1 on each thread $\tau_{i,j} \in \tau_i \in \tau$ individually. The tardiness of a job of a parallel task is the maximum tardiness among its threads, and then the tardiness of a parallel task is the maximum tardiness among its jobs.

It is worth noticing that the upper bound of tardiness is computed for sporadic implicit-deadline tasks, while the fully-stretched transformation generates at most two threads that scheduled using gEDF and may be delayed, which are τ'_{cd} and τ'_{imp}. As a solution to this problem, and in order to use the tardiness bound from Theorem 1, we propose a modification to the constrained deadline threads τ'_{cd} to be executing completely using gEDF, and it is converted to implicit-deadline threads. An example of this modification is shown in the example in Fig. 1(d).

Let the tardiness of a parallel task $\tau_k \in \tau$ be denoted by x_k when it executes in the parallel scenario described above (all threads are activated in parallel). If task τ_k is partially stretched, then the threads of the parallel tasks will be stretched which will increase the utilization and execution time of threads. On another hand, the number of threads to be scheduled using gEDF is reduced on m processors. So, after the partially-stretched scenario, the values of C_{min}, ε and μ will increase. Also, when task τ_k is fully-stretched, the resulted fully-stretched threads (their utilization equals to 1) will be assigned dedicated processors, and at most 2 threads from each parallel task will be scheduled using gEDF only. As a result, the total

---

[6] A processor sharing is an idle fluid schedule in which each task executes at a precisely uniform rate given by its utilization (from [13]).

utilization of the taskset τ will be reduced and also the number of processors on which gEDF algorithm is used, in addition to the effects of the partially-stretched scenario. The stretching scenarios have the advantage of reducing the number of threads that may cause a tardiness due to deadline misses when compared to the parallel scenario. Hence, the tardiness of the parallel tasks will be reduced as a result.

Based on these effects, we can conclude that the tardiness bound of parallel tasks is not comparable with the bound after stretching. Because stretching scenarios change the taskset in a way that can increase and decrease the tardiness bound at the same time. Hence, the theoretical tardiness bound of Theorem 1 cannot determine the performance of parallel and stretched tasks in the scheduling problem using gEDF, and it cannot be used as an indication to the performance of parallelism in real-time systems. As a result, we will use experimental analysis to simulate the scheduling of the different scenarios of parallel task execution and to give us an indication on the performance.

4 Experimental Analysis

In this section, we show the simulation results of the experiments conducted using randomly-generated tasksets to evaluate the performance of parallel execution in comparison with the stretching execution scenarios described in Sect. 2. The results are obtained by simulating the scheduling of a large number of parallel tasksets with different utilization on a platform of 16 identical processors when global EDF is used.

The simulation process is based on an event-triggered scheduling. This means that at each event in the interval $[0, 3 * H)$, where H denotes the hyper period of the scheduled taskset τ and is defined as the least common multiple of periods, the scheduler is awakened and it decides which jobs have the highest priorities to execute on the available processors. According to EDF, the job with the earliest absolute deadline has the highest priority. We consider that a parallel job is blocked either by the execution of a higher priority thread or by an earlier job that has been delayed. During the simulation process, we calculate the tardiness of each job of parallel tasks, in order to calculate the average tardiness of tasks in the set, while varying three parameters: the execution behavior of parallel tasks (either Parallel "Par", Fully-Stretched "F-Str" or Partially-Stretched "P-Str"), the utilization of tasks within each taskset (either High "Hi" or Low "Lo"), this is done by varying the number of tasks of each taskset, and finally the number of parallel threads within each parallel task (maximum of 3 or 10 threads/task).

We used a simulation tool called YARTISS [14], which is a multiprocessor real-time scheduling simulator developed by our research team. It contains many scheduling algorithms and task models (including parallel tasks), and it can be used easily for both hard and soft real-time systems.

For each system utilization from 1 to 16, we generated $50,000$ tasksets randomly. The number of parallel tasks within each taskset is varied from 3 to 12 tasks/taskset. This variation affects the structure of tasks because, for a fixed utilization, increasing the number of tasks means that the taskset's utilization will

be distributed on a larger number of tasks, which will lower the average utilization of tasks within the taskset. Also, we can control the percentage of parallelism
within a taskset by varying the number of parallel threads of each task during
task generation. This can help in analyzing the effect of parallelism on scheduling
as we will see below.

Regarding the generation of parallel tasksets, our task generator is based on
the Uunifast-Discard algorithm [15] for random generation of tasks. This algorithm is proposed by Davis and Burns to generate randomly a set of tasks of
a certain total utilization on multiprocessor systems. The number of tasks and
their utilization are inputs of this algorithm. The taskset generator is described
briefly as follows:

- The algorithm takes two parameters n and U, where n is the number of parallel
  tasks in the set and U is the total utilization of the taskset ($U > 0$).
- The Uunifast-Discard algorithm distributes the total utilization on the taskset.
  A parallel task τ_i can have a utilization U_i greater than 1 which means that
  its threads cannot be stretched completely, and it has to execute in parallel.
- The number of threads and their WCET of each parallel tasks are generated
  randomly based on the utilization of the tasks. The maximum number of
  threads is fixed to be either 3 or 10 threads per parallel task.

In order to limit the simulation interval and reduce the time needed to perform the simulation, which is based on the length of the hyper period of each
taskset, we used the limitation method proposed in [16], which relays on using a
considerate choice of periods of the tasks while generation so as to reduce their
least common multiple. Using this method, we implemented our task generator
to choose periods of tasks in the interval $[1, 25200]$.

Analysis of Experimental Results. For each taskset, the average of the maximum tardiness of all tasks is computed. The results are showed in Fig. 4, which
consists of 2 insets. Inset 4(a) shows the comparison of average tardiness of
tasksets for the three types of execution behaviors, while Inset 4(b) focuses on
the comparison between the parallel and the fully-stretched execution behavior.

The average tardiness is calculated by considering the schedulable tasks (their
tardiness equal to zero), so as to give us an indication on the number of deadline
misses happened during simulation. Moreover, the x-axis of the insets of Fig. 4
represents the utilization of the scheduled tasksets (from 1 to 16 on a system of
16 identical processors), while the y-axis represents the average tardiness of the
tasksets.

The rest of this section discusses the results in details.

The Effect of Utilization of Tasksets on Tardiness. Referring to Fig. 4,
most of the tasksets have negligible tardiness when tasksets have utilization less
than 4. Then the tardiness increases differently (based on the used scenario) for
higher utilization. These results are quite logical, since the number of processors
in the simulation is always considered to be $m = 16$. Hence, lower utilization

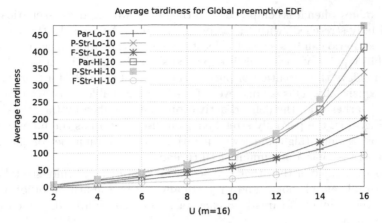

(a) Comparison of the average tardiness of taskset when executing on $m = 16$ using all execution scenarios for parallel tasks.

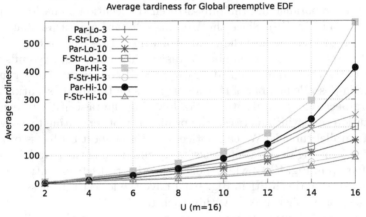

(b) Comparison of the average tardiness of taskset when executing on $m = 16$ focusing on the parallel and the Full-stretch execution scenarios.

Fig. 4. Simulation results of average tardiness of parallel tasks by varying their execution behavior (Parallel "Par", Full-stretch "F-Str" and Partially-stretch "P-Str"), the utilization of tasks within tasksets (high "Hi" and Low "Lo") and the maximum number of threads within each parallel task (either 3 or 10 threads/task).

tasksets mean lower execution demand from processors which increases schedulability and reduces deadline misses. Starting from $U_{taskset} > 4$, we can notice an increase in tardiness for the average tardiness values which varies based on the execution scenario.

However, we can conclude by looking at these results, and specially when $U_{taskset} = 16$, that the partially-stretched transformation has always the highest tardiness values when it is compared with the other two execution scenarios (parallel and fully-stretched) with the same parameters. As a result, the partially-stretched scenario can be seen as the least appealing execution scenario from the schedulability point of view. This is expected since the partially-stretched transformation delays the execution of part of the parallel threads of a task so as to execute sequentially. This is done even if there are available processors for them to execute earlier than the defined activation time specified by the transformation. In Fig. 4(a), the partially-stretched scenario (P-Str) has the highest tardiness in both groups (high and low utilization) when the number of threads of each parallel task has a maximum of 10 threads.

The performance of the other two scenarios (parallel and fully-stretched) is not comparable at this point, and they are affected by the utilization of parallel tasks and the number of threads in each task, and this will be discussed in the next paragraph.

The Effect of the Number of Tasks per Taskset on Tardiness. The difference between the parallel and the fully-stretched execution scenarios of parallel tasks is shown in Fig. 4(b). Since the Uunifast-Discard algorithm that we used for generating tasksets divides the total utilization of taskset on the number of tasks per taskset, varying the number of tasks while fixing the system's utilization will vary the utilization assigned for each task. In our parallel task generator, the maximum possible number of threads depends on the total execution time of the task (respectively, its utilization). So, lowering the task utilization means a lower execution time which increases the probability of generating tasks with low number of parallel threads. We can notice that the highest tardiness of tasksets is caused from the high-utilization tasksets executed using the parallel execution scenario (Par-Hi in Fig. 4(b)), while their respective tasksets executing using the fully-stretched scenario (F-Str in Fig. 4(b)) have the lowest tardiness, regardless of the number of parallel threads within each task.

Regarding the low-utilization tasks, we can notice that the tardiness of the tasksets depends on the number of parallel threads within each task. As shown in Fig. 4(b), the fully-stretched tasksets whose tasks consist of 3 threads (F-Str-Lo-3) have lower but relatively close tardiness than the parallel scenario (Par-Lo-3). However, the parallel executing tasksets whose tasks consist of 10 threads (Par-Lo-10) are behaving better than the fully-stretched scenario (F-Str-Lo-10).

In this case, the scheduling of the parallel scenario is clearly better than the fully-stretched scenario as shown in Fig. 4(b). This can be explained by noticing that in this case the number of parallel threads in a task is high while its utilization is low. Since the threads inherit the deadline and period of their original task, then the threads have low utilization as well. The parallel scenario gives the scheduling algorithm more freedom in scheduling the parallel threads, by activating them all at the same time, and choosing their execution order based on the availability of processors. While the fully-stretched scenario forces the parallel tasks to execute sequentially even if this approach is not work-conserving and it might cause delays in the scheduling process.

From the results conducted by simulation, we have now an experimental indication on the effect of parallelism on the scheduling of real-time systems. It is possible now to overrule the typical assumption that parallelism has always negative effects on scheduling. As we have shown above, the parallel scheduling is better than its sequential alternatives when tasks have low number of parallel threads. According to this, the scheduler can get better scheduling decisions while parallelizing the execution of certain tasks on multiple processors than the sequential execution. This result matches the motivation of parallelism and its practical uses in non-real time systems.

5   Conclusion

In this paper, we were interested in studying the effect of parallelism in real-time systems. The problem is summarized as the scheduling of sporadic implicit-deadline parallel tasks on multiprocessors using global earliest deadline first (gEDF) as scheduling algorithm. The parallel tasks are either executed in a parallel scenario in which all the threads of the parallel tasks execute in parallel as soon as possible, or in a stretching scenario, in which the threads are executed as sequentially as possible. We proposed two stretching scenarios based on the number of thread migrations and preemptions required by the transformation: partially and fully stretched. In the latter, threads are stretched to form transformed threads with utilization equal to 1, but it requires higher number of migrations and preemptions between processors and jobs.

Using extensive simulation, we showed that parallelism did not cause major negative effects on the scheduling of real-time systems. Admitting that sequential execution of tasks has better results in general than parallelism, There are certain cases where parallelism behaves better and has lower tardiness values than stretching. Based on these remarks and results, we can overrule the common assumption in real-time systems against parallelism, and that tries to avoid parallel structure in order to get better scheduling results.

In the future, we aim at extending our work, and provide theoretical analyses to support our experimental results, by providing an upper bound of tardiness adapted to parallel real-time tasks on multiprocessor systems. Also, we are looking forward to analyze scheduling algorithms other than gEDF algorithm that we used in this paper. Based on this, we can classify the common scheduling algorithms in real-time systems based on their ability to schedule parallel tasks with low tardiness bounds.

Finally, we aim at generalizing our task model of parallel tasks, so as to include more complicated structures of parallel threads, such as the multi-threaded segment model and the Directed Acyclic Graphs. Such task models are used to represent practical parallel programming APIs.

References

1. Mixed criticality systems. European Commission Workshop on Mixed Criticality Systems, Brussels, Belgium, February 2012
2. Posix threads programming. https://computing.llnl.gov/tutorials/pthreads/
3. OpenMP. http://www.openmp.org
4. Davis, R.I., Burns, A.: A survey of hard real-time scheduling algorithms and schedulability analysis techniques for multiprocessor systems. ACM Comput. Curveys **43**, 1–44 (2011)
5. Saifullah, A., Ferry, D., Agrawal, K., Lu, C., Gill, C.: Real-time scheduling of parallel tasks under a general DAG model. Technical report, Washington University in St Louis (2012)
6. Baruah, S.K., Bonifaciy, V., Marchetti-Spaccamela, A., Stougie, L., Wiese, A.: A generalized parallel task model for recurrent real-time processes. In: Proceedings of the 33rd IEEE Real-Time Systems Symposium (RTSS), December 2012, pp. 63–72 (2012)
7. Lakshmanan, K., Kato, S., (Raj) Rajkumar, R.: Scheduling parallel real-time tasks on multi-core processors. In: Proceedings of the 31st IEEE Real-Time Systems Symposium (RTSS), pp. 259–268. IEEE Computer Society (2010)
8. Ha, R., Liu, J.: Validating timing constraints in multiprocessor and distributed real-time systems. In: 14th International Conference on Distributed Computing Systems, pp. 162–171. IEEE Computer Society Press (1994)
9. Dhall, S.K., Liu, C.L.: On a real-time scheduling problem. Oper. Res. **26**(1), 127–140 (1978)
10. Phillips, C.A., Stein, C., Torng, E., Wein, J.: Optimal time-critical scheduling via resource augmentation (extended abstract). In: Proceedings of the Twenty-Ninth Annual ACM Symposium on Theory of Computing, ser. STOC 1997, pp. 140–149 (1997)
11. Valente, P., Lipari, G.: An upper bound to the lateness of soft real-time tasks scheduled by edf on multiprocessors. In: 26th IEEE International Real-Time Systems Symposium, 2005, RTSS 2005, pp. 10–320 (2005)
12. Valente, P., Lipari, G.: An upper bound to the lateness of soft real-time tasks scheduled by EDF on multiprocessors. Technical report RETIS TR05-01, Scuola Superiore S.Anna (2005)
13. Devi, U.: Soft real-time scheduling on multiprocessors. Ph.D. dissertation, University of North Carolina at Chapel Hill, Chapel Hill, Sweden (2006)
14. YaRTISS simulation tool. http://yartiss.univ-mlv.fr/
15. Davis, R., Burns, A.: Improved priority assignment for global fixed priority preemptive scheduling in multiprocessor real-time systems. Real-Time Syst. **47**(1), 1–40 (2011)
16. Goossens, J., Macq, C.: Limitation of the hyper-period in real-time periodic task set generation. In: Proceedings of the 9th International Conference on Real-Time Systems (RTS), March 2001, pp. 133–148 (2001)

Multi-resource Aware Fairsharing
for Heterogeneous Systems

Dalibor Klusáček[1][(⊠)] and Hana Rudová[2]

[1] CESNET z.s.p.o., Zikova 4, Prague, Czech Republic
xklusac@fi.muni.cz
[2] Faculty of Informatics, Masaryk University,
Botanická 68a, Brno, Czech Republic
hanka@fi.muni.cz

Abstract. Current production resource management and scheduling systems often use some mechanism to guarantee fair sharing of computational resources among different users of the system. For example, the user who so far consumed small amount of CPU time gets higher priority and vice versa. However, different users may have highly heterogeneous demands concerning system resources, including CPUs, RAM, HDD storage capacity or, e.g., GPU cores. Therefore, it may not be fair to prioritize them only with respect to the consumed CPU time. Still, applied mechanisms often do not reflect other consumed resources or they use rather simplified and "ad hoc" solutions to approach these issues. We show that such solutions may be (highly) unfair and unsuitable for heterogeneous systems. We provide a survey of existing works that try to deal with this situation, analyzing and evaluating their characteristics. Next, we present new enhanced approach that supports multi-resource aware user prioritization mechanism. Importantly, this approach is capable of dealing with the heterogeneity of both jobs and resources. A working implementation of this new prioritization scheme is currently applied in the Czech National Grid Infrastructure MetaCentrum.

Keywords: Multi-resource fairness · Fairshare · Heterogeneity

1 Introduction

This paper is inspired by our cooperation with the Czech National Grid Infrastructure MetaCentrum [18]. MetaCentrum is highly heterogeneous national Grid that provides computational resources to various users and research groups. Naturally, it is crucial to guarantee that computational resources are shared in a fair fashion with respect to different users and research groups [12,14]. Fairness is guaranteed by the *fairshare algorithm* [2,11], which is implemented within the applied resource manager, in this case the TORQUE [3].

For many years the fairshare algorithm considered only single resource when establishing users priorities. The fairshare algorithm measured the amount of consumed CPU time for each user and then calculated users priorities such that

© Springer International Publishing Switzerland 2015
W. Cirne and N. Desai (Eds.): JSSPP 2014, LNCS 8828, pp. 53–69, 2015.
DOI: 10.1007/978-3-319-15789-4_4

the user with the smallest amount of consumed CPU time obtained the highest priority and vice versa [14]. However, with the growing heterogeneity of jobs and resources, it quickly became apparent that this solution is very unfair since it does not reflect other consumed resources [16,17].

An intuitive solution is to apply a more complex, multi-resource aware fair-share algorithm. However, as we will demonstrate in Sect. 2, existing solutions are not very suitable for truly heterogeneous workloads and systems. Often, these solutions either use unrealistic system models or fail to provide fair solutions in specific, yet frequent usage scenarios.

In this paper we present a new fair sharing prioritization scheme which we have proposed, implemented and put into daily service. It represents a rather unique multi-resource aware fairshare mechanism, which was designed for truly heterogeneous workloads and systems. Based on an extensive analysis of pros and cons of several related works (see Sect. 2) we have carefully extended widely used *Processor Equivalent (PE)* metric which is available in Maui and Moab schedulers [1,2,11]. The extension guarantees that the prioritization scheme is not sensitive to job and machine parameters, i.e., it remains fair even when the jobs and resources are (highly) heterogeneous. Importantly, the scheme is insensitive to scheduler decisions, i.e., the computation of priorities is not influenced by the job-to-machine mapping process of the applied job scheduler. Also, jobs running across different nodes are supported, and the solution reflects various speeds of machines and performs corresponding walltime normalization to capture the effects of slow vs. fast machines on resulting job walltime[1].

This paper is structured as follows. In Sect. 2 we discuss the pros and cons of existing works covering both classical CPU-based and multi-resource aware fairness techniques using several real life-based examples. In Sect. 3 we describe the newly proposed multi-resource aware fairness technique. Section 4 evaluates the proposed solution using historic MetaCentrum workload. We conclude the paper and discuss the future work in Sect. 5.

2   Related Work

Before we start, we would like to stress out that there is no widely accepted and universal definition concerning fairness. In fact, different people and/or organizations may have different notion of "what is fair" when it comes to multiple resources [9,13]. In our previous work [17], we have shown how different reasonable fairness-related requirements may interact together, often resulting in conflicting situations. Therefore, in the following text we present approaches and viewpoints that were established and are currently applied in MetaCentrum.

2.1   Fairshare

All resource management systems and schedulers such as TORQUE [3], PBS-Pro [19], Moab, Maui [1], Quincy [10] or Hadoop Fair and Capacity Schedulers [4,6]

---

[1] Walltime is the time a job spends executing on a machine(s). It is an important parameter used in the fairshare algorithm as we explain in Sect. 2.

support some form of fairshare mechanism. Nice explanation of Maui fairshare mechanism can be found in [11]. For many years, the solution applied in Meta-Centrum TORQUE was very similar to Maui or Moab. It used the well known *max-min* approach [9], giving the highest priority to a user with the smallest amount of consumed CPU time and vice versa.

For the purpose of this paper, we assume that a user priority is established by Formula 1 [11]. Here, F_u is the resulting priority of a given user u. F_u is computed over the set J_u, which contains all jobs of user u that shall be used to establish user priority. The final value is computed as a sum of products of job penalty $P(j)$ and the job walltime ($walltime_j$). As soon as priorities are computed for all users, the user with the smallest value of F_u gets the highest priority in a job queue.

$$F_u = \sum_{j \in J_u} walltime_j \cdot P(j) \tag{1}$$

Formula 1 is a general form of a function that can be used to establish ordering of users. It represents the simplest version, that does not use so called decay algorithm [11]. Decay algorithm is typically applied to determine the value of F_u with respect to aging, i.e., it specifies how the effective fairshare usage is decreased over the time[2]. For simplicity, we will not consider the decay algorithm in the formulas as its inclusion is straightforward and can be found in [11] or [17].

When computing F_u, a proper computation of the job penalty $P(j)$ is the key problem. Commonly, fairshare algorithms only consider a single resource, typically CPUs. In such a case, the penalty function $P(j)$ for a given job j is simply $P(j) = reqCPU_j$, where $reqCPU_j$ is the number of CPUs allocated to that job[3]. Clearly, the penalty of a given user's job j is proportional to the number of CPUs it requires. To illustrate the problems related to a CPU-based penalty we provide following real life-based Example 1 [17], which is based on a workload coming from Zewura cluster, a part of MetaCentrum.

Example 1. Zewura consists of 20 nodes, each having 80 CPUs and 512 GB of RAM. Figure 1 (left) shows the heterogeneity of CPU and RAM requirements of jobs that were executed on this cluster. Clearly, there are many jobs that use a lot of RAM while using only a fraction of CPUs. Similarly, Fig. 1 (right) shows an example of CPUs and RAM usage on a selected node within the Zewura cluster. For nearly two weeks in July 2012, jobs were using at most 10 % of CPUs while consuming all available RAM memory. Those remaining 90 % of CPUs were

---

[2] A *fairshare usage* represents the metric of utilization measurement [11]. Typically, it is the amount of consumed CPU time of a given user.

[3] In MetaCentrum, resources allocated (i.e., reserved) to a given job cannot be used by other jobs even if those resources are not fully used. Therefore, when speaking about CPU, RAM, etc., requirements we mean the amount of a given resource that has been allocated for a job, even if actual job requirements were smaller. Similarly, a job CPU time is the number of allocated CPUs multiplied by that job walltime.

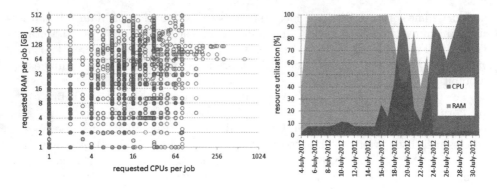

Fig. 1. Heterogeneity of jobs CPU and RAM requirements (left) and an example of CPU and RAM utilization on one Zewura node (right).

then useless because no new job could have been executed there due to the lack of available RAM. More importantly, using the standard fairshare algorithm, the owner(s) of these memory-demanding jobs were only accounted for using 10 % of available CPU time. However, as intuition suggests, they should have been accounted as if using 100 % of machine CPU time because they effectively "disabled" whole machine by using all its RAM [17].

Apparently, the classical — single resource-based — fairshare mechanism computed according to consumed CPU time may be considered unfair as the users with high RAM requirements are not adequately penalized with respect to those users who only need (a lot of) CPUs. Of course, similar findings can be done concerning other resources such as GPUs or HDD storage. For simplicity, we only consider CPUs and RAM in the rest of the paper. The addition of additional resources is possible and it is a part of our future work (see Sect. 5).

Although the single resource-based fairshare algorithm may seem inadequate, many systems are still using it today [5,10,19]. Let us now discuss multi-resource aware solutions that are already available in several mainstream resource managers and schedulers.

2.2 Standard Job Metric

The latest documentation of PBS-Pro [19] suggests that an administrator must select exactly one resource to be tracked for fairshare purposes, therefore it is not possible to combine multiple consumed resources in fairshare. We have discussed this issue with people from PBS Works[4] and according to their advice, it is possible to use so called *standard job* metric. It works as follows. First, a system administrator defines resource requirements of so called "standard job".

---

[4] PBS Works is a division of Altair which is responsible for PBS-Pro development. The meeting took place at the Supercomputing 2013 conference in Denver, CO, USA.

These requirements should correspond to a typical small job, e.g., *standard* $CPU = 1$ CPU and *standardRAM* $= 1$ GB of RAM. Next, a job penalty of any actual job is computed by Formula 2, i.e., $P(j)$ is the number of standardized jobs that are needed to cover resource requirements of a considered job j.

$$P(j) = \max \left(\frac{reqCPU_j}{standardCPU}, \frac{reqRAM_j}{standardRAM} \right) \tag{2}$$

Although this metric is simple, we see an apparent problem — it is highly sensitive with respect to the used setup of "standard job". At the same time, our existing workloads indicate that there is no "standard job" as is also visible in Fig. 1 (left). Therefore, it is quite questionable to use this metric across all users and the whole system.

2.3 Processor Equivalent Metric

Moab and Maui provide different, yet still simple solution called *processor equivalent (PE)* [1,2,11], which allows to combine CPU and, e.g., RAM consumptions, translating multi-resource consumption requests into a scalar value. PE is based on the application of *max* function that determines the most constraining resource consumption of a job and translates it into an equivalent processor count using Formula 3, where *availCPU* and *availRAM* are the total amounts of CPUs and RAM in the system, respectively.

$$P(j) = PE(j) = \max \left(\frac{reqCPU_j}{availCPU}, \frac{reqRAM_j}{availRAM} \right) \cdot availCPU \tag{3}$$

Moab documentation illustrates the processor equivalent functionality using following Example 2.

Example 2. Consider a situation that a job requires 20 % of all CPUs and 50 % of the total memory of a 128-processor system. Only two such jobs could be supported by this system. The job is essentially using 50 % of all available resources since the most constrained resource is memory in this case. The processor equivalents for this job should be 50 % of the processors, or $PE = 64$ [2].

Although the documentation states that "the calculation works equally well on homogeneous or heterogeneous systems" [2], this is not true as problems may appear once the system and workload become heterogeneous. Let us demonstrate MetaCentrum-inspired Example 3 where PE fails to produce reasonable job penalties.

Example 3. Consider a heterogeneous system with 2 types of nodes. First type of nodes has 8 CPUs and 16 GB of RAM. Second type of nodes has 80 CPUs and 512 GB of RAM. The system contains 10 nodes of type 1 and 1 nodes of type 2. Together, the system has 160 CPUs (*availCPU*) and 672 GB of RAM (*availRAM*). Now a user submits a RAM-constrained job requiring 1 CPU and 512 GB of RAM per node. This scenario emulates the situation discussed in Example 1 which is depicted in Fig. 1 (right). The resulting job processor equivalent (using Formula 3) is $PE(j) = \max(1/160, 512/672) \cdot 160 = 121.9$. Using the interpretations of PE as found in Moab documentation [2], we can say that memory is the most constrained resource for this job, thus $PE(j) = 121.9$ which means that approximately 76 % of all available resources are used by this job. However, this is not entirely true. Since that job requires 512 GB of RAM per node, it can only be executed on that large (type 2) machine. At the same time, the job uses all RAM of that (type 2) machine. As a result, this job "occupies" all 80 CPUs of this machine. The question is, whether it is fair to "charge" the user as if using 121.9 CPUs, as suggests the PE-based penalty. We think that this is not fair.

Still, one may suggest that since the job is really using 76 % of all available RAM, it should be penalized by $PE(j) = 121.9$ (an equivalent of 76 % CPUs). As it turns out this interpretation is not correct, as we can easily construct following counter example.

Example 4. Let us consider a scenario with a CPU-constrained job requiring 80 CPUs per node and 80 GB of RAM. The resulting job processor equivalent is $PE(j) = \max(80/160, 80/672) \cdot 160 = 80$. It indicates that 50 % of all available resources are used by this job. Since that job requires 80 CPUs per node, it can only be executed on that large (type 2) machine. At the same time, the job uses all CPUs of that (type 2) machine. Then, also all RAM on this machine (512 GB of RAM) must be considered as unavailable. Using the same argumentation as in case of Example 3, we must say that this job is occupying 76 % of all RAM. However, in this case the $PE(j)$ is only 80 (an equivalent of 50 % CPUs).

To sum up, Examples 3 and 4 show how two different jobs (RAM vs. CPU-constrained) that *occupy the same resources* (one type 2 node) may obtain highly different penalties. From our point of view, it means that the use of PE in heterogeneous environments does not solve fairly the problem observed in Fig. 1 (right) and described in Example 1.

2.4   Other Approaches

So far, we have discussed solutions that are available within several mainstream systems. However, there are also several works that propose novel multi-resource aware scheduling methods. We have provided a detailed survey of those methods in our previous work [17], so we only briefly recapitulate here. For example, *Dominant Resource Factor (DRF)* [9] suggests to perform max-min fairshare algorithm over so called dominant user's share, which is the maximum share that a user has been allocated of any resource. Recently, DRF has been included into the new *Fair Scheduler* in Hadoop Next Generation [6]. Simultaneous fair allocation of multiple continuously divisible resources called *bottleneck-based fairness (BBF)* is proposed in [8]. In BBF, an allocation of resources is considered fair if all users either get all the resources they wished for, or else get at least their entitlement on some bottleneck resource, and therefore cannot complain about not receiving more. The tradeoffs of using multi-resource oriented fairness algorithms including newly proposed *Generalized Fairness on Jobs (GFJ)* are discussed in [13]. Especially, the overall utilization is of interest. Unlike DRF, GJF measures fairness only in terms of the number of jobs allocated to each user, disregarding the amount of requested resources [13]. From our point of view, such a notion of fairness is impractical as it allows to cheat easily by "packing" several small jobs as a one large job. Also, all these approaches make the assumption that all jobs and/or resources are continuously divisible [7]. However, for common grid and cluster environments, this is rarely the case, thus these techniques are rather impractical for our purposes. In our recent short abstract [16], we have presented a possible extension of the fairshare algorithm to cover heterogeneity of resources. However, the abstract provided neither detailed analysis of related work, neither a detailed explanation or an evaluation of the solution itself. Moreover, the proposed techniques did not support some important features, e.g., computation of penalties for multi-node jobs.

In the previous text we have illustrated several problems that complicate the design of a proper multi-resource aware job penalty function (a key part of the fairshare algorithm). Existing mainstream solutions often rely on too simplified and sensitive approaches ("standard job"-based metric) or they fail to provide reliable results for heterogeneous systems and workloads (PE metric). Other works such as DRF, GFJ or BBF then use system models that are not suitable for our purposes.

3 Proposed Multi-resource Aware Fairshare Algorithm

In this section we describe the newly developed multi-resource aware fairshare mechanism which is currently used to prioritize users in MetaCentrum. It has several important features that we summarize in the following list:

(1) **multi-resource awareness:** The solution reflects various consumed resources (CPU and RAM by default) using modified processor equivalent metric.
(2) **heterogeneity awareness:** Processor equivalent metric is used in a new way, guaranteeing the same penalties for jobs that occupy the same resources. This modification solves the problems related to the heterogeneity of jobs and resources described in Sect. 2.3.
(3) **insensitivity to scheduler decisions:** Job penalty is not sensitive to scheduler decisions, i.e., a given job penalty is not influenced by the results of the job-to-machine mapping process being performed by the job scheduler.
(4) **walltime normalization:** We reflect various speeds of machines and perform so called *walltime normalization* to capture the effects of slow vs. fast machines on resulting job walltime.
(5) **support for multi-node jobs:** The solution calculates proper job penalties for multi-node jobs that may have different per-node requirements.

In the following text we describe how these features are implemented, starting with the new penalty function that allows features 1-3, then proceeding to walltime normalization (feature 4). For simplicity, we first describe how the scheme works for single node jobs and then proceed to the description of multi-node job support (feature 5). Finally, we briefly describe how the solution has been implemented in TORQUE.

3.1 Proposed Penalty Function

The newly proposed penalty function is based on an extension of processor equivalent (PE) metric (see Formula 3) presented in Sect. 2.3. As we have shown in Examples 3 and 4, PE cannot solve the problems observed in Example 1. It may provide misleading and unfair results when measuring the usage of the system, by producing different penalties for jobs that occupy the same resources. The origin of the problem observed in Examples 3 and 4 is that the system and jobs are heterogeneous, thus only a subset of nodes may be suitable to execute a job. Then, it is questionable to compute job penalty with respect to all available resources. A simple solution addressing this problem is to compute PE only with respect to a machine i that has been used to execute that particular job j as shows Formula 4. Instead of using global amounts of CPUs and RAM, here the $availCPU_i$ and the $availRAM_i$ are the amounts of CPUs and RAM on that machine i, respectively[5].

$$PE(j, i) = \max \left(\frac{reqCPU_j}{availCPU_i}, \frac{reqRAM_j}{availRAM_i} \right) \cdot availCPU_i \cdot node\_cost_i \quad (4)$$

This reformulation solves the problem observed in Examples 3 and 4 as those RAM and CPU-heavy jobs now obtain the same penalties ($PE(j, i) = 80$). Sadly, $PE(j, i)$ brings a new disadvantage. Now, the PE calculation is *sensitive to scheduler decisions* [16]. Consider following example.

Example 5. Let a job j requests 1 CPU and 16 GB of RAM. Clearly such job can be executed both on type 1 and type 2 nodes. However, when j is executed on a type 1 node, then $PE(j, 1) = \max(1/8, 16/16) \cdot 8 = 8$ while if j is executed on a type 2 node, then $PE(j, 2) = \max(1/80, 16/512) \cdot 80 = 2.5$.

Since a user has limited capabilities to influence scheduler behavior, such metric is highly unfair as it may assign highly variable penalties for identical jobs. Therefore, we use this metric in a different way. In the first step, we construct the set M_j which is the set of all machines that are suitable to execute job j. Then we compute the "local" processor equivalent $PE(j, i)$ for each machine i such that $i \in M_j$ using Formula 4. Finally, we compute the job penalty $P(j)$ using Formula 5.

---

[5] The additional parameter $node\_cost_i$ is optional and can be used to express (real) cost and/or importance of machine i, e.g., GPU-equipped nodes are less common (i.e., more valuable) in MetaCentrum. By default, $node\_cost_i = 1.0$.

$$P(j) = queue\_cost_j \cdot \min_{i \in M_j} PE(j, i) \tag{5}$$

Job penalty $P(j)$ is based on the minimal $PE(j, i)$, i.e., it uses the cheapest "price" available in the system. It is important to notice, that it represents the best possible fit and $P(j)$ *remains the same disregarding the final job assignment.* Therefore, we can guarantee that $P(j)$ is *insensitive to scheduler decisions.* At the same time, we avoid the problems related to heterogeneity, since we only consider those machines (M_j) that are suitable for that job j. The use of this penalty has one major benefit — our users are satisfied as we always choose the best price for them, disregarding the final scheduler decision. Therefore, they are not tempted to fool the system by "playing" with job parameters or with job-to-machine mapping, which could otherwise degrade, e.g., the system throughput.

As can be seen in Formula 5, we also use *queue_cost* parameter. It can be used to further increase or decrease job penalty depending on the user's choice of queue. By default, all queues have the same cost (1.0). However, it is sometimes useful to increase the price for, e.g., those queues that are used for very long jobs or provide access to some specialized/expensive hardware. To sum up, the proposed penalty shown in Formula 5 is multi-resource aware, reflects heterogeneity of jobs and resources, and provides results that are not sensitive to scheduler decisions, i.e., it supports the features 1, 2 and 3 described at the beginning of Sect. 3.

3.2 Walltime Normalization

Job walltime is a very important parameter that is used along with the job penalty to establish the final user ordering (see Formula 1). However, in heterogeneous systems like MetaCentrum, the walltime of a job may depend on the speed of machine(s) where that job is executed. Figure 2 illustrates this situation by showing the per-CPU-core results of the Standard Performance Evaluation Corporation's SPEC CPU2006 benchmark (CFP2006 suite/fp_rate_base2006) for major MetaCentrum clusters. In order to further illustrate the heterogeneity of resources, the figure also shows the total number of CPU cores on each cluster, as well as the number of CPU cores per node and the amount of RAM per node.

The figure demonstrates large differences in machine performance. Especially those "flexible" jobs that can be executed on many clusters can end up with highly variable walltimes. In addition, if a job ends up on a slow machine, its walltime will be higher, thus the fairshare usage of its owner will increase even more. Clearly, this scheduler-dependent job assignment results in a highly unfair behavior of the fairshare algorithm and explains the importance of walltime normalization. As far as we know, walltime normalization is not typically applied and it is not even mentioned in the documentation of PBS-Pro, TORQUE, Maui or Moab. Therefore, we have decided to apply simple walltime normalization, where the resulting walltime of a job j is multiplied by the SPEC result ($SPEC_j$) of the machine that was used to execute that job j. We assume that the resulting job walltime is inversely proportional to the $SPEC_j$. Since this is not true for

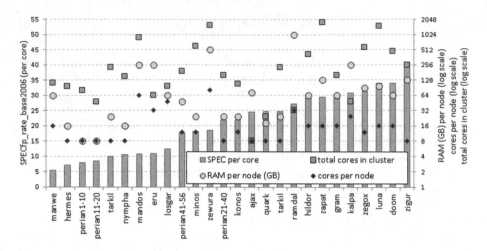

Fig. 2. Heterogeneity of SPEC CPU2006 results, CPU cores and RAM for major Meta-Centrum clusters.

some applications, our users can directly specify a desired speed of machine(s) upon each job submission, by providing the minimum and the maximum eligible SPEC. In that case, only those machines satisfying these constraints remain in the set of eligible machines M_j. Once the walltime normalization is applied, the resulting priority of a given user u is now computed using Formula 6.

$$F_u = \sum_{j \in J_u} walltime_j \cdot SPEC_j \cdot P(j)$$

$$= \sum_{j \in J_u} walltime_j \cdot SPEC_j \cdot queue\_cost_j \cdot \min_{i \in M_j} PE(j, i) \qquad (6)$$

Beside features 1-3, this formula also supports feature 4. Still, it is only suitable for single node jobs. In practice, users may submit jobs that require several nodes to execute. Moreover, the specifications concerning each requested node may be different. Such a situation requires more complex function which we describe in the next section.

3.3 Multi-node Jobs

The last feature 5 mentioned at the beginning of Sect. 3 enables us to correctly compute fairshare priority with respect to multi-node jobs, that may have heterogeneous per-node requirements. We assume that a given multi-node job j requests r nodes. For each such node, there is a separate resource specification[6]. Resource requests concerning k-th node ($1 \leq k \leq r$) are denoted as $reqCPU_{k,j}$

---

[6] It is obtained by parsing node specification requests obtained by `qsub` command.

and $reqRAM_{k,j}$. To compute the job penalty, following steps are performed for all requested nodes. At first, we find the set of machines that meet the k-th request and denote it as $M_{k,j}$. Then, for every suitable machine i such that $i \in M_{k,j}$ we compute the corresponding "local" processor equivalent, denoted as $PE_k(j,i)$ (see Formula 7). Then, the "price" for the k-th request is the minimal (cheapest) $PE_k(j,i)$. The resulting job penalty $P(j)$ is the sum of minimal prices, multiplied by the $queue\_cost$ as shown in Formula 8. In the next step, we normalize the walltime of the job. Since the job uses r different machines, we have r (possibly different) SPEC values, where the k-th value is denoted as $SPEC_{j,k}$. As the walltime is the time when the whole job completes, it is most likely influenced by the slowest machine being used, i.e., the machine with lowest SPEC result. Therefore, the walltime is normalized by the minimal $SPEC_{j,k}$. Together, the fairshare priority F_u is computed as shows Formula 9.

$$PE_k(j,i) = \max \left(\frac{reqCPU_{k,j}}{availCPU_i}, \frac{reqRAM_{k,j}}{availRAM_i} \right) \cdot availCPU_i \cdot node\_cost_i \quad (7)$$

$$P(j) = queue\_cost_j \cdot \sum_{k=1}^{r} \min_{i \in M_{k,j}} PE_k(j,i) \quad (8)$$

$$F_u = \sum_{j \in J_u} walltime_j \cdot \min_{1 \le k \le r} (SPEC_{j,k}) \cdot P(j) \quad (9)$$

3.4   Implementation in TORQUE

To conclude this section, we just briefly describe computation of the proposed multi-resource aware fairshare priority function (see Formula 9) within the TORQUE deployed in MetaCentrum[7].

The computation is done in two major steps. In the first step, a job penalty $P(j)$ is computed upon each job arrival, i.e., prior to a job execution. This computation is performed by the scheduler. $P(j)$ is refreshed during each scheduling cycle until a job starts its execution. As soon as a job starts, the TORQUE server obtains information about machine(s) being used by that job, especially those corresponding value(s) of SPEC and node cost(s). At this point, the server has all information required to recompute a fairshare priority F_u of a corresponding user. If needed, job queues are then reordered according to a newly computed fairshare priority.

It is important to notice, that a fairshare priority F_u of a user is updated immediately after his or her job starts its execution. Otherwise, a priority of that user would remain the same until at least one of his or her jobs completes, which is potentially dangerous. Since an exact walltime of a running job is not known until that job completes, the maximum walltime limit is used instead as an approximation. As soon as that job completes, its actual walltime is used accordingly and a fairshare priority F_u of a corresponding user is recomputed

---

[7] This enhanced TORQUE can be obtained at: https://github.com/CESNET/torque.

from scratch (replacing previous approximation). If needed, job queues are then reordered accordingly.

4   Experimental Analysis

In this section we describe how the new multi-resource aware fairshare works on a real workload. For the purpose of evaluation we have used workload from MetaCentrum which covers first six months of the year 2013. This log contains 726,401 jobs, and is available at: http://www.fi.muni.cz/~xklusac/jsspp/. We have used *Alea* [15] job scheduling simulator to demonstrate the effects of our new prioritization mechanism. Alea is commonly used in MetaCentrum to evaluate suitability of newly developed solutions. Using the simulator, we have emulated both previous (CPU-based) as well as the new multi-resource aware fairshare mechanism and then analyzed their differences. The proposed prioritization scheme consists of two main parts—the new penalty function $P(j)$ and the walltime normalization. Therefore, we have performed two major experiments that cover these main parts of the proposed solution.

First, we have analyzed which jobs are affected by the new penalty function (see Formula 8). We have plotted all jobs from the workload according to their heterogeneous CPU and RAM requirements (see Fig. 3), and we have highlighted those jobs that have different (higher) value of the new penalty function compared to the old (CPU-based) version.

The results correspond to our expectations, i.e., the new $P(j)$ assigns higher penalties to those jobs with high RAM to CPU ratio. Such jobs represent less than 2 % of all jobs, and generate more than 5 % of the overall CPU utilization.

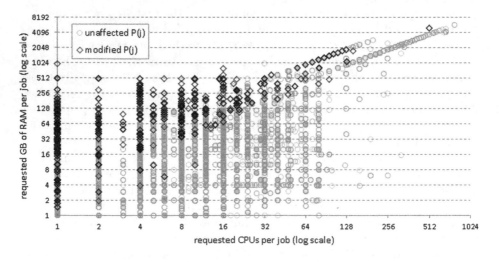

Fig. 3. The heterogeneity of CPU and RAM requirements of jobs from the workload. Dark boxes highlight those jobs that are affected by the new penalty function.

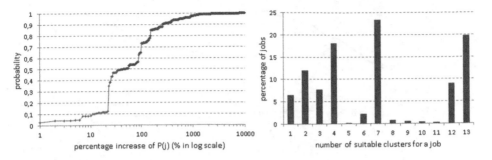

Fig. 4. CDF of resulting changes in $P(j)$ value (left) and the histogram of job-to-cluster suitability (right).

Also, approximately 40 % of users now have at least one job that would obtain higher penalty, compared to the original solution.

Next, we took those jobs with higher penalty (those affected by the new $P(j)$) and measured the percentage increase of the new $P(j)$ (with respect to the old, CPU-based version). Figure 4 (left) shows the results using a cumulative distribution function (CDF). In this case, the CDF is a $f(x)$-like function showing the probability that the percentage increase of $P(j)$ for given job j is less than or equal to x. In another words, the CDF represents the fraction of jobs having their $P(j)$ less than or equal to x. As can be seen, the improvement is mostly significant. For example, for nearly 90 % of considered jobs their new $P(j)$ has increased at least by 20 %. Also, 40 % of considered jobs have their $P(j)$ at least two times higher (≥ 100 %).

In the next step, we have measured the influence of the new $P(j)$ on the overall performance of the system. For this purpose we have measured the distribution of job wait times and bounded slowdowns when the original and the new $P(j)$ has been used, respectively. Jobs were scheduled from a single queue that was dynamically reordered according to continuously updated job priorities. Only the job at the head of the queue was eligible to run, i.e., we intentionally did not use backfilling. The reason is that backfilling can dilute the impact of the job prioritization algorithm [11], and therefore make it much harder to analyze the effect of new prioritization scheme. For similar reasons, walltime normalization has not been used in this experiment. Our results in Fig. 5 show that there is no danger when using the new priority function. In fact, the cumulative distribution functions (CDF) of wait times and slowdowns were slightly better for the new $P(j)$.

While the wait times and slowdowns were generally lower for the new prioritization scheme (see Fig. 5), this was not true for those jobs that — according to the new $P(j)$ — now obtain higher penalties. This is an expected and desirable behavior. For example, in this experiment the wait times of such jobs have increased by 33 min on average.

In the final experiment, we have measured the possible influence of walltime normalization. As was demonstrated in Fig. 2, there are significant differences in

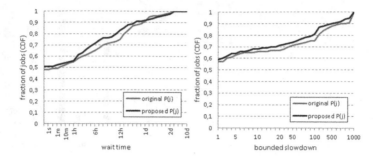

Fig. 5. Comparison of wait times (left) and bounded slowdowns (right) distributions.

the performance of clusters in MetaCentrum. At first, we have analyzed a job-to-cluster suitability by measuring how many clusters can be used to execute a given job. A cluster is capable to execute a job if it satisfies all job requirements as specified upon job submission. Typically, a job requires a set of CPUs, a fixed amount of RAM (per node), and data storage capacity. Moreover, it may require additional properties such as geographical locality of cluster(s), operating system, CPU architecture, etc[8]. Figure 4 (right) shows the histogram of job-to-cluster suitability. The x-axis shows the number of suitable clusters and y-axis shows the percentage of jobs that can run on this number of clusters. There are 26 main clusters in MetaCentrum, but there are no jobs that can be executed on every cluster. Therefore, the x-axis is bounded by 13, which is the maximum number of clusters that some jobs can use (approximately 20 % of jobs). Most jobs in the workload (93.6 %) can execute on at least 2 clusters and more than 50 % of jobs can use at least 7 clusters.

Since we have observed that many jobs are rather flexible, we have decided to measure the possible effect of walltime normalization on a job. For each job we have found the set of suitable clusters. Next, we have found the cluster(s) with the minimum and the maximum SPEC (denoted as $SPEC_{j,min}$ and $SPEC_{j,max}$), and $SPEC_j$ of the original cluster that has been used to execute that job (this information is available in the original workload log). Figure 6 (left) shows the CDFs of $SPEC_{j,min}$, $SPEC_{j,max}$ and $SPEC_j$, respectively. It clearly demonstrates how large can be the differences among the original, the "slowest" and the "fastest" suitable cluster, i.e., how important is to perform some form of walltime normalization. Without doing so, we can significantly handicap those jobs (and users), that were assigned to slow machines. Beside poorer performance, slow machines also imply higher walltimes, thus further increasing the fairshare usage of corresponding job owners.

To further highlight this issue, we have computed the absolute difference between the "slowest" and the "fastest" suitable cluster ($SPEC_{j,max} - SPEC_{j,min}$) for every job j. The results are shown in the CDF in Fig. 6 (right). We can clearly

---

[8] Detailed description is available at: https://wiki.metacentrum.cz/wiki/Running_jobs_in_scheduler.

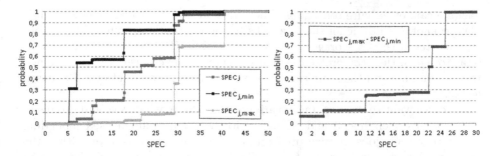

Fig. 6. CDFs of the minimal ($SPEC_{j,min}$), the maximal ($SPEC_{j,max}$) and the actual SPEC values ($SPEC_j$) as observed in the workload (left). The CDF showing the maximum possible differences in SPEC values (right).

see how large the differences are. For example, the maximal possible difference in SPEC values is greater than 11 for 89 % of jobs, while the maximal possible difference is greater than 22 for 50 % of jobs. Again, this example demonstrates how important is to perform some form of walltime normalization. Otherwise, the resulting priority ordering of users is likely to be (very) unfair.

5   Conclusion and Future Work

This paper addresses an urgent real life job scheduling problem, focusing on fair sharing of various resources among different users of the system. The novelty of our work is related to the fact that we consider *multiple consumed resources in heterogeneous systems* when establishing users priorities. We have discussed the pros and cons of several existing approaches, using real life-based examples. Next, we have provided the description and the analysis of the multi-resource aware fairshare technique which is currently used in the Czech National Grid Infrastructure MetaCentrum. The main features of this solutions are the ability to reflect both CPU and RAM requirements of jobs, the ability to handle heterogeneity of jobs and resources, the insensitivity to scheduler decisions, walltime normalization, and the support of multi-node jobs.

We plan to further analyze the performance and suitability of the production solution as well as possible problems that may appear in the future. The proposed solution is used for about 6 months (from November 2013) in the production system with 26 clusters and no significant comments from the users were recorded so far. It is important that the solution is capable of working in the real production environment, even tough we still need to extend the set of implemented features (e.g., GPU-awareness, peer-to-peer fairshare synchronization) to become fully functional in larger scale. Therefore, our further development will focus on more complex usage scenarios that are based on MetaCentrum needs. For example, it is quite obvious that the PE-based metric may be too severe for jobs requiring special resources that are not needed by all jobs, e.g., GPUs. If a given job consumes all GPUs on a machine, it does not mean that such a machine cannot execute other jobs. Therefore, we will try to find some suitable relaxation of this metric for such special situations. Another example of a "problematic" resource is a storage capacity (e.g., local HDD/SSD or (hierarchical) data storages). Here the problem is that consumed capacity is rarely constrained by a job lifetime and therefore cannot be simply incorporated into the PE-based metric.

Also, we want to develop a new variant of fairshare, where selected groups of users can have their "local" and "global" priorities, that would be used depending on whether their jobs are executed on their own infrastructure or within the public pool of resources, respectively. Finally, as MetaCentrum is planning to use several TORQUE servers simultaneously using a peer-to-peer model, we will need to synchronize computations of fairshare priorities among several servers.

Acknowledgments. We highly appreciate the support of the Grant Agency of the Czech Republic under the grant No. P202/12/0306. The support provided under the programme "Projects of Large Infrastructure for Research, Development, and Innovations" LM2010005 funded by the Ministry of Education, Youth, and Sports of the Czech Republic is highly appreciated. The access to the MetaCentrum computing facilities and workloads is kindly acknowledged.

References

1. Adaptive Computing Enterprises, Inc. Maui Scheduler Administrator's Guide, version 3.2, January 2014. http://docs.adaptivecomputing.com
2. Adaptive Computing Enterprises, Inc. Moab workload manager administrator's guide, version 7.2.6, January 2014. http://docs.adaptivecomputing.com
3. Adaptive Computing Enterprises, Inc. TORQUE Admininstrator Guide, version 4.2.6, January 2014. http://docs.adaptivecomputing.com
4. Apache.org. Hadoop Capacity Scheduler, January 2014. http://hadoop.apache.org/docs/r1.2.1/capacity_scheduler.html
5. Apache.org. Hadoop Fair Scheduler, January 2014. http://hadoop.apache.org/docs/r1.2.1/fair_scheduler.html
6. Apache.org. Hadoop Next Generation Fair Scheduler, January 2014. http://hadoop.apache.org/docs/r2.2.0/hadoop-yarn/hadoop-yarn-site/FairScheduler.html
7. Blazewicz, J., Drozdowski, M., Markiewicz, M.: Divisible task scheduling - concept and verification. Parallel Comput. **25**(1), 87–98 (1999)
8. Dolev, D., Feitelson, D.G., Halpern, J.Y., Kupferman, R., Linial, N.: No justified complaints: on fair sharing of multiple resources. In: Proceedings of the 3rd Innovations in Theoretical Computer Science Conference, ITCS 2012, pp. 68–75. ACM, New York (2012)
9. Ghodsi, A., Zaharia, M., Hindman, B., Konwinski, A., Shenker, S., Stoica, I.: Dominant resource fairness: fair allocation of multiple resource types. In: 8th USENIX Symposium on Networked Systems Design and Implementation (2011)
10. Isard, M., Prabhakaran, V., Currey, J., Wieder, U., Talwar, K., Goldberg, A.: Quincy: fair scheduling for distributed computing clusters. In: ACM SIGOPS 22nd Symposium on Operating Systems Principles, pp. 261–276 (2009)

11. Jackson, D.B., Snell, Q.O., Clement, M.J.: Core algorithms of the maui scheduler. In: Feitelson, D.G., Rudolph, L. (eds.) JSSPP 2001. LNCS, vol. 2221, pp. 87–102. Springer, Heidelberg (2001)
12. Jain, R., Chiu, D.-M., Hawe, W.: A quantitative measure of fairness and discrimination for resource allocation in shared computer systems. Technical report TR-301, Digital Equipment Corporation (1984)
13. Joe-Wong, C., Sen, S., Lan, T., Chiang, M.: Multi-resource allocation: fairness-efficiency tradeoffs in a unifying framework. In: 31st Annual International Conference on Computer Communications (IEEE INFOCOM), pp. 1206–1214 (2012)
14. Kleban, S.D., Clearwater, S.H.: Fair share on high performance computing systems: what does fair really mean? In: Third IEEE International Symposium on Cluster Computing and the Grid (CCGrid2003), pp. 146–153. IEEE Computer Society (2003)
15. Klusáček, D., Rudová, H.: Alea 2 - job scheduling simulator. In: Proceedings of the 3rd International ICST Conference on Simulation Tools and Techniques (SIMUTools 2010). ICST (2010)
16. Klusáček, D., Rudová, H.: New multi-resource fairshare prioritization mechanisms for heterogeneous computing platforms. In: Cracow Grid Workshop, pp. 89–90. ACC Cyfronet AGH (2013)
17. Klusáček, D., Rudová, H., Jaroš, M.: Multi resource fairness: problems and challenges. In: Desai, N., Cirne, W. (eds.) JSSPP 2013. LNCS, vol. 8429, pp. 81–95. Springer, Heidelberg (2014)
18. MetaCentrum, January 2014. http://www.metacentrum.cz/
19. PBS Works. PBS Professional 12.1, Administrator's Guide, January 2014. http://www.pbsworks.com

Priority Operators for Fairshare Scheduling

Gonzalo P. Rodrigo$^{(\boxtimes)}$, Per-Olov Östberg, and Erik Elmroth

Department of Computing Science, Umeå University, SE-901 87 Umeå, Sweden
{gonzalo,p-o,elmroth}@cs.umu.se
www.cloudresearch.org

Abstract. Collaborative resource sharing in distributed computing requires scalable mechanisms for allocation and control of user quotas. Decentralized fairshare prioritization is a technique for enforcement of user quotas that can be realized without centralized control. The technique is based on influencing the job scheduling order of local resource management systems using an algorithm that establishes a semantic for prioritization of jobs based on the individual distances between user's quota allocations and user's historical resource usage (i.e. intended and current system state). This work addresses the design and evaluation of priority operators, mathematical functions to quantify fairshare distances, and identify a set of desirable characteristics for fairshare priority operators. In addition, this work also proposes a set of operators for fairshare prioritization, establishes a methodology for verification and evaluation of operator characteristics, and evaluates the proposed operator set based on this mathematical framework. Limitations in the numerical representation of scheduling factor values are identified as a key challenge in priority operator formulation, and it is demonstrated that the contributed priority operators (the Sigmoid operator family) behave robustly even in the presence of severe resolution limitations.

1 Introduction

Distributed computing environments, such as high throughput computing [1] and grid computing [2] environments, share a common challenge: distributed collaborative resource sharing requires some form of coordination mechanism for control of resource capacity distribution. Compute grids address this problem through establishment of virtual organizations [3], abstract organizations that define hierarchies and quota allocations for users, and delegate to participating resource sites to enforce user quotas in local resource scheduling.

Fairshare scheduling is a scheduling technique derived from an operating system task scheduler algorithm [4] that prioritizes tasks based on the historical resource usage of the task owner (rather than that of the task itself). This technique defines a "fair" model of resource sharing that allows users to receive system capacity proportional to quota allocations irrespective of the number of tasks they have running on the system (i.e. preventing starvation of users with few tasks).

© Springer International Publishing Switzerland 2015
W. Cirne and N. Desai (Eds.): JSSPP 2014, LNCS 8828, pp. 70–89, 2015.
DOI: 10.1007/978-3-319-15789-4_5

In local resource management (cluster scheduler) systems such as SLURM [5] and Maui [6], this prioritization technique is extended to job level and fairshare prioritization is used to influence the scheduling order of jobs based on the job owner's historical resource capacity consumption. At this level, fairshare is typically treated as one scheduling factor among many and administrators can assign weights to configure the relative importance of fairsharing in systems.

For distributed computing environments such as compute grids, a model for decentralized fairshare scheduling based on distribution of hierarchical allocation policies is proposed in [7], and a prototype realization and evaluation of the model is presented in [8]. Based on this work a generalized model for *decentralized prioritization* in distributed computing is discussed in [9], and the practical integration of the fairshare system in local resource management systems is demonstrated and evaluated in [10]. This paper extends on this line of work and addresses design and evaluation of *priority operators*: mathematical functions to determine the distance between individual users' quota allocations and historical resource consumption. As priority operators lie at the heart of the model, priority operator design can have a great impact on system performance. As a consequence, the desirable properties of priority operators are studied, the challenges arising from limitations in the numerical representation of operator values are identified, and an analysis method for formal classification of operator behavior is defined.

2 Decentralized Prioritization

As illustrated in Fig. 1, the decentralized prioritization model defines a computational pipeline for calculation and application of prioritization. From a high level, the pipeline can be summarized in three steps: distribution of prioritization information (historical usage records and quota allocations), calculation of prioritization data, and domain-specific application of prioritization (e.g., fairshare prioritization of jobs in cluster scheduling).

To model organizational hierarchies, the system expresses prioritization target functions (quota allocations or intended system behavior) in tree formats, and prioritization calculation is performed using an algorithm that uses tree structures to efficiently calculate prioritization ordering for users. The tree calculation part of the algorithm is illustrated in Fig. 2, where the distance between the intended system state (target tree) and the current system state (measured tree) is calculated via node-wise application of a priority operator (in Fig. 2 subtraction). The algorithm produces a priority tree - a single data structure containing all priority information needed for prioritization.

Fig. 1. A computational pipeline for decentralized prioritization. Illustration from [9].

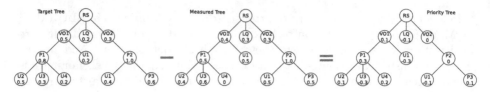

Fig. 2. A tree-based priority calculation algorithm. The user organizational hierarchy is represented in the tree structure (two virtual organizations and a local resource queue). Illustration from [9].

For application of prioritization (the last step in the pipeline), priority vectors are extracted from the priority tree and used to infer a prioritization order of the items to be prioritized. In fairshare prioritization of jobs in grid scheduling for example, the target tree contains quota information for users, the (measured) state tree contains a summation of historical usage information for users, and the resulting priority tree contains a measurement of how much of their respective quota each user has consumed. As each user is represented by a unique node in the trees, the values along the tree path from the root to the user node can be used to construct a priority vector for the user. Full details of the prioritization pipeline and computation algorithm are available in [8,9].

2.1   Challenges and Resolution Limitations

Decentralized fairshare prioritization systems are meant to serve large numbers of resource management systems in environments created from complex multilevel organizations. Access to resources is governed by policies which structure is mapped from those organization and, as a consequence, these policies have the shape of large (deep and wide) trees. After using the priority operators to create the priority tree (as seen in Fig. 2), the tree is traversed from top to bottom extracting a set of priority vectors (Fig. 3) that have independent components representing each "level" of corresponding subgroups in the tree. The vector with the highest value at the most relevant component is the one chosen. For two or more vectors with the same component value, subsequent components are used to determine priority order.

However, the dimension of the overall system is translated to the length of the vector. To simplify comparison, vectors are mapped on lexicographic strings.

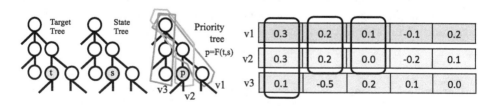

Fig. 3. Construction of priority tree and priority vectors

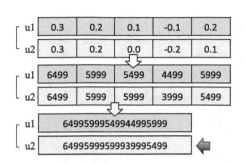 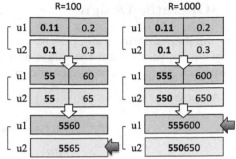

Fig. 4. Priority vector serialization, resolution r = 10000.

Fig. 5. Resolution limitation impact on the ordering process.

As seen in Fig. 4, for an example scalar resolution of 10000, each component of the vector is (using Eq. 1) mapped linearly to a scalar in the range of 0 to 9999, where -1 is translated to 0 and 1 to 9999.

$$scalar(p,r) = floor\left(\left(\frac{p+1}{2}\right) * r\right) \tag{1}$$

Then, the values are concatenated to construct the final string. In this example, by comparing the scalar with a simple numeric operation it can be determined that $u2$ has a greater priority than $u1$ (full process described in [8]). It is important to note that the full final string is needed, because any transformation of the vectors (that would not preserve the individual element order or magnitude) would reduce the system's ability to divide shares hierarchically.

Mapping the priority vectors to a scalar space with a limited domain has consequences. In particular, resolution limitations in scalar values may cause multiple priority values to be mapped to the same scalar, potentially impacting the ordering semantics of prioritization. For example, in Fig. 5 two users have different priority vectors. However, when the scalar resolution is 100, the first components of both vectors map to the same scalar, although $u1$ has a greater priority. The result is that $u2$ gets a final bigger scalar value, and thus is selected over $u1$. When the resolution is increased to 1000 the ordering becomes correct.

At the same time, it is also important to remember that it is desirable to use the smallest possible resolution. The overall size of the system, with thousands of users organized in deep trees, increases the number of comparisons and elements in each priority vector. Any small reduction in the resolution may have a significant impact on the resources needed to compute the priority vectors.

This demonstrates that the behaviors of the operators in low resolution have to be understood and modeled. The second part of this work investigates the impact of representation resolution on operator performance and the trade-offs between operator resolution and other characteristics of the system.

3   Operator Design

For fairshare prioritization, priority operators are defined as functions operating only on the values from the target and state tree that correspond to the same position in the tree. These operators must comply with the following:

1. An operator is a function with two input variables such that

$$t \in [0,1], s \in [0,1] \Rightarrow F(t,s) \in [-1,1] \tag{2}$$

$$\begin{aligned}
F(t,s) = 0 &\iff t = s \\
F(t,s) > 0 &\iff t > s \\
F(t,s) < 0 &\iff t < s
\end{aligned} \tag{3}$$

where t represents a target value, s a (normalized) state value and $t = s$ is the ideal balance axis transecting the operator value space.

2. The function is strictly increasing on target and strictly decreasing on state:

$$\begin{aligned}
\forall t_j, t_i, s_j, s_i, t, s &\in (0,1], \\
F(t_j, u) > F(t_i, u) &\iff t_j > t_i \\
F(t_j, s_i) > F(t_j, s_j) &\iff s_j < s_i \\
F(t_j, s) = F(t_i, s) &\iff t_j = t_i \\
F(t, s_i) = F(t, s_j) &\iff s_j = s_i
\end{aligned} \tag{4}$$

3. Operator functions are idempotent and deterministic.

3.1   Operator Characteristics

Desirable operator characteristics are dependent on application scenarios.

In the context of ordering prioritization (ranking) problems it is considered desirable for operators to:

1. Have well-defined boundary behaviors:

$$\begin{aligned}
\forall s \in (0,1], t = 0 &\implies F(t,s) = -1 \\
\forall t \in (0,1], s = 0 &\implies F(t,s) = 1
\end{aligned} \tag{5}$$

so users with target 0 always gets the lowest possible priority (-1) and users with some target but state 0 gets the highest possible priority (1).

2. Operate in subgroup isolation: priority operator values should depend only on the target and state values of subgroup member nodes.

3. Bring the system to redistribute unused resource capacity among users in the same subgroup proportional to their allocations.

4. Be computationally efficient and have minimal memory footprints.

5. Abide by the principle of equivalence: Two operators are equivalent if they produce the same priority ordering. Equivalent operators share the same priority ordering characteristics.

3.2 Operators

This section presents generalizations of the operators already used in fairshare prioritization, a set of new contributions (Sigmoid operators), as well as an adaptation of an operator from the open source cluster scheduler SLURM.

1. Absolute: Expresses the absolute difference between target and state.

$$d_{Absolute} = t - s \tag{6}$$

2. Relative: Expresses what proportion of the user's allocation is available.

$$d_{Relative} = \begin{cases} \dfrac{t - s}{t} & s < t \\ 0 & s = t \\ -\dfrac{s - t}{s} & s > t \end{cases} \tag{7}$$

3. Relative exponential: Increases the effects of the Relative.

$$d_{Relative-n} = \begin{cases} \left(\dfrac{t - s}{t}\right)^n & s < t \\ 0 & s = t \\ -\left(\dfrac{s - t}{s}\right)^n & s > t \end{cases} \tag{8}$$

4. Sigmoid: Designed to understand the output resolution problem.

$$d_{Sigmoid} = \begin{cases} \sin\left(\dfrac{\pi}{2}\dfrac{t - s}{t}\right) & s < t \\ 0 & s = t \\ -\sin\left(\dfrac{\pi}{2}\dfrac{s - t}{s}\right) & s > t \end{cases} \tag{9}$$

5. Sigmoid Exponential: Increases the effects of the Sigmoid.

$$d_{Sigmoid-n} = \begin{cases} \sqrt[n]{\sin\left(\dfrac{\pi}{2}\dfrac{t - s}{t}\right)} & s < t \\ 0 & s = t \\ -\sqrt[n]{\sin\left(\dfrac{\pi}{2}\dfrac{s - t}{s}\right)} & s > t \end{cases} \tag{10}$$

6. Combined: Controlled aggregation of the Absolute and Relative operators.

$$d_{Combined} = k \cdot d_{Absolute} + (1 - k)d_{Relative-2} \; \forall k \in [0, 1] \tag{11}$$

7. SLURM: The operator used by the SLURM scheduling system [11].

$$d_{SLURMOriginal} = 2^{\left(\frac{-s}{t}\right)} \tag{12}$$

Modified to the operator output value range $[-1, 1]$

$$d_{SLURM} = 2^{\left(1 + \frac{-s}{t}\right)} - 1 \tag{13}$$

4 Operator Evaluation

Each operator is investigated for each desirable operator characteristic.

4.1 Operator Definition

The first evaluation covers the second point of the definition. For each operator the sign of the first derivative when $t \neq s$ is observed. For all operators F:

$$\forall s, t \in [0,1] \wedge t \neq s :$$
$$\frac{d(F(t,s))}{d(p)} > 0, \frac{d(F(t,s))}{d(s)} < 0 \tag{14}$$

assuring the compliance of this part of the definition. Then, as all $F(t,s)$ are strictly increasing on t and strictly decreasing on s, by studying the upper and lower bounds of the input space, the compliance for the output value space can be assured:

$$F(1,0) \leq 1, F(0,0) = 0, F(0,1) \geq -1$$
$$t, s \in [0,1] \wedge t = s \Leftrightarrow F(t,s) = 0 \tag{15}$$

4.2 Boundary Behavior

Table 1 presents the priority values in the boundary cases for each operator:

Table 1. Boundary behavior for each operator

Operator	$t = 0$	$s = 0$
Absolute	$-s$	t
Relative	-1	1
Relative-2	-1	1
Combined	$-0.5 - \frac{s}{2}$	$0.5 + \frac{t}{2}$
Sigmoid	-1	1
Sigmoid-2	-1	1
SLURM	-1	1

The Absolute and Combined operator fail to comply with this property. For the Absolute, the maximum and minimum possible priority are limited in each case by the target value. The Combined operator inherits this behavior from the Absolute component of the operator.

4.3   Subgroup Isolation

This property is assured by the definition of the operators: They take into account only the state and target of the corresponding nodes, which are related to the values of the nodes in the same subgroup. The first represents what share of the usage of this subgroup corresponds to this node and the latter what share of the usage should correspond to it. No data outside of the subgroup is used to calculate these values.

4.4   Proportional Distribution of Unused Share

The situation in which a subset of users in a subgroup are not submitting jobs can be understood as an scenario with a new set of target values (virtual target): Eliminating the non-submitting users and recalculating the target of the submitting users (dividing the non-used share among them in proportion to their original targets). If the system would operate with only the virtual target as the input for the operator, it would converge to that new target. If an operator produces the same ordering with the virtual target (all users submitting jobs) and the old target (but with some users not submitting jobs), then it can be stated that the operator brings the system to the virtual target (even if the input is the old target), spreading the unused share proportionally to the user's targets. By defining $\mathbb{T} = \{$set of indexes of the users submitting jobs$\}$, the condition to be complied with by the operator can be expressed as:

$$i, j \in \mathbb{T} : t'_i = \frac{t_i}{\sum_{i \in \mathbb{T}} t_i}, \sum_{i \in \mathbb{T}} t_i \leq 1, t'_i \geq t_i$$

$$\forall t'_i, t'_j, s_i, s_j \in [0, 1] : \qquad (16)$$

1. $F(t'_j, s_j) > F(t'_i, s_i) \Rightarrow F(t_j, s_j) > F(t_i, s_i)$
2. $F(t'_j, s_j) = F(t'_i, s_i) \Rightarrow F(t_j, s_j) = F(t_i, s_i)$

where t_i is the target of user i, s_i is the normalized state of user i and t'_i is the virtual target of user i after adding the proportional part of the unused share. This reasoning is fully developed in [12] where it is proved that the Relative operator complies with this property and that any operator which would produce the same ordering would also comply with this property.

As seen in the following section, the Relative-2, Sigmoid, Sigmoid-2 and SLURM operators are equivalent to the Relative, so they also distribute unused shares among the active users of the same subgroup proportionally.

4.5   Computational Efficiency

Looking into the formulation of the operators it is obvious that the ones including power, root, or trigonometric operations have higher computational complexity, but all of them have similar memory requirements. Still, the real performance of this operators largely depends on the final implementation. As a consequence, this matter is left for the evaluation of implemented systems.

4.6   Equivalence

A theorem is formulated in [13] that allows to state that two operator are equivalent under one condition: if two operators F, F' have the same $G(F, t_j, s_j, t_i) = s_i$ so $F(t_j, s_j) = F(t_i, s_i)$, then, they are equivalent and thus, produce the same ordering. It is observed that G for the Relative operator is:

$$G(F, t_j, s_j, t_i) = s_j \frac{t_i}{t_j} \qquad (17)$$

As the operators are analyzed, it can be stated that the Relative, Relative exponential, Sigmoid, Sigmoid exponential, and SLURM operators share the same G and thus are equivalent (sharing the same ordering characteristics: proportional distribution of unused shares among active subgroup members). The Absolute and Combined operators have a different G and thus, they are not equivalent.

5   Limitations in Output Resolution

In the problem definition, resolution r will represent the number of possible scalar priority values. Also, under a certain resolution, each priority value p has a resulting effective priority value $S(p, r)$, understood as the minimum priority value that has the same corresponding scalar as p. By applying the scalar formula from Fig. 4 and composing it with its own inverse function, this effective priority value can be calculated as:

$$S(p, r) = \frac{scalar(p, r)}{r} * 2 - 1 \qquad (18)$$

5.1   Methodology

The output resolution problem is studied in three steps for each operator. The first step presents a coarse grained study of how all the possible input pairs (t, s) are divided into sets which elements map on the same priority value. It could be argued that, for an operator, the bigger the set corresponding to a priory value p, the smaller resolving power (capacity to distinguish between two users) around p and vice versa. This is referred as the input density study.

The second step is a fine grained extension of the previous one. As it is presented in the following sections, the input density analysis hides some details in the operator behavior. To avoid this, each target value is studied, analyzing the sizes of the sets of state values that map on the same output priority value. For a given operator, priority p and target t, the bigger the set of state values corresponding to that p under t, the smaller resolving power and vice versa. This is denominated the input local density study.

Finally, the input local density study is brought to a semi-real scenario: A grid scenario with a time window, resource dimension, and an average job size estimated from production systems. The final target is to calculate the minimum output resolution required for a job to be significant for a certain user to make sure that its corresponding priority value changes. This study is based on the previous step, as the input local density of a priority, target values can be understood as the minimum amount of normalized state that has to be added to the history of a user to assure that its corresponding priority value changes. This is denominated the jobs size analysis.

In all cases the study is focused on certain output ranges that are significant to the system: around balance, where the state value of the user is close to its target; under-target, when the state is far under the target; and over-target, when the state is far over the target.

5.2 Input Density Analysis

Calculation Method. This analysis requires to calculate the relationship between the input values corresponding to an effective priority value and the complete input range. The method uses polygon surface calculation formulas when possible and relies on surface size sampling when not. Figure 6 presents the effect of the discretization on the output of the Absolute operator: for each priority value p there is one horizontal surface related to the set of (t, s) that produces that effective priority value. The area of each surface represents the relative size of that set, as a consequence, what is investigated: the input density corresponding to p. When the geometrics of the surface are not simple enough, sampling is used to study the range of input values corresponding the same priority value.

Input Density Results. Experiments are run for resolution values between 8 and 1048576 to generate all the input density maps. In order to ease the results analysis, the discussions will focus on the bits needed to represent a

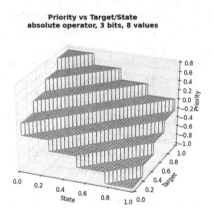

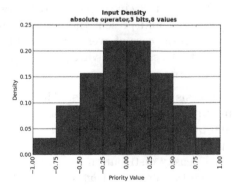

Fig. 6. 3D Representation of effective priorities for the Absolute operator, output resolution 3 bits.

Fig. 7. Input density, Absolute operator, 3 bits, 8 values.

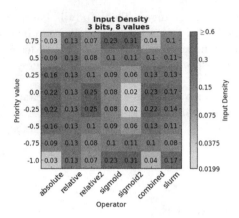

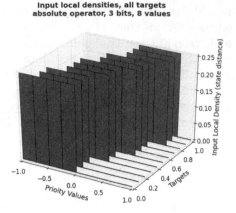

Fig. 8. Input density comparison among all operators, 3 bits, 8 values.

Fig. 9. Aggregation of the input density analysis for different target values, Absolute operator. Resolutions 3 bits.

given resolution, in this case from 3 to 20 bits. Also, as resolution is increased, the differences between the priority values become less significant. However, for the lower resolutions the operators kept a similar relationship in the same priority value areas. 3 bits (8 values) is chosen to present the results as it is clear enough to show the effects of low resolution on each operator.

The results for each individual operators are represented in the format shown in Fig. 7. The data of all operators is presented in the heat map on Fig. 8. Several things can be observed in this graph. There is a symmetric behavior around balance for most of the operators (except for the Combined and SLURM). Also, the Relative operator presents the same input density for all its priority values. The Sigmoid-2 presents the lowest density around balance while the highest around the over/under-target cases. The Absolute operator is the one presenting the lowest density in the over/under-target cases. This implies that the Sigmoid-2 operator should present the highest resolving power around balance while the lowest in the case of over usage and under usage. In the case of the Relative, it presents the same resolving power along the whole output spectrum.

Analysis Considerations. The input density analysis gives a coarse grained picture of the resolution characterization, it presents how the whole input is mapped to the output. However, it fails to demonstrate the particularities of the operators. As described in the next section, the operators present different input local density distribution for different target values. As the density of a priority value is the normalized aggregation of the local input densities in the whole target ranges. Higher values are combined with lower ones, averaging the final result, even more significant as the operators are not covering the full output range for all the target values. Let us illustrate this with an example: the Absolute operator. According to the results in this section, it presents a high resolving power around the over/under-target areas and low around balance. However, let us look into what happens for each target value (results derived from next section), Fig. 9 presents the aggregation of input local densities for 11 different targets between 0.0 and 1.0. The first observation is that, as expected, not all targets can generate the full priority range. However, what is more important is that, the resolving power is the same in all cases. This result seems contradictory to the one observed in Fig. 7. This apparent divergence comes from the fact that the input density is the aggregation of the input local density along the target range, hiding the local behavior, best cases scenarios and worst case scenarios. It can be concluded that the input density view gives an overall picture of the operator behavior but it is incomplete without the per-target input local density study.

5.3   Input Local Density Analysis

Calculation Methods. An inverse method is used to calculate the input local density of an operator. The lowest and highest state values which produce the effective priority p for target t are computed for an operator F, a priority p, target t and resolution r. The local density is the difference between them. This can be expressed as:

$$D(F, p, t, r) = |s_j - s_i| : S(p, r) = p \quad \wedge$$
$$(\forall s_i \leq s \leq s_j, F(t, s) = p) \quad \wedge \qquad (19)$$
$$(\forall s < s_i \wedge s_j < s, F(t, s) \neq p)$$

The inverse expression of the operators on the input s and the set of possible effective priority values for resolution r, $\mathbb{P}_r$ are used to calculate s_j and s_i. The resulting operation is:

$$D(F, p_i, t, r) = s_{i+1} - s_i = I_s(F, p_{i+1}, t) - I_s(F, p_i, t) \qquad (20)$$

where:

$$\mathbb{P}_r = \{p_i : i \in \mathbb{N}_r, p_i = -1 + (i - 1) \cdot \frac{2}{r}\} \qquad (21)$$

For example if $r = 4$ then $\mathbb{P}_4 = \{-1, -0.5, 0, 0.5\}$). The inverse function on s of operator F is:

$$I_s(F, p, t) = s : F(t, s) = p \qquad (22)$$

Input Local Density Results. Experiments for resolutions between 3 and 20 bits are run. The target value range is divided by 10 equidistant values, $[0, 0.1, ..., 0.9]$, which should be sufficient to appreciate the general trend as the functions are strictly increasing on target. This translates into 180 operator profiles to be analyzed. An example of the aggregation of all profiles (for the Absolute operator with a resolution of 3 bits) is illustrated in Fig. 9. As the resolution increases, local densities are becoming more similar for a given operator, policy, and target.

However, for lower resolutions, operators keep a similar relationship in the same priority areas. Here, the behavior of operators under low resolution using 3 bit resolutions and target values of 0.1 and 0.5 (as these represent one extreme and middle point) is illustrated.

Figure 10 shows one way to represent this data, the operator profile: an overlap between the corresponding input local density and the operator plot for the defined target value. It graphically correlates the priority value, input target, input state and input density, where lower input local densities are considered as something desirable since they indicate higher resolving power. This is the way to interpret them: The horizontal axis represents normalized state from 0.0 to 1.0 while the vertical axis is composed by a range of priority values from −1 to 1. The graph represents the overlay of different operators in different colors: The priority values and their corresponding state values in the shape of a plotted line in the corresponding color. On the vertical axis the input density is illustrated for each priority value in the shape of an horizontal bar, in the corresponding color (its unit is normalized state). It is possible to observe the different operator function shapes while comparing the different density inputs. Figure 11 shows the contraposition of the Sigmoid-2 and Relative-2: how the Sigmoid shape is designed to offer the bigger slope (and thus, smaller local density) around balance, and is more flat in the extremes.

By comparing the graphs in Figs. 10 and 11 it is observed that the range of priority values present in the graphs is smaller as the target increases. This is due to how the operator functions are built: none of them fully cover the range $[-1, 1]$. As the target value increases the most negative value possible for over-state becomes closer to 0.0 (for example, with the Absolute operator, at target $= 0.5$ and state $= 1.0$, the minimum possible priority value is -0.5). This

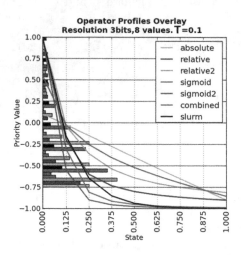

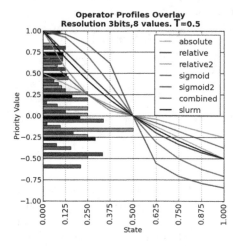

Fig. 10. Operator Profile overlay, all operators. Resolution 3 bits. target value 0.1

Fig. 11. Operator Profile overlay, all operators. Resolution 3 bits. target value 0.5

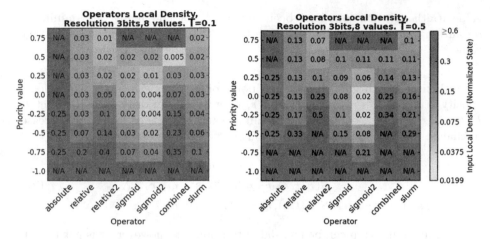

Fig. 12. Input local density heat map. **Fig. 13.** Input local density heat map.
Resolution 3 bits. target value 0.1   Resolution 3 bits. target value 0.5

has a first consequence on some of operators: as the target value increases, the same input range of $[0, 1]$ is mapped onto a smaller output range, increasing the overall input local density, increasing the average size of the bars in the graphs. One interesting point is that the Absolute operator presents a constant density in all the graphs and all the priority values, due to the subtraction-only operation that composes it.

In order to ease the density analysis the density values are mapped on a heat map which opposes the priority values and the operators. The result are Figs. 12 and 13. Darker color indicates a higher local density (and lower resolving power) for a pair or operator and target value while a lighter color implies a lower local density (and higher resolving power). As it can be observed in the graphs, it is confirmed that certain operators have a lower input local density behavior for different cases. In balance situations the Sigmoid and Sigmoid-2 presents smaller densities. In under-target situations, the Relative-2 operators present smaller densities. In situations of over-target, again the Sigmoid and Sigmoid-2 operators present lower densities, although not much lower. One immediate conclusion of this section is that the Sigmoid family presents a higher resolving power for the balance cases and over usage cases, while the Relative operator presents a higher resolving power for the under usage cases.

5.4   Job Size Analysis

In this study the analysis is brought to a semi-real environment: a grid scenario with a time window (representing the total historical usage taken into account) and a set of resources. The motivation is to understand how big a job has to be to be significant and force a change the effective priority. This is equivalent to understanding how many decisions would be made with the same priority values (although new jobs have been completed) or how many bits (minimum resolution) would be required for a certain job to affect the effective priority value.

Calculation Method. The starting point of this analysis is the input local density study. For a given resolution r, operator F, priority p, and target t, $D(F, p, t, r)$ can be seen as the minimum amount that the state has to increase to change the output effective priority. This step can be expressed as:

$$M(F, t, s, r) = m : m \in (0, 1] \qquad \wedge$$
$$S(F(t, s), r) \neq S(F(t, s + m), r) \qquad \wedge \qquad (23)$$
$$\nexists n : 0 < n < m \wedge S(F(t, s), r) \neq S(F(t, s + n), r)$$

This minimum step can be translated to a job size, however, it is not trivial: The impact of a job size on the normalized state depends on the normalized state itself, as it represents how much of the state pool corresponds to this user. One job of a certain size has a bigger impact for a user with a smaller normalized state than for one with a bigger one. The current state and the state of a user after adding the length of a job can be expressed as:

$$s_i^d = \frac{\sum_{0<j\leq d} J_i^j}{U^d}, J_i^{d+1} = k \cdot U^d$$
$$s_i^{d+1} = \frac{\sum_{0<j\leq d} J_i^j + J_i^{d+1}}{U^d + J_i^{d+1}} = \frac{\sum_{0<j\leq d} J_i^j + k \cdot U^d}{U^d + k \cdot U^d} \qquad (24)$$
$$= \frac{(1+k)(\sum_{0<j\leq d} J_i^j + k \cdot U^d)}{U^d} = (1+k)(s_i^d + k)$$

where s_i^d is the normalized state of a user i at a time d, J_i^j is the size of a job submitted by user i in the time j, U^d is all the state recorded for all users until time d and k is the proportion between the job submitted in time d and the total state recorded until d. This equation is an expression of the new state as a function of the previous state and the proportion between the job and the time window. The target is to obtain a function that calculates how big that proportion has to be to jump from one state values (s_i^d) to the next ($s_i^d + 1$). Those states are taken as the boundaries for the local density calculation and expressed as $s_i^{d+1} - s_i^d$ where s_i^{d+1} is substituted by the result in the Eq. 24:

$$D(F, p_i, t, r) = s_i^{d+1} - s_i^d = (1+k)(s_i^d + k) - s_i^d$$
$$k^2 + (1 + s_i^d)k - D(F, p_i, t, r) = 0 \qquad (25)$$

Which can be solved by using the quadratic equations solving formula:

$$k = K(F, p_i, t, r, s_i^d) = \frac{-(1 + s_i^d) + \sqrt{(1 + s_i^d)^2 + 4 \cdot D(F, p_i, t, r)}}{2} \qquad (26)$$

This finally results in the expression of k as a function of the operator, previous state, target priority value, and resolution. This is used to calculate what the minimum job size to be submitted is, in order to change one user's priority value according to its current state and target, and the corresponding operator and resolution. Knowing the job size in any case, a strategy is established for the calculations on each operator in each resolution: for each priority, among all the possible k on each target, which is the biggest one (as a bigger k means smaller job). This allows to calculate what would be the minimum job size that would assure a change in the effective priority value.

Job Size Analysis Results. Using a workload trace from the Swegrid [14], a synthetic example is created, in which the time window is 1 year and the system manages 600 resource nodes. This implies a total state pool (time window) of $U^d = 8760 \cdot 600 = 5,256,000\,\mathrm{h}$. By using that U^d and the obtained k, a corresponding average job size is calculated. A bigger job size implies a lower resolving power and a smaller job size implies a higher resolving power. For the priority value to study, the calculations are focused in 3 contexts: around balance, where the state is close to the target and the priority values are in the range $[-0.25, 0.25]$; under-target, where priority values are in the range $[0.6, 0.9]$; and over-target, where the priorities values are in the range $[-0.9, -0.6]$.

The results of the around balance study can be observed in Fig. 14. This heat map represents the worst case among the minimum job size required to make a difference in the priority value for each resolution with each operator. Bigger jobs (and thus lower resolving power) are represented with darker color while smaller jobs (and thus higher resolving power) imply a lighter color. The color range is limited at jobs size 10,000 h and a logarithmic scale is applied

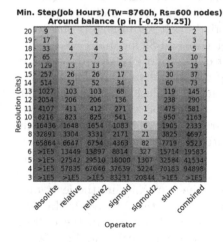

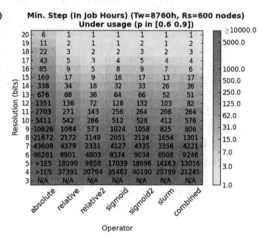

Fig. 14. Job size in hours required to alter user's priority value when state is close to target.

Fig. 15. Job size in hours required to alter user's priority value when state is under-target.

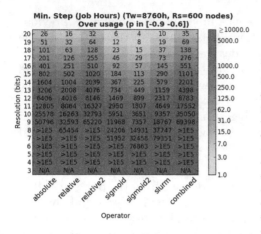

Fig. 16. Job size in hours required to alter user's priority value when state is over-target.

Table 2. Output resolution bits required for a job of 2,000 h to be significant for a Tw = 1 year and Rs = 600 nodes. Less is better.

Operator	Balance	Over t.	Under t.	Overall
Absolute	13	14	12	14
Relative	9	14	9	14
Relative-2	9	15	8	15
Sigmoid	9	12	9	12
Sigmoid-2	5	11	9	11
SLURM	9	13	8	13
Combined	10	15	8	15

for the color distribution. It is observed that the results are independent of the resolution: the Absolute operator needs bigger jobs to make a difference, while the Sigmoid-2 has enough resolving power around balance to always require a smaller job than the rest operators. If operators are ordered by job sizes from higher to lower resolving power, the following ordering is observed: Sigmoid-2, Sigmoid, SLURM, Relative, Relative-2, Combined, Absolute. This ordering does not change as resolution increases, although, as expected, the job size decreases as the resolution increases.

In the over-target scenario presented in Fig. 16 the following ordering from higher to lower resolving power in all resolutions is observed: Sigmoid-2, Sigmoid, SLURM, Relative, Absolute, Relative-2 and Combined. In the under-target scenario presented in Fig. 15 the following ordering in all resolutions is observed: Relative-2, Combined, SLURM, Sigmoid, Relative, and Sigmoid-2.

At this point it is possible to infer impact of a certain job for each operator in the studied cases. However, a way to bring this insight to a running scenario is needed. For a given job size, what is the minimum resolution in bits needed for an operator to make a difference? The chosen average job size is 2,000 h (200 h, 10 nodes). This parameter only affects to the gross value of bits obtained for each operator however, it does not change the relative relationship of the operators.

The outcome of the analysis of the results in Figs. 14, 15 and 16 is summarized in Table 2. The first result is that the Sigmoid-2 presents a clear advantage around situations of balance. The Sigmoid-2 is the one requiring the least bits in the case of balance and over-target. For under-target, the Relative-2, SLURM and Combined perform better but only with small difference. In the overall picture, the Sigmoid-2 operator is the one which requires least bits in balance and over-target while for under-target it is just one bit away from the best.

6 Prior and Related Work

The motivation for this work arose from findings in earlier efforts. In [8] and [10], the family of Relative and Combined operator are added to the Aequus fairshare scheduling system. The system's robustness and capabilities are evaluated and it is discovered that the absolute operator and relative operator generate different ordering semantics when some users do not submit jobs. Also, convergence delays appeared when using low priority value resolutions (required for large scale experiments). These findings are part of the motivation for this paper.

Fairshare priority is present as a decision factor in well known schedulers. SLURM ([10] shows how this system can substitute SLURM's fairshare engine), as the rest of schedulers, is not meant to deal with as deep hierarchies as Karma [9,11] so the output resolution of its operator is not constrained. The SLURM operator, as studied in this paper, complies with all the desired characteristics. Maui [15] presents similar characteristics but uses a version of the Relative as its operator. Other well known example is LSF used by the CERN [16], which choses the absolute operator [17]. Still, the Karma hierarchical system is prepared for much deeper tree schemas than current schedulers.

Work related to the priority resolution is found in another scheduling field in which memory is limited: real time schedulers for communication and embedded systems. During the study of the monotonic scheduling algorithm in [18], this problem is named *priority granularity*: "fewer priority levels available than there are task periods", similar to the idea of a number of users with very similar priority and limited resolution around it. In [19], a solution is proposed by creating an exponential grid to distribute the priorities increasing the resolving power around a certain desired area, very similar to the design intent of the Sigmoid operator. Finally, [20] presents how the low output resolution can affect negatively the utilization of resources, as it would alter the best possible decisions, for this case a logarithmic grid is presented. This studies are focused on the final priority value without taking into account the relationship of the input of the prioritization system and its output. In this work, the effect of the resolution limitations on the different system states (input to the priority operator) is investigated, which allows modification of system behavior towards the desired resolving power behavior.

7 Future Work

This study is a mathematical understanding of the operators in the fairshare prioritization scheduling. It allows to establish boundaries on the mathematical behavior of the functions, however, it would be desired to confront the results with the Karma [9] system: To establish a simulation environment in which all the operators are tested in a close to real situation, with different output resolutions, tree models (different target values, target tree shapes and depths) and sources of system noise (as presented in [8]). In this context it would interesting to study a possible adaptive operator: a dynamic recommendation of the best suited operator and minimum output resolution depending on the overall state of the system.

Testing the Relative and Sigmoid operator family on the SLURM scheduling system would be also worth exploring. The results presented in this work indicate that these operators may have a better resolving power than the SLURM operator, while similar general characteristics. Bringing those conclusion to SLURM, which has a different data pipeline than Karma, would bring light on the compatibility of our operators with other scheduling strategies.

In a different line of thinking, as presented in [9], the Karma prioritization engine can be used to deal with scenarios that are not strictly concerned about the ordering of elements, but also about the magnitude of the priority values produced by the system. It would be desirable to understand what is the impact of the different operator output value distribution on this magnitude aware systems.

8   Conclusions

This paper presents the role of priority operators in fairshare prioritization scheduling. It establishes a formal operator definition and a set of desired characteristics for priority operators, and reviews a set of operators (including a proposed new one) using these definitions. To evaluate the desired characteristics a set of methods and mathematical proofs are defined. They allow to test the compliance of existing and future operators. Following this method, the presented operators are evaluated to determine compliance with the desired operator characteristics. Results indicate that the Relative, Relative-n, Sigmoid, Sigmoid-n and SLURM operators all comply with all desired operator characteristics, whereas the Absolute and Combined operators do not.

In addition, the impact of limitations in output resolution on fairshare prioritization is investigated. A three-step methodology is developed to evaluate the impact on the resolving power of each operator; study of the input density, the input local density, and the significant job size; and the need to go through all three steps in order to get an overall view of the behavior of a fairshare operator is demonstrated. Using the proposed methodology, the operator set is evaluated and the Sigmoid family of operators, a contribution of this paper, is shown to present the best overall characteristics as fairshare priority operators.

Acknowledgments. The authors extend their gratitude to Daniel Espling for prior work and technical support, Cristian Klein for feedback, and Tomas Forsman for technical assistance. Financial support for the project is provided by the Swedish Government's strategic research effort eSSENCE and the Swedish Research Council (VR) under contract number C0590801 for the project Cloud Control.

References

1. Raman, R., Livny, M., Solomon, M.: Matchmaking: distributed resource management for high throughput computing. In: Proceedings of the Seventh International Symposium on High Performance Distributed Computing, pp. 140–146. IEEE (1998)

2. Foster, I., Kesselman, C.: The Grid: Blueprint for a New Computing Infrastructure. Morgan Kaufmann, San Francisco (2004)
3. Foster, I., Kesselman, C., Tuecke, S.: The anatomy of the grid: enabling scalable virtual organizations. Int. J. Supercomput. Appl. **15**(3), 200–222 (2001)
4. Kay, J., Lauder, P.: A fair share scheduler. Commun. ACM **31**(1), 44–55 (1988)
5. Yoo, A.B., Jette, M.A., Grondona, M.: SLURM: simple linux utility for resource management. In: Feitelson, D., Rudolph, L., Schwiegelshohn, U. (eds.) JSSPP 2003. LNCS, vol. 2862, pp. 44–60. Springer, Heidelberg (2003)
6. Maui Cluster Scheduler, January 2014. http://www.adaptivecomputing.com/products/open-source/maui/
7. Elmroth, E., Gardfjäll, P.: Design and evaluation of a decentralized system for Grid-wide fairshare scheduling. In: Stockinger, H., et al. (eds.) Proceedings of e-Science 2005, pp. 221–229. IEEE CS Press (2005)
8. Östberg, P-O., Espling, D., Elmroth, E.: Decentralized scalable fairshare scheduling. Future Gener. Comput. Syst. **29**(1), 130–143 (2013)
9. Östberg, P-O., Elmroth, E.: Decentralized prioritization-based management systems for distributed computing. In: 2013 IEEE 9th International Conference on eScience (eScience), pp. 228–237. IEEE (2013)
10. Espling, D., Östberg, P-O., Elmroth, E.: Integration and evaluation of decentralized fairshare prioritization (aequus). In: Proceedings of PDSEC 2014 - The 15th IEEE International Workshop on Parallel and Distributed Scientific and Engineering Computing (PDSEC 2014), pp. 1198–1207. IEEE (2014)
11. SLURM: Multifactor priority plugin - simplified fair-share formula, January 2014. https://computing.llnl.gov/linux/slurm/priority_multifactor.html
12. Rodrigo, G.P.: Proof of compliance for the relative operator on the proportional distribution of unused share in an ordering fairshare system, January 2014. http://urn.kb.se/resolve?urn=urn:nbn:se:umu:diva-89298
13. Rodrigo, G.P.: Establishing the equivalence between operators, January 2014. http://urn.kb.se/resolve?urn=urn:nbn:se:umu:diva-89297
14. Swegrid: Swegrid organization, January 2014. http://snicdocs.nsc.liu.se/wiki/SweGrid
15. Jackson, D., Snell, Q., Clement, M.: Core algorithms of the Maui scheduler. In: Feitelson, D.G., Rudolph, L. (eds.) JSSPP 2001. LNCS, vol. 2221, pp. 87–102. Springer, Heidelberg (2001)
16. CERN: It services - batch service, January 2014. http://information-technology.web.cern.ch/services/batch
17. LSF: Fairshare scheduling, January 2014. http://www.ccs.miami.edu/hpc/lsf/7.0.6/admin/fairshare.html
18. Lehoczky, J., Sha, L., Ding, Y.: The rate monotonic scheduling algorithm: exact characterization and average case behavior. In: Proceedings of the Real Time Systems Symposium, pp. 166–171. IEEE (1989)
19. Sha, L., Lehoczky, J.P., Rajkumar, R.: Task scheduling in distributed real-time systems. In: Robotics and IECON 1987 Conferences, International Society for Optics and Photonics, pp. 909–917 (1987)
20. Lehoczky, J.P., Sha, L.: Performance of real-time bus scheduling algorithms. ACM SIGMETRICS Perform. Eval. Rev. **14**(1), 44–53 (1986)

User-Aware Metrics for Measuring Quality of Parallel Job Schedules

Šimon Tóth and Dalibor Klusáček$^{(\boxtimes)}$

Faculty of Informatics, Masaryk University, Brno, Czech Republic
{toth,xklusac}@fi.muni.cz

Abstract. The work presented in this paper is motivated by the challenges in the design of scheduling algorithms for the Czech National Grid MetaCentrum. One of the most notable problems is our inability to efficiently analyze the quality of schedules. While it is still possible to observe and measure certain aspects of generated schedules using various metrics, it is very challenging to choose a set of metrics that would be representative when measuring the schedule quality. Without quality quantification (either relative, or absolute), we have no way to determine the impact of new algorithms and configurations on the schedule quality, prior to their deployment in a production service. The only two options we are left with is to either use expert assessment or to simply deploy new solutions into production and observe their impact on user satisfaction. To approach this problem, we have designed a novel user-aware model and a metric that can overcome the presented issues by evaluating the quality on a user level. The model assigns an expected end time (*EET*) to each job based on a fair partitioning of the system resources, modeling users expectations. Using this calculated *EET* we can then compare generated schedules in detail, while also being able to adequately visualize schedule artifacts, allowing an expert to further analyze them. Moreover, we present how coupling this model with a job scheduling simulator gives us the ability to do an in-depth evaluation of scheduling algorithms before they are deployed into a production environment.

Keywords: Grid · Performance evaluation · Metrics · Queue-based scheduling · Fairness · User-aware scheduling

1 Introduction

The Czech National Grid MetaCentrum is a highly heterogeneous environment currently composed of 26 clusters with heavily varying configurations (GPU clusters, RAM heavy clusters, machines with large SSD disks, clusters with infiniband, high speed NFS access, etc.). MetaCentrum currently contains over 10000 CPU cores, servicing 800 concurrently running jobs on average.

The heterogeneous character of the system is mirrored in its users base. User requirements range from instantaneous access requests, through large job

© Springer International Publishing Switzerland 2015
W. Cirne and N. Desai (Eds.): JSSPP 2014, LNCS 8828, pp. 90–107, 2015.
DOI: 10.1007/978-3-319-15789-4_6

submissions (thousands of jobs in a single batch), long workflows (large batches of jobs that need to be run in sequence) to extremely unbalanced requests (single CPU core, 1TB of memory). To deal with these various challenges present in this environment we are employing a multitude of software/middleware solutions. These range from our virtualized infrastructure [22] to a locally maintained fork of the Torque [2] batch system coupled with a custom scheduler [26].

Specifically for testing the impact of various changes in the scheduler employed in the MetaCentrum we are using an advanced job scheduling simulator *Alea* [14]. Unfortunately, it is rather hard to correctly evaluate schedules generated by the simulator. This mainly stems from the dichotomy of the simulated workloads. Workloads that can be evaluated using human experts are too simple to be applicable for the production environment and real workloads are to complex to be evaluated in any manner beyond easily understood performance metrics. Similar problem occurs when evaluating job traces recorded in Meta-Centrum, as these are usually extremely complex.

We have found that commonly used performance metrics and optimization criteria like average response time, wait time or slowdown [8] do not really reflect what we actually need to optimize. Although these metrics are widely used in the literature, their use is rather questionable. For example, the use of mean values to measure (highly) skewed distributions is a problem in itself [18]. Even though we are capable of complex analysis based on user-agnostic metrics [17,18], this analysis still does not provide satisfactory results. User-agnostic metrics do not consider whether different users are treated in a fair fashion by the system, which is a very important part of MetaCentrum scheduling algorithm.

In this work we propose a new user-aware metric that allows us to measure the suitability of applied scheduling algorithms. In a natural fashion, it models user expectations concerning system performance using individually computed expected end times (EET). We demonstrate the gain of this solution over evaluation using classical and widely used metrics [8], using both synthetic examples as well as experimental evaluation where real workload and the simulator are used. It demonstrates that our solution provides truly detailed insight into the behavior of the scheduling algorithm, highlighting how suitable, i.e., efficient and fair, are various algorithms with respect to specific users demands.

2   Schedule Evaluation

It must be said that there is no general agreement about measuring schedule quality. This is understandable as the proper measure is inherently heavily environment dependent. The most common approach when determining the quality of a schedule is to use a combination of various metrics. There are several well established groups of metrics. Firstly, we have user-agnostic metrics. These can be either related to a system itself (machine usage, power consumption, etc.) or related to jobs in a system (slowdown, response time, wait time, etc.). Secondly, we have user-aware metrics, mostly represented by some form of fairness-related metric. We will now closely discuss several categories of metrics that are used to evaluate the suitability of scheduling algorithms.

2.1 User-Agnostic Metrics

Typical and widely used metrics are those that do not consider users of the system. Among them, the most popular are the *average response time, average wait time* or the *average slowdown.* Average response time measures the mean time from job submission to its termination. The average wait time is the mean time that jobs spend waiting before their execution starts. The slowdown is the ratio of an actual response time of a job to a response time if executed without any waiting. While the response time only focuses on a time when a job terminates, the slowdown measures the responsiveness of the system with respect to a job length, i.e., jobs are completed within the time proportional to jobs demands [8]. Wait time supplies the slowdown and the response time. Short wait times prevent the users from feeling that the scheduler "ignores" their jobs.

Although widely used, these job-related metrics are based on several assumptions that no longer hold in heterogeneous, grid-like environments, as we explain in the following text.

Problems with Job Priority. One of the main assumptions of standard job-related metrics is that a shorter job should receive higher priority in the system (see, e.g., the slowdown or the response time). Shorter jobs are easier to schedule and users with more complex (longer) requests are therefore required to expect longer wait times.

This assumption is problematic on several levels. Firstly, as long as we are measuring the total job penalty or the average value (e.g., total/average slowdown/response time) this "shortest job first" priority advantage will remain absolute. This can very easily lead to huge starvation of (few) long jobs[1]. The grid is indeed a dynamic system and the number of jobs submitted by a single user is, to a certain degree, proportional to the number of jobs successfully processed. Given the total job length dispersion (from several minutes to a month) [5,20], users with extremely long jobs would hardly ever get their requests satisfied.

Secondly, the correlation between the absolute job length and the job urgency is little to none. Again, due to the large dispersion of job lengths, the notion of a "short job" has very different meaning to different users. The increased benevolence toward wait times for long jobs is simply due to the increased absolute users runtime estimation error (10 % imprecision on a month long job equates to 3 days).

Problems with Resource Requirements. Similar issues occur when dealing with different job resource requirements. If one can split a large CPU demanding job into a set of smaller jobs, these will obtain higher priority. This problem was previously addressed by normalizing the selected metric using the number of CPU cores a job is requesting [7,13], as a weight.

---

[1] Production systems (including MetaCentrum) usually employ a certain type of anti-starvation technique. Since this approach goes directly against the order suggested by the job-related metric, it naturally leads to skewed results.

Unfortunately, nearly no metric is designed to reflect combined consumption of multiple resources [15] such as CPUs, RAM, GPUs, HDD, etc. When multiple resources are concerned, further measures need to be employed, like dominant resource [10] or processor equivalent [12] to properly reflect other than CPU-related job requirements.

Why Users Matter. Last but not least, we now demonstrate the major problem which causes that user-agnostic metrics are impractical in real systems.

Let us consider an example of a schedule optimized according to average wait time (see Fig. 1a). In this schedule we have two users (bright-orange and dark-blue) and the optimization criterion favors the jobs of the blue user due to their shorter length[2]. The total penalty for this schedule according to average wait time would be $\frac{0+0+1+1+2+2}{6} = 1$. Unfortunately, the orange user will clearly not consider this schedule optimal. He or she is requesting the same amount of resources as the blue user, but has to wait until all jobs of the blue user are processed.

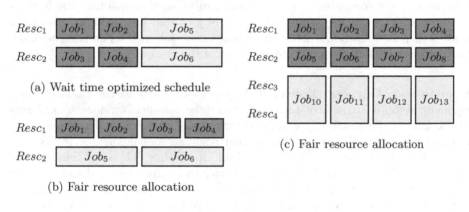

(a) Wait time optimized schedule

(b) Fair resource allocation

(c) Fair resource allocation

Fig. 1. Examples of optimal schedules

Let us consider a different schedule, this time using fair resource allocation among the blue and the orange user (see Fig. 1b). In this case both users receive one resource exclusively for their jobs and both users receive the complete results of their jobs at the same time. The total penalty for this schedule according to average wait time would be $\frac{0+1+2+3+0+2}{6} = \frac{4}{3}$, which is more than in the previous example. Indeed, we would get similar results for both response time and slowdown.

An analogous problem occurs when we simulate similar situation where, instead of job runtimes, overall resource requirements are considered (see Fig. 1c). Again the presented fair resource allocation among the blue and the orange user is not considered optimal according to user-agnostic metrics.

---

[2] $Resc_1$ and $Resc_2$ represent resources, e.g., CPU cores.

2.2 User-Aware Metrics

User-aware metrics aim at maximizing "benefits" regarding the users of the system. Very often, the metric applied for such goal is related to fairness. In production environments, some type of fairness guaranteeing process/metric is usually provided. These measures are highly dependent on the system itself and range from simple measures that try to maintain the order in which the requests entered the system [23] to much more complicated measures concerned with the combined consumption of various resources [10].

Job-to-job Fairness. Fairness is often understood and represented as a *job-related* metric, meaning that every job should be served in a fair fashion with respect to other jobs [19,23,24]. For example, a *fair start time* (*FST*) metric [19,23] measures the influence of later arriving jobs on the execution start time of currently waiting jobs. *FST* is calculated for each job, by creating a schedule assuming no later jobs arrive. The resulting "unfairness" is the difference between *FST* and the actual start time. Similar metric is so called *fair slowdown* [24]. The fair slowdown is computed using *FST* and can be used to quantify the fairness of a scheduler by looking at the percentage of jobs that have a higher slowdown than is their fair slowdown [24]. Sadly, these job-to-job metrics do not guarantee fair behavior with respect to different users of the system.

User-to-user Fairness. Instead of the job-to-job fairness, the resource management systems frequently prefer to guarantee fair performance to *different users*. One of the commonly employed techniques is *fairshare*. Fairshare-based fairness is supported in many production resource management systems such as in PBS [21], TORQUE [2], Moab, Maui [1], Quincy [11] or in Hadoop Fair and Capacity Schedulers [3,4]. Fairshare tries to balance the mid-to-long term resource usage among *users* of the system[3]. More precisely, if a user A and a user B have identical priorities, they will receive the same amount of resources, when averaged over a reasonably long time period [12]. This is of course only true when both user A and user B actually request these resources.

Fairshare can also be expressed using the following equation:

$$\forall u; \lim_{time \to \infty} Usage(u) = AvailableResources \cdot time \cdot DesignatedFraction(u)$$

Simply put, if we take a large enough time period, the total used resources by one user ($Usage(u)$) will equate to the amount of resources designated for this user. Or formulated in a different manner, the amount of used resources will converge toward the amount designated by a user priority.

While the methods applied in production fairshare algorithms are well documented [12], there is — surprisingly — no common agreement about how to actually measure, i.e., evaluate, analyze or even compare, the level of (un)fairness for such user-to-user approaches. Authors that need to employ such methods

---

[3] Depending on the implementation, fairshare can also prevent usage spikes.

usually rely on measuring the variability (using, e.g., the standard deviation) of user-agnostic metrics [27].

Therefore, in the following text we propose a novel user-aware model and a metric that can overcome previous issues by evaluating the schedule quality on a user level. In a natural fashion, the model represents user expectations concerning system performance, using individually computed *EET*s and allows us to compare quality of different schedules in a reasonably detailed manner.

3 Proposed User-Aware Model

As we discussed in the previous section, commonly used metrics may provide misleading results. Moreover, production-based anti-starvation and fairshare mechanisms can further delay executions of certain jobs, thus confusing those metrics even more. Therefore, we can no longer rely on these metrics when evaluating the quality of generated schedules.

This situation leads us to the formulation of a new user-aware model that can be used instead. The model is designed with several important features in mind: the model needs to be simple enough, so that its output remains easy to analyze; the model needs to provide information-rich output; the model needs to be robust enough to ignore irrelevant differences, e.g., in particular job resource specifications (see next Sect. 3.1).

3.1 The Model of User Expectations

Our model tries to capture the expectations of users concerning the target system and then it evaluates the quality of a given schedule by determining how well were these expectations satisfied.

User Expectations on Job Wait Times. As we have observed during the past years in MetaCentrum, there are some common expectations of the users toward the (expected) behavior of the scheduling system. User expectations toward job wait time mainly correlate with the complexity of the job requirements and the number of jobs present in the batch. The more resources a job requires, the more tolerant a user tends to be toward its wait time. Similar correlation exists when considering a set of jobs as a group, the expected response time (of the whole group) correlates with the total amount of required resources. On the other hand, users exhibit very little tolerance in situations when their jobs are waiting, while jobs of other users with similar requirements are starting regularly.

In order to follow these expectations, we have decided to model each user separately, independent of other users in the system. Our model is also built to disregard insignificant differences, e.g., in the specification of resource requirements. For example, if 4 simultaneously submitted jobs require 1 CPU and 4 GB RAM each, then we consider this to be equal to 1 job that requires 4 CPUs and 16 GB of RAM.

User Expectations on Available Capacity. According to our experience, user expectations toward the capacity the system can provide for a single user tend to be rather reasonable. Users understand that they cannot allocate the entire system for themselves. Therefore, we are matching the capacity expectation by giving each user a virtual share of the system, following the idea of the well known fairshare principle [12].

As we have already mentioned, our model has been designed in order to match user expectations. Similarly, the proposed metric is designed to determine whether these expectations were fulfilled in the provided schedule. Let us now closely describe the proposed expected end time (*EET*) metric.

3.2   Proposed *EET*-based Metric

The proposed *EET*-based metric works in a simple but robust fashion. Simply put, specific *EET* expressing user expectations is calculated for every arriving job and then it is checked against the provided schedule[4] analyzing which of the calculated *EET*s are satisfied and which are violated.

Simply put, *EET* for a particular job is calculated by assigning the job to a given resource of predefined capacity. This capacity represents the share of real resources a user is expecting to receive from the system (at any time). We can assign different capacity of this resource to different users, thus modeling more or less demanding users (users with different priorities). User's jobs are then inserted into the available capacity in a "tetris-like" fashion. It means that we need to rearrange jobs that do not fit into the remaining capacity of this resource, essentially treating them as moldable/malleable [9]. Just like moldable jobs, a runtime of a job is proportionally increased if the amount of available resources is smaller than requested by that job. On the other hand, unlike moldable jobs, a job cannot allocate more resources than it requires, i.e., its runtime cannot be decreased by using more resources. This approach has been adopted based on our experiences concerning users expectations, as were discussed in Sect. 3.1. However, such transformations are only done for the purposes of the *EET* calculation and the job scheduling algorithms we are considering in this paper only work with non-moldable jobs that have constant resource usage.

Algorithm for *EET* Calculation. The computation of *EET* is described in Algorithm 1 and works as follows. Based on the expectations we mentioned in Sect. 3.1, each user is assigned a resource with a predefined capacity, that he or she expects to have access to (Line 1). Each job is then allowed to consume this resource starting from its arrival time. Available share is being allocated in blocks, where 1 block has duration ("length") of 1 time unit and size ("height") equal to 1 resource unit. In this paper, 1 block equals to 1 s × 1 CPU. Of course, a job may require more resources per time unit than is available. In such situation, a job is rearranged to fit within available blocks in that share.

---

[4] By default, we assume that this provided schedule is a historic schedule as found in a workload trace. If needed, it can be extended for a use within "live" scheduler.

Simply put, such job is then "longer" and "narrower". On the other hand, if the available share is larger than the resources requested per time unit ($RescReq_j$), we do not rearrange such job. Simply put, jobs that are "long" and "narrow" cannot become "shorter" and "higher", since they are still limited by the amount of resources requested ($RescReq_j$) in each time unit.

Algorithm 1. Calculation of EET for a given user

1: **for** $time = 0$ **to** $SheduleEnd$ **do**
2:     $capacity_{time} = ExpectedCapacity$
3: **end for**
4: $sort\_arrival(jobs)$
5: **for** $j = 0$ **to** $JobCount$ **do**
6:     $jobCapacity = rescReq_j \cdot runtime_j$
7:     $time = arrival_j$
8:     **while** $jobCapacity > 0$ **do**
9:         $consumedCapacity = \min(capacity_{time}, rescReq_j)$
10:        $capacity_{time} = capacity_{time} - consumedCapacity$
11:        $jobCapacity = jobCapacity - consumedCapacity$
12:        $time = time + 1$
13:    **end while**
14:    $EET_j = time$
15: **end for**

The presented Algorithm 1 will calculate the EET for a single resource type (e.g., CPU cores requested), but extending this algorithm for multiple resources (e.g., Memory, GPU cards, ...) is relatively straightforward. After calculating an EET for each resource separately, we then select the latest/maximum EET, thus the final EET is dictated by the scarcest and/or most utilized resource.

Processing one job after another in order of arrival (Line 1), each job is represented by the product ($jobCapacity$) of its resource requirements ($rescReq_j$) over time ($runtime_j$). In a loop, we determine the capacity that will be consumed ($consumedCapacity$) in the user share at a given $time$ by the job j (Line 1). The capacity of user share could be already (partially) consumed by previously added jobs, therefore the $consumedCapacity$ at given $time$ is either the remaining share capacity at that $time$ ($capacity_{time}$) or the $rescReq_j$ (when a job requests less resources than is the current $capacity_{time}$). Next, we allocate this $consumedCapacity$ and update both the remaining $capacity_{time}$ (Line 1) and the remaining $jobCapacity$, i.e., the "job remainder" that remains unallocated (Line 1). Finally we increase the $time$ (Line 1) and proceed to next iteration. Once the whole job is allocated ($jobCapacity \leq 0$), the inner while loop ends and the job EET_j is equal to the $time$.

As designed, the EET-based Metric is used in a "post mortem" fashion, meaning that it is used offline using historic workload trace as an input. Therefore, an exact $runtime_j$ is known for every job. If properly modified, it can also be used online, e.g., inside a job scheduling heuristic. So far, we have not use it in such a way, and we only use it for offline analysis of various scheduling algorithms.

Example of *EET* Calculation. For simplicity, let us consider a user having two jobs with parameters specified in Table 1. We have decided to grant this user share $ExpectedCapacity = 3$. The first job of this user only requires two units. Since no units were consumed yet and $ExpectedCapacity > rescReq$ the EET will trivially correspond to job runtime. The second job will arrive at $time = 1$. There is only one unit of share remaining from $time = 0$ to $time = 4$ and the job requires two units of share. The job will therefore consume one unit of share at time $time = 1$ and the second unit of share at $time = 2$, ending up with $EET = 3$. This process is illustrated in Fig. 2.

Table 1. Calculated EET for a user with two jobs and $ExpectedUserCapacity=3$.

	arrival	rescReq	runtime	EET
Job_1	0	2	4	4
Job_2	1	2	1	3

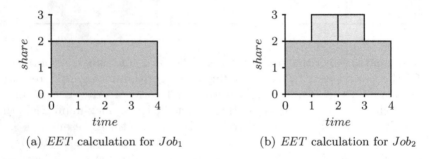

(a) *EET* calculation for Job_1 (b) *EET* calculation for Job_2

Fig. 2. Visualization of EET calculation

For two such users, presented in the example, we can construct an optimal schedule with no broken EETs using a system with $capacity = 6$ (see Fig. 3). This example also demonstrates the fundamental difference between performance metrics and our model. Using performance metrics, Job_4 would receive penalty according to most metrics, since it was delayed by one time unit. Our model makes such distinction irrelevant by only considering the violated EETs.

3.3   Application of the Proposed Model

Critical part of the model is of course our ability to extract important information out of it. This is directly related to the robustness and simplicity of the model, which allows us to draw direct links between the generated schedule and the output of the model.

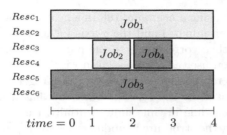

Fig. 3. Optimal schedule (all *EET*s satisfied) for two identical users that both have those two jobs from Table 1.

Violated *EET* and Tardiness. First layer of information output is related directly to the violated *EET*s. We can measure how many *EET*s were violated, as well as to what extent. For a crude comparison, we measure the number of violated *EET*s (*violatedEET$_u$*) for each user u, and transform it to percentage of jobs that did not meet their *EET*s (*VEET$_u$*) as shown in Formula 1.

$$VEET_u = \frac{violatedEET_u}{jobCount_u} \cdot 100\,\% \tag{1}$$

Using a statistical box-plot, we can then examine the distribution of this value across all users and visually compare the results across multiple algorithms. An example of such a comparison is presented in Fig. 6a.

If we want to examine how significantly were those *EET*s violated we use a simple metric based on tardiness. First, we compute job tardiness using Formula 2, where C_j is the actual completion time of a job and EET_j is the expected end time of job j. Next, we compute the total weighted tardiness for a given user (WT_u) using Formula 3. Here, J_u is the set of jobs belonging to that user u and w_j is the number of CPUs used by a job j, representing the "weight" of that job.

$$T_j = \max(0,\ C_j - EET_j) \tag{2}$$

$$WT_u = \sum_{j \in J_u} (w_j \cdot T_j) \tag{3}$$

Again, we then plot the distribution of this value across all users and visually compare the results across multiple algorithms. An example of such a comparison is presented in Fig. 6b. The interpretation however does still require further analysis due to the nature of value distributions themselves[5].

EET Heatmaps. For a more in-depth analysis we can analyze how *EET*s are violated throughout the schedule. This is done by plotting the number of violated

---

[5] What is better, a more disperse distribution with a better median, or a less disperse distribution?

*EET*s during the time using a *heatmap* [18]. In a heatmap, we use x-axis for time (samples are taken each minute) and the y-axis for users of the system. A color at given coordinates then corresponds to the number of violated *EET*s at that point in time and given user as can be seen in Fig. 7.

Such a heatmap is represented as a 2D array of integers. It has m rows where m is the number of users of the system. Each row has a length of t, where t is the length of the schedule in time units. Initially, each cell is equal to 0 (no violated *EET*s). Next, the structure is updated according to the actual schedule and calculated *EET*s. To illustrate the process, let us consider a situation when a given user job is executed so that its *EET* (calculated using Algorithm 1) is violated by 2 min ($T_j = 2$). Since the resolution (sampling rate) of the heatmap is 1 min, and the *EET* has been violated by 2 min, two consecutive horizontal cells in the data structure will be incremented by 1. For example, $[x][y]$ and $[x + 1][y]$ will be both incremented by 1. Here, y is the index of given user. Clearly, such a heatmap captures both the number of violated *EET*s at given time, as well as the tardiness ($T_j = 2$ implies that two consecutive cells are incremented). The question is how to determine the x, i.e., what should be used as the "start time" of that violated *EET*. There are, of course, several possible approaches for determining this time. In our case, we set the "start time" x of the violated *EET* as: $x = EET_j - runtime_j$, i.e., x is the latest possible job start time that enables us to meet the job *EET*. An illustration of the aforementioned example is shown in Fig. 4. When the violated *EET*s are plotted in this way, they are usually aligned with the areas of high system usage, which are frequently the root cause of such a violation.

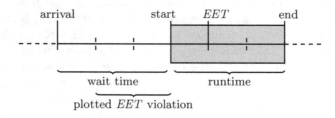

Fig. 4. An example of a violated *EET* plotting.

When such a heatmap is used in conjunction with the actual schedule it allows us to better understand "what is happening" in the system and why. We will provide such an example in the following section.

4   Experiments

In the experimental part of this work, we demonstrate how the proposed model can be used to deeply evaluate the suitability of several scheduling algorithms with respect to a given computing system.

4.1   Experimental Setup

For the purpose of evaluation, the proposed model and the *EET*-based metric has been implemented within the *Alea* job scheduling simulator [14]. To simulate the system workload, we have used a real historical workload trace coming from MetaCentrum which covered 5 months of job execution on the *zewura* cluster. Zewura contains 7 shared memory computing nodes, each consisting of 80 CPUs and 504 GB of RAM. The log contains 17,250 jobs belonging to 70 distinct users. These jobs are either sequential (1 CPU required only) or (highly) parallel. Also, job runtimes as well as memory requirements are highly heterogeneous with some jobs running only few minutes while others running up to 30 days. Concerning RAM, jobs are requesting anything between few MBs of RAM up to 504 GBs of RAM. This workload log is freely available at: http://www.fi.muni.cz/~xklusac/workload.

In order to demonstrate how the proposed model and metric can be used to evaluate the behavior of scheduling algorithms, we have applied two widely used scheduling algorithms — the trivial *First In First Out (FIFO)* and the well known *backfilling* [20]. FIFO always schedules the first job in the queue, checking the availability of the resources required by such job. If all the resources required by the first job in the queue are available, it is immediately scheduled for execution, otherwise FIFO waits until all required resources become available. While the first job is waiting for execution none of the remaining jobs can be scheduled, even if required resources are available. In practice, such approach often implies a low utilization of the systems resources, that cannot be used by some "less demanding" job(s) from the queue [20,23]. To solve this problem algorithms based on *backfilling* are frequently used [20].

Backfilling is an optimization of the FIFO algorithm that tries to maximize resource utilization [20]. It works as FIFO but when the first job in the queue cannot be scheduled immediately, backfilling calculates the earliest possible starting time for the first job using the processing time estimates of running jobs. Then, it makes a reservation to run the job at this pre-computed time. Next, it scans the queue of waiting jobs and schedules immediately every job not interfering with the reservation [20]. This increases resource utilization, as idle resources are utilized by suitable jobs, while decreasing the mean job wait time.

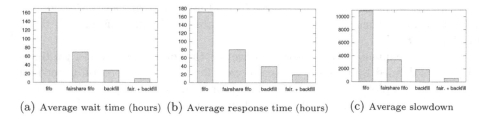

(a) Average wait time (hours) (b) Average response time (hours)   (c) Average slowdown

Fig. 5. Experimental results when measured by classical user-agnostic metrics.

In our experiments, both FIFO and backfilling were applied either with or without fairshare-based priorities enabled. If fairshare-based priorities are enabled, it means that the jobs waiting in the queue are periodically reordered according to actual users' fairshare priorities. Fairshare priorities are updated continuously as jobs are being processed. In other words, those jobs belonging to less active users obtain higher priority and vice versa as was discussed in Sect. 2.2. Further details can be found in, e.g., [1,12,15].

As a result of such a simulation setup, we have obtained four different job schedules, which are marked according to the applied scheduling algorithm as: *fifo, fairshare fifo, backfill* and *fair. + backfill.*

4.2   Experimental Results

In the Fig. 5 we show a simple comparison of applied scheduling algorithms using the popular user-agnostic metrics (wait time, response time and slowdown) that have been described in Sect. 2.1.

As we can see, the results suggests that backfilling algorithm (both with fairshare enabled or disabled) is much better than both FIFO versions. This is not surprising and sounds with results from the literature [20] (see FIFO and backfilling comparison in Sect. 4.1). What remains unclear is whether the application of fairshare priorities results in better, i.e., more fair performance for the users of the system. As we have explained in Sect. 3.1, good fairness and a high performance are the two most important factors that make the system users satisfied — at least this is the case in MetaCentrum.

Therefore, let us now demonstrate how the *EET*-based metric that emulates user expectations can be used for much more detailed analysis. For a very crude comparison of these algorithms, we can use the percentage of violated *EET*s (*VEET_u*). This information is calculated for each user by Formula 1 and plotted using a box-plot[6] as shown in Fig. 6a. In our case, the y-axis denotes the percentage of violated *EET*s and the boxes show how the users are distributed according to the percentage of violated *EET*s. This gives us immediate information about the quality of the algorithms with respect to both performance (small percentage of violated *EET*s indicates good performance) and fairness (bigger deviation equates less fairness). As can be seen, only algorithms with enabled fairshare-based priorities (fairshare fifo, fair. + backfill) are able to provide at least some fairness to the users (75 % of users have at most 35 % violated *EET*s). On the other hand, no algorithm was able to eliminate users with 100 % of violated *EET*s.

For a more quantitative comparison, we use the total weighted user tardiness (*WT_u*) as defined by Formula 3. Again, we calculate this metric on a per-user basis and then plot these values as a box-plot as shown in Fig. 6b. Here, y-axis represents the calculated total weighted user tardiness (seconds in log. scale).

---

[6] Box-plot maintains information on the distribution of *VEET_u* values by showing their minimum, lower quartile, median, upper quartile and the maximum, plus possible extreme outliers marked as dots.

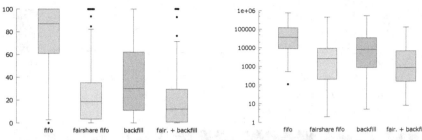

(a) Percentage of users (boxes) having at most $y\%$ of violated EETs (y-axis).

(b) Total weighted tardiness in seconds (y-axis, log. scale) according to users (boxes).

Fig. 6. Simple comparison of different scheduling algorithms

This figure provides further details to the results observed in Fig. 6a, by showing that fair. + backfill significantly decreases those job delays observed by users.

For an in-depth analysis we plot a time overview of violated EETs using so called heatmap [18]. For each user (y-axis) and a point in time (x-axis) we plot a color corresponding to the number of violated EETs at that coordinates. Moreover, we also plot actual CPU and RAM usage bellow each heatmap, to put the results in context with the resource utilization. Such graphs are available in Fig. 7. It gives us the ability to evaluate the behavior of the algorithms with respect to each user of the system and analyze the specific artifacts that may appear in the schedule. For example, for those algorithms using fairshare there are clear artifacts created by the fairshare algorithm, appearing as long lines of violated EETs (second and fourth row in Fig. 7). This is an expected behavior for workload-heavy users, as their priority is decreased proportionally to the amount of resources they consume. Concerning system usage, we can see that FIFO algorithms (first and second row in Fig. 7) performs worse than backfilling. Plain FIFO not only suffers from a large number of violated EETs (which indicates poorer usage) but we can also clearly see the gaps in the system usage (bottom part of the top graph). The overall bad impact on EETs is a natural effect of poor resource utilization. From this point of view, backfilling should perform very well. However, as we can see in case of plain backfilling, it increases the system utilization at the expense of some users. In this context, plain backfilling performs worse than FIFO with fairshare, which sounds with the results from Fig. 6. Only the backfilling algorithm with fairshare-based priorities (bottom row) performs better, decreasing the number of violated EETs and increasing the system utilization. This direct "high resolution" comparison provides clear evidence how fairshare-based priorities and backfilling improve the performance and fairness of the system with respect to its users. It is worth noticing that these issues and characteristics cannot be captured by classical user-agnostic metrics as we have discussed in Sect. 2.1 and demonstrated in Fig. 5. For example, according to user-agnostic metrics, plain backfilling is much better than FIFO with fairshare, while our results show the exact opposite.

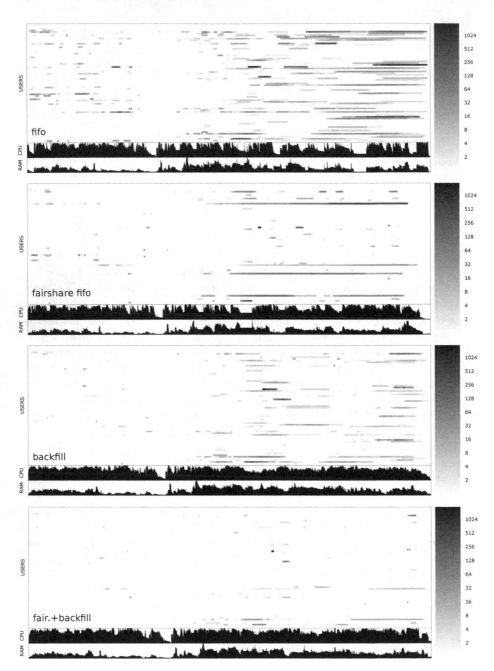

Fig. 7. Heatmaps showing the number of violated *EET*s comparing *fifo* (first row) and *fairshare fifo* (second row) against *backfill* (third row) and *fair. + backfill* (fourth row).

4.3 Summary

In this section we have demonstrated how the proposed model and the metric can be used to better understand the behavior of various scheduling algorithms. Using a real workload and a simulator, we have shown how different scheduling approaches can be tested and their results compared in a "high resolution" manner. Using our approach, we now better understand how various scheduling setups influence the impact on system users. It is worth noticing that the widely used user-agnostic performance metric are neither suitable for real-life multi-user oriented systems nor are able to provide such a detailed insight.

The tool used here for workload processing and visualization [25] is available at: http://happycerberus.github.io/Deadline-Schedule-Evaluator under the MIT license. This tool is capable of processing standard accounting format-based workload data, it also supports SWF-like workload traces from workload archives, or it can even use a trace coming from a job scheduling simulator. This way we can either analyze the current performance of our systems, or do a fast, iteration-like development and analysis of new scheduling algorithms using a simulator. Beside the general, system-wide views presented in Sect. 4.2, the tool can also provide more detailed views. For example, we can filter out specific users (e.g., system administrators) and queues (high/low priority), or even generate a heatmap for single queue or user.

5 Conclusion and Future Work

In this paper we have presented a novel model for measuring the quality of schedules, based on user expectations. The main purpose of this model is to provide an alternative to popular job metrics that capture certain aspects of the schedule but do not properly represent the suitability of the schedule as a whole. Our experiments on real workload from the Czech National Grid MetaCentrum have shown that this model does indeed provide expected level of detail and explains clearly the pros and cons of selected scheduling algorithms. We have shown how the model-based results can be represented both in a simple comparison (Fig. 6) and in an in-depth heatmap representation of the generated schedule (Fig. 7). This model has been already successfully used in practice [16] when searching for a new, more efficient, queue setup in MetaCentrum.

In the future, we aim to refine current simple EET model. For example, the EET calculation should reflect previous user activity. Clearly, if a user utilized a lot of resources in the (near) past, the EET shall be higher (i.e., less strict) as such a user is typically having smaller priority compared to less active users. This is a normal situation in systems using fairshare approach, thus we should not penalize it by our metric. Second, many users are executing workflows or so called "bag of tasks" [6] applications and they are interested in the performance of an entire batch of jobs, rather than focusing on the performance of a single job/task within their workload. For such a workflow or bags of tasks we should therefore generate single EET rather than compute separate EET for each job/task. This will require more complex data sets as our current workload traces do not make any distinction among normal jobs and workflows and/or bag of tasks-like applications.

Acknowledgments. We highly appreciate the support of the Grant Agency of the Czech Republic under the grant No. P202/12/0306. The access to the MetaCentrum workloads is kindly acknowledged.

References

1. Adaptive Computing Enterprises, Inc., Maui Scheduler Administrator's Guide, version 3.2, January 2014. http://docs.adaptivecomputing.com
2. Adaptive Computing Enterprises, Inc., TORQUE Admininstrator Guide, version 4.2.6, January 2014. http://docs.adaptivecomputing.com
3. Apache.org. Hadoop Capacity Scheduler, January 2014. http://hadoop.apache.org/docs/r1.1.1/capacity_scheduler.html
4. Apache.org. Hadoop Fair Scheduler, January 2014. http://hadoop.apache.org/docs/r1.1.1/fair_scheduler.html
5. Cirne, W., Berman, F.: A comprehensive model of the supercomputer workload. In 2001 IEEE International Workshop on Workload Characterization (WWC 2001), pp. 140–148. IEEE Computer Society (2001)
6. Cirne, W., Brasileiro, F., Sauvé, J., Andrade, N., Paranhos, D., Santos-neto, E., Medeiros, R., Gr, F.C.: Grid computing for bag of tasks applications. In: 3rd IFIP Conference on E-Commerce, E-Business and EGovernment (2003)
7. Ernemann, C., Hamscher, V., Yahyapour, R.: Benefits of global Grid computing for job scheduling. In: Proceedings of the 5th IEEE/ACM International Workshop on Grid Computing, GRID 2004, pp. 374–379. IEEE (2004)
8. Feitelson, D.G., Rudolph, L., Schwiegelshohn, U., Sevcik, K.C., Wong, P.: Job scheduling strategies for parallel processing. In: Feitelson, D.G., Rudolph, L. (eds.) Theory and practice in parallel job scheduling. LNCS, vol. 1291, pp. 1–34. Springer, Heidelberg (1997)
9. Frachtenberg, E., Feitelson, D.G.: Pitfalls in parallel job scheduling evaluation. In: Feitelson, D.G., Frachtenberg, E., Rudolph, L., Schwiegelshohn, U. (eds.) Job Scheduling Strategies for Parallel Processing. LNCS, vol. 3834, pp. 257–282. Springer, Heidelberg (2005)
10. Ghodsi, A., Zaharia, M., Hindman, B., Konwinski, A., Shenker, S., Stoica, I.: Dominant resource fairness: fair allocation of multiple resource types. In: 8th USENIX Symposium on Networked Systems Design and Implementation (2011)
11. Isard, M., Prabhakaran, V., Currey, J., Wieder, U., Talwar, K., Goldberg, A.: Quincy: Fair scheduling for distributed computing clusters. In: SOSP 2009 (2009)
12. Jackson, D., Snell, Q., Clement, M.: Core algorithms of the Maui scheduler. In: Feitelson, D.G., Rudolph, L. (eds.) Job Scheduling Strategies for Parallel Processing. LNCS, vol. 2221, pp. 87–102. Springer, Heidelberg (2001)
13. Karatza, H.D.: Performance of gang scheduling strategies in a parallel system. Simul. Model. Pract. Theory **17**(2), 430–441 (2009)
14. Klusáček,D., Rudová, H.: Alea 2 - job scheduling simulator. In: Proceedings of the 3rd International ICST Conference on Simulation Tools and Techniques (SIMU-Tools 2010). ICST, 2010

15. Klusáček, D., Rudová, H., Jaroš, M.: Multi resource fairness: problems and challenges. In: Desai, N., Cirne, W. (eds.) Job Scheduling Strategies for Parallel Processing (JSSPP 2013). LNCS. Springer, Heidelberg (2013)
16. Klusáček, D., Tóth, Š.: On interactions among scheduling policies: finding efficient queue setup using high-resolution simulations. In: Silva, F., Dutra, I., Costa, V.S. (eds.) Euro-Par 2014. LNCS, vol. 8632. Springer, Heidelberg (2014)
17. Krakov, D., Feitelson, D.: High-resolution analysis of parallel job workloads. In: Cirne, W., Desai, N., Frachtenberg, E., Schwiegelshohn, U. (eds.) Job Scheduling Strategies for Parallel Processing. LNCS, vol. 7698, pp. 178–195. Springer, Heidelberg (2013)
18. Krakov, D., Feitelson, D.G.: Comparing Performance Heatmaps. In: Desai, N., Cirne, W. (eds.) Job Scheduling Strategies for Parallel Processing. LNCS. Springer, Heidelberg (2013)
19. Leung, V.J., Sabin, G., Sadayappan, P.: Parallel job scheduling policies to improve fairness: a case study. Technical Report SAND2008-1310, Sandia National Laboratories (2008)
20. Mu'alem, A.W., Feitelson, D.G.: Utilization, predictability, workloads, and user runtime estimates in scheduling the IBM SP2 with backfilling. IEEE Trans. Parallel Distrib. Syst. 12(6), 529–543 (2001)
21. PBS Works. PBS Professional 12.1, Administrator's Guide, January 2014. http://www.pbsworks.com/documentation/support/
22. Ruda, M., Šustr, Z., Sitera, J., Antoš, D., Hejtmánek, L., Holub, P., Mulač, M.: Virtual clusters as a new service of MetaCentrum, the Czech NGI. In: Cracow 2009 Grid Workshop (2010)
23. Sabin, G., Kochhar, G., Sadayappan, P.: Job fairness in non-preemptive job scheduling. In: International Conference on Parallel Processing (ICPP 2004), pp. 186–194. IEEE Computer Society (2004)
24. Srinivasan, S., Kettimuthu, R., Subramani, V., Sadayappan, P.: Selective reservation strategies for backfill job scheduling. In: Feitelson, D.G., Rudolph, L., Schwiegelshohn, U. (eds.) Job Scheduling Strategies for Parallel Processing. LNCS, vol. 2537, pp. 55–71. Springer, Heidelberg (2002)
25. Tóth, Š., Klusáček, D.: Tools and methods for detailed analysis of complex job schedules in the Czech National Grid. In: Bubak, M., Turała, M., Wiatr, K. (eds.) Cracow Grid Workshop, pp. 83–84. ACC CYFRONET AGH, Cracow (2013)
26. Tóth, Š., Ruda, M.: Practical experiences with torque meta-scheduling in the Czech National Grid. Comput. Sci. 13(2), 33–45 (2012)
27. Vasupongayya, S., Chiang, S.-H.: On job fairness in non-preemptive parallel job scheduling. In: Zheng, S.Q. (ed.) International Conference on Parallel and Distributed Computing Systems (PDCS 2005), pp. 100–105. IASTED/ACTA Press, San Diego (2005)

Prediction of Queue Waiting Times
for Metascheduling on Parallel Batch Systems

Rajath Kumar and Sathish Vadhiyar[⊠]

Supercomputer Education and Research Center,
Indian Institute of Science, Bangalore, India
rajath.kumar@gmail.com, vss@serc.iisc.in

Abstract. Prediction of queue waiting times of jobs submitted to production parallel batch systems is important to provide overall estimates
to users and can also help meta-schedulers make scheduling decisions.
In this work, we have developed a framework for predicting ranges of
queue waiting times for jobs by employing multi-class classification of
similar jobs in history. Our hierarchical prediction strategy first predicts
the point wait time of a job using dynamic k-Nearest Neighbor (kNN)
method. It then performs a multi-class classification using Support Vector Machines (SVMs) among all the classes of the jobs. The probabilities
given by the SVM for the class predicted using k-NN and its neighboring classes are used to provide a set of ranges of predicted wait times
with probabilities. We have used these predictions and probabilities in a
meta-scheduling strategy that distributes jobs to different queues/sites in
a multi-queue/grid environment for minimizing wait times of the jobs.
Experiments with different production supercomputer job traces show
that our prediction strategies can give correct predictions for about
77–87 % of the jobs, and also result in about 12 % improved accuracy
when compared to the next best existing method. Experiments with
our meta-scheduling strategy using different production and synthetic
job traces for various system sizes, partitioning schemes and different
workloads, show that the meta-scheduling strategy gives much improved
performance when compared to existing scheduling policies by reducing
the overall average queue waiting times of the jobs by about 47 %.

1 Introduction

Production parallel systems in many supercomputing sites are batch systems
that provide space sharing of available processors among multiple parallel applications or jobs. Well known parallel job scheduling frameworks including IBM
Loadleveler [1] and PBS [2] are used in production supercomputers for management of jobs in the batch systems. These frameworks employ batch queues in
which the jobs submitted to the batch systems are queued before allocation by a
batch scheduler to a set of available processors for execution. Thus, in addition
to the time taken for execution, a job submitted to a batch queue incurs time
due to waiting in the queue before allocation to a set of processors for execution.

© Springer International Publishing Switzerland 2015
W. Cirne and N. Desai (Eds.): JSSPP 2014, LNCS 8828, pp. 108–128, 2015.
DOI: 10.1007/978-3-319-15789-4_7

Predicting queue waiting times of the jobs on the batch systems will be highly beneficial for users. The predictions can be used by a user for various purposes including planning management of his jobs and meeting deadlines, considering migrating to other queues, systems or sites at his disposal for application execution when informed of possible high queue waiting times on a queue, and investigating alternate job parameters including different requested number of processors and estimated execution times. Such predictions can also be efficiently used by a meta-scheduler to make automatic scheduling decisions for selecting the appropriate number of processors and queues for job execution to optimize certain cost metrics, and help reduce the complexities associated with job submissions for the users. The decisions by the user and meta-scheduler using the predictions can in turn result in overall load balancing of jobs across multiple queues and systems. Such predictions are also highly sought after in production batch systems. For example, predictions of queue waiting times are available in production systems of TeraGrid [3]. These show the importance of accurate queue wait time prediction mechanisms for the users submitting their jobs to batch systems.

Prediction of queue waiting times is challenging due to various factors including diverse scheduling algorithms followed by the job scheduling frameworks, time-varying policies applied for a single queue, and priorities for the jobs. In our previous work [4], we have developed a framework called PQStar (Predicting Quick Starters) for identification and prediction of jobs with short actual queue waiting times. We refer to these jobs as *quick starters*. The basis of our method for identifying a quick starter job is to establish boundaries in the history of prior job submissions, and to use the similar jobs within the boundaries for prediction. Thus, the most relevant and recent history is used for predicting the target quick starter job. For our work, we defined quick starters as those jobs with actual waiting times of less than one hour, since these formed the majority in many real supercomputing traces. The prediction strategies lead to correct identification of up to 20 times more quick starters and resulted in up to 64 % higher overall prediction accuracy than existing methods.

In this work, we extend our framework with strategies for predicting ranges of queue waiting times for all classes of jobs, and use these stochastic predictions to build a top-level meta-scheduler to reduce the overall average wait times of the jobs submitted to the queues. We have developed a machine learning based framework that identifies for a target job, similar jobs in history using job characteristics and system states, and employs multi-class classification method to provide predictions for the jobs. Our hierarchical prediction strategies first predict the point wait time of a job using the *Dynamic-k Nearest Neighbor* (kNN). It then performs a multi-class classification using *Support Vector Machines (SVMs)* among all the classes of the jobs. The probabilities given by the SVM for the predicted class obtained from the kNN, along with its neighboring classes, are used to provide a set of ranges of wait times with probabilities. An important aspect of our prediction model is that it considers the processor occupancy state and the queue state at the time of the job submission in addition to the job characteristics including the requested number of processors and the estimated runtime. The processor and queue states include the current number of free nodes, number of jobs with large request sizes currently executing in the system, and relative difference between the current job and other jobs in the queue in terms of request size and estimated run time. These states are obtained by using a simulator that updates the states during job arrivals and departures.

We have also developed a meta-scheduling framework which uses the predictions of queue waiting times to select a queue for job submission and execution. The primary objective of our meta-scheduler is to distribute jobs to different queues/sites in a multi-queue/grid environment for minimizing average wait times of the jobs submitted to the queues. For a given target job, we first identify the queues/sites where the job can be a quick starter to obtain a set of candidate queues/sites and then compute the expected value of the wait time in each of the candidate queues/sites using the ranges of queue waiting times and probabilities. Our meta-scheduler then schedules the job to the queue with minimum expected value for job execution.

Our experiments with different production supercomputer job traces show that our prediction strategies can give correct predictions for about 77–87 % of the jobs, and also result in about 12 % improved accuracy when compared to the next best existing method. Our experiments with our meta-scheduling strategy using different production and synthetic job traces for various system sizes, partitioning schemes and different workloads, show that our meta-scheduling strategy gives much improved performance when compared to existing scheduling policies by reducing the overall average queue waiting times of the jobs by about 47 %.

2   Related Work

In the works by Smith et al. [5,6], runtime predictions are derived using similar runs in the history, and these estimates are further used to simulate the scheduling algorithms like FCFS, LWF (Least Work First) and Backfilling [7] to obtain the queue wait times predictions. Some statistical methods use time series analysis of queue waiting times for jobs in the history to predict waiting times for submitted jobs. QBETS [8,9] is a system that predicts the bounds on the queue wait times with a quantitative confidence level. However, QBETS gives conservative upper bound predictions, which leads to large prediction errors for most of the jobs. Also it considers only the job characteristics and not the state of the system.

The efforts by Li et al. [10,11] consider the system states for the prediction of queue waiting times. In their method known as Instance Based Learning (IBL), they use weighted sum of Heterogeneous Euclidean-Overlap Distances between different attributes of two jobs to find the similarities between the jobs. Their work gives only point predictions for wait times while we provide ranges of wait times with probabilities which we show as more useful than the point predictions.

One common strategy for scheduling jobs in a multi-queue environment is to use *redundant requests*, where the users submit several requests simultaneously to multiple batch schedulers on behalf of a single job submission. Once, one of these requests is granted access to compute nodes, the others are canceled by the user. In the work by Casanova et al. [12], the effect of redundant batch requests on different aspects has been discussed. While redundant requests have been shown to improve response times of jobs, it was also shown that batch system middleware may not be able to handle high loads due to the redundant requests, and may be complex to implement for practical purposes. We use redundant requests strategy as a baseline for evaluating our methods. In the work by Subramani et al. [13], scheduling by the meta-scheduler is done based on the current load in the system for homogeneous systems. They define load as the ratio of (sum of the cpu times of the queued jobs + sum of the remaining cpu times of the running jobs) and the total system size. They first propose a "least loaded" scheme in which a greedy strategy is followed and the job is submitted to a particular queue/site with the least load. They also propose a "k-distributed" scheme in which the job is submitted to k least loaded queues/sites. This is similar to the redundant batch requests, except that, the job is submitted to some subset of the total number of queues/sites, based on the load on the system. While considering the load on the systems, their work does not consider the characteristics of the job to be scheduled. In our method, we explicitly consider the predictions of the queue waiting times for the scheduling of the job to the appropriate queue/site. Hence, the fitness of the current job to the queue/site is evaluated. The efforts by Sabin et al. [14] and Li et al. [15] discuss meta-scheduling in heterogeneous grid environments assuming knowledge of execution times on different systems. Our work focuses on homogeneous systems in which all processors associated with all the queues have the same speed, and hence response times of jobs are minimized by minimizing only the queue waiting times.

3 Predictions of Queue Waiting Times

3.1 Identifying Quick Starters

In our previous work [4], we have developed strategies for predictions of quick starters. For a given target job, our method splits the history for a target job into near, mid and long term history based on similarity of processor occupancy states. A processor occupancy state at a given instance denotes the allocation of the processors to the jobs executing at that instance. The method then finds similar jobs in the near, mid and long term history in terms of request size and estimated run time. The basis of identifying quick starters using near-term history is that by looking at jobs with similar characteristics in the near-term history with similar processor occupancy states and checking if those jobs have potentially been backfilled, it can be predicted if the target job can be backfilled and hence marked as a quick starter. For mid-term history, our method also considers the availability of free nodes for accommodating the request of the target job, and position of the job in the queue in terms of request size and estimated runtime.

3.2   Predicting Queue Waiting Time Ranges

In this work, we propose a method which predicts either continuous or disjoint ranges of wait times for a job, with each range associated with the probability of the actual wait time lying in that range. The wait time prediction problem can be formulated as a supervised machine learning problem, which uses the history jobs, their feature vectors and their wait times as training set for future wait time predictions. Any job submitted to the system is defined by a set of features associated with the job. This set of features forms the *feature vectors*. The features associated with the job can be broadly classified into three categories. 1. Job Characteristics: These are the core characteristics associated with the job and are provided by the user at the time of target job submission. These include request sizes and estimated run times for the jobs. 2. Queue States: These are the properties associated with the batch queues and the jobs currently waiting for execution at the time of the arrival of the target job. 3. Processor States: These are the properties associated with the processor occupancies by the jobs currently executing in the system at the time of the arrival of the target job. In our work, we define a total of 19 features for a job's feature vector. Table 1 shows the list of 19 features along with the categories of the features.

From the table, we can see that we consider an extensive set of features to represent a job. We consider features related to the system states in addition to the job characteristics. We also consider features that rank the target job in relation to the jobs in the queue and the jobs in execution. These include:

- $queue\_jobrank_{req\_size}$,
- $queue\_jobrank_{ert}$,
- $queue\_jobrank_{cputime}$,
- $proc_{remain\_cputime\_lower\_req\_size}$,
- $proc_{remain\_cputime\_lower\_ert}$, and
- $proc_{remain\_cputime\_lower\_cputime}$.

While considering a small feature space would reduce the time taken for training and predictions, we found that the features we consider are essential in describing the job and system properties and to adequately capture similarities between two jobs. We arrived at this feature list by starting with only the features related to request sizes and estimated run times, and found that the resulting set leads to false similarities between two jobs. Hence, we included other features including job ranks and demand cpu times. While considering features to be included in the feature vector, we exclude features which are derivable from or dual of the already existing features in the feature set. For example, free nodes is derivable from the feature, occupied nodes, while the sum of the elapsed times of running jobs in the system is a dual feature of the sum of the remaining times of running jobs.

Defining Job Similarity. In order to define similarity between a target job and the history job, we use their respective feature vectors and a distance metric

Table 1. Job features

Feature	Type	Description
$request\_size$	Job	No of processors requested by the user for the target job
ert (estimated run time)	Job	The approximate estimation of runtime provided by the user for the target job
$queue\_jobrank_{req\_size}$	Queue	The position of the target job in the list of waiting jobs in the queue at the time of its entry sorted in increasing order of request sizes
$queue\_jobrank_{ert}$	Queue	The position of the target job in the list of waiting jobs in the queue at the time of its entry sorted in increasing order of ert's
$queue\_jobrank_{cputime}$	Queue	The position of the target job in the list of waiting jobs in the queue at the time of its entry sorted in increasing order of cpu times ($ert*requestsize$)
$queue_{demand\_cputime}$	Queue	The sum of the demand cpu times ($ert*requestsize$) of the waiting jobs in the queue
n_{queue}	Queue	The number of jobs waiting in the queue
$queue_{demand\_cputime\_lower\_req\_size}$	Queue	The sum of the demand cpu times ($ert*requestsize$) of the waiting jobs in the queue with lower $requestsize$ than the target job
$queue_{demand\_cputime\_lower\_ert}$	Queue	The sum of the demand cpu times ($ert*requestsize$) of the waiting jobs in the queue with lower ert than the target job
$queue_{demand\_cputime\_lower\_cputime}$	Queue	The sum of the demand cpu times ($ert*requestsize$) of the waiting jobs in the queue with lower cpu times ($ert*requestsize$) than the target job
$proc\_jobrank_{req\_size}$	Processor	The position of the target job in the list of running jobs in the system at the time of its entry sorted in increasing order of request sizes

(*Continued*)

Table 1. (*Continued*)

Feature	Type	Description
$proc\_jobrank_{ert}$	Processor	The position of the target job in the list of running jobs in the system at the time of its entry sorted in increasing order of ert's
$proc\_jobrank_{cputime}$	Processor	The position of the target job in the list of running jobs in the system at the time of its entry sorted in increasing order of cpu times ($ert*requestsize$)
$proc_{remain\_cputime}$	Processor	The sum of the remaining cpu times ($ert*requestsize$ - $elapsed_{time}*$ $requestsize$) of the running jobs in the system
n_{proc}	Processor	The number of jobs running in the system
$proc_{remain\_cputime\_lower\_req\_size}$	Processor	The sum of the remaining cpu times ($ert*requestsize$ - $elapsed_{time}*$ $requestsize$) of the running jobs in the system with lower $requestsize$ than the target job
$proc_{remain\_cputime\_lower\_ert}$	Processor	The sum of the remaining cpu times ($ert*requestsize$ - $elapsed_{time}*$ $requestsize$) of the running jobs in the system with lower ert than the target job
$proc_{remain\_cputime\_lower\_cputime}$	Processor	The sum of the remaining cpu times ($ert*requestsize$ - $elapsed_{time}*$ $requestsize$) of the running jobs in the system with lower cpu times ($ert*requestsize$) than the target job
$occupied\_nodes$	Processor	The total number of nodes in the system that has been occupied by the running jobs

called *Heterogeneous Euclid Overlap Metric (HEOM)* [16] for computing the distance between the target and the history job. Given two feature vectors, X and Y, each of size n, the HEOM distance between the two vectors is computed as $HEOM_{distance} = \dfrac{\sum\limits_{i=1}^{n} ||X_i - Y_i||}{\sum\limits_{i=1}^{n} (X_i + Y_i)}$. Instead of normalizing every element of the feature vector by its maximum value, the $HEOM_{distance}$ uses the original feature vectors and obtains a distance between 0 and 1. Hence, the $HEOM_{distance}$ metric can be efficiently used to find the difference between two feature vectors where each element in a vector can have different ranges.

Dynamic k-Nearest Neighbors. The k-Nearest Neighbors is a popular learning algorithm in which the nearest k history jobs, in terms of their distance from the target job, are chosen as similar jobs. The wait times of the similar jobs are used for predictions for the target job. An important aspect of this learning algorithm is choosing of the value of k. In our method, we choose the value of k dynamically for every target job.

For a given target job, we compute the $HEOM_{distance}$ between the target job and each job in the history. We define the value of k as the number of history jobs within 5 % of the distance from the target job. Thus, k is equal to the number of jobs in the history with a $HEOM_{distance}$ of less than or equal to the value of 0.05. If we do not find any jobs in the history within 0.05, we look for job within 0.1, 0.15 and so on until we find at least one similar job within any one of these thresholds. The higher the threshold value, the lower will be the similarity between the target and the history jobs.

Wait times of these k nearest neighbors are used to obtain a point wait time prediction for the target job. We explored three primary techniques for computing the point wait time of the target job.

1. Avg_{Wt}: Weighted Average using the inverse of the HEOM distance as a function of weight. This is computed using Eq. 1.

$$Avg_{Wt} = \frac{\sum_{i=1}^{k} Weight_i * Wait_i}{\sum_{i=1}^{k} Weight_i} \qquad (1)$$

where, $Weight_i$ = inverse of HEOM distance between the target job and the ith history job, and $Wait_i$ = actual wait time of the ith history job.
2. Reg_{lin}: Linear Regression of the feature vectors and the wait times.
3. Reg_{non_lin}: Non Linear Regression of the feature vectors and the wait times using a non-linear kernel function of degree equal to the number of features (which is 19 in our case). We have explored three different kernel functions in our work, namely, polynomial, sigmoid and the radial basis functions.

For performing the linear and non-linear regressions we use the python libraries provided for regression methods in [17]. The weighted average and regression techniques assign weights, explicitly and implicitly, respectively, for each job in the history depending on the similarity of the job to the target job.

Multi-class Probabilities. The point predictions obtained using kNN method can generally be highly inaccurate for queue waiting times due to several factors including small number of similar jobs in the history, large distance between the target job and the most similar job or the fact that even the most similar jobs in the history can have high variations in wait times. Hence we attempt to provide predictions of ranges of queue waiting times. For providing a range of wait times, we divide the wait times of a job into multiple classes. In our work, we use the classes shown in Table 2 since these classes are commonly observed in many supercomputing traces [18]. For a given target job, we first compute the predicted class based on the predicted point wait time obtained from using k-NN. For example, if the predicted point wait time is 1 h and 15 min, the predicted class is class 2 since its range is 1 to 3 h.

Table 2. Class ranges

Class	Wait time ranges
1	less than or equal to 1 h
2	1 h to 3 h
3	3 h to 6 h
4	6 h to 12 h
5	12 h to 24 h
6	greater than 24 h (or 1 day)

As a next step, we use another machine learning technique, *Support Vector Machine (SVM)*, for multi-class classification of a target job. SVM is one of the most popular classification based learning algorithms. SVMs can efficiently perform non-linear classification using the "kernel trick", implicitly mapping their inputs into high-dimensional feature spaces. SVMs are also computationally less expensive, and handles over-fitting better than the other methods. It is a supervised learning algorithm which takes as input the training set consisting of history jobs, their feature vectors and the classes of the jobs based on their actual waiting times. It also takes as input the target jobs and their feature vectors. For a target job, based on the training model, it outputs the probabilities of the target job's waiting time belonging to the different classes. In order to get the class probabilities, we feed the entire set of jobs in the history to the SVM Multi-Class Classification library [17] for the training set. Since SVM training can be time consuming (order of few tens of seconds for each target job), we use SVM training only at regular intervals and not for every target job. For our experiments, SVM training was done after every 5000 jobs.

Our next goal is to convert the point wait time obtained from the kNN method into more reliable ranges. This is done in two steps. In the first step, we consider the predicted class, X, corresponding to the point wait time predicted by kNN. This class gives a single range of wait times. As reported in our experiments in Sect. 5, this single class prediction results in prediction errors in large number of cases. Hence we attempt to provide two class ranges by considering the two immediate neighboring classes of X. We obtain the probabilities of these three classes using the SVM classifier. Two of these three classes with the two highest probabilities are given as the ranges of wait times for the target job, along with their normalized probabilities. The normalized probability of a class is obtained by the ratio of its probability given by SVM and the sum of the probabilities of the two classes. It has to be noted that our method only gives the ranges of wait times as the output for the user. The probabilities are used internally by the meta-scheduler described in the next section. If the class X is either the first or last class (i.e. less than or equal to one hour or greater than 1 day), then our method provides only two class ranges.

Two primary reasons guide our methodology of using the predicted class obtained by the dynamic k-NN method and its neighboring classes for the selection of the output predicted classes (or ranges). Using the SVM probabilities directly can at times lead to a situation in which the top two or three classes with highest probabilities may be separated by more than one class, i.e., widely separated, and hence may not be intuitive to the user. Hence, we obtain a predicted class using the dynamic k-NN and only try to make some minor corrections in the predictions using the SVM class probabilities. Another reason is that in some cases the SVM class probabilities may not give a unanimous choice of a class as a clear leader. In such scenarios, choosing two or three classes with highest probabilities may not prove to be effective as the absolute probabilities for each of them may be quite low. Hence, we reduce the candidate classes for prediction to three using k-NN, and use only the probabilities among the three.

The entire algorithm followed in our *Multi-Class Wait time ranges* method is illustrated in the flowchart shown in Fig. 1.

4   Metascheduling

A single supercomputing system typically consists of multiple batch queues that differ in terms of the processor and execution time requirements of the jobs to cater to the needs of different jobs. A user chooses a batch queue among the many available batch queues when submitting a high performance computing job for problem solving. This choice is typically made by the user based on his limited experience with the application on some of the systems available. The user mostly chooses the system on which he has had the experience of best performance or minimum queue waiting time. Most of the supercomputing systems have static scheduling policy of distributing the jobs among the queues. This is primarily done based on the request size and the estimated run time of the job provided by the user.

Meta-scheduler is a top-level scheduler that distributes jobs among multiple systems to optimize costs including execution time or system utilization. We have developed a meta-scheduler that uses the quick starter identification and stochastic predictions of the queue wait times for selecting an appropriate queue/site among a given set of queues for the job. The primary objective of

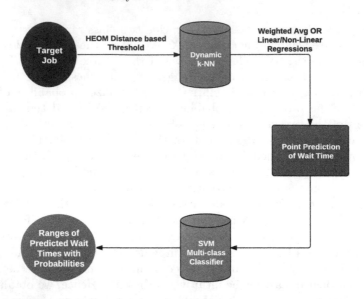

Fig. 1. Multi-Class Methodology for providing predicted wait time ranges with probability

our meta-scheduler is to reduce the average wait times of the jobs submitted to the queues. The system model considered in this work is that all the processors corresponding to the queues are homogeneous, i.e., the execution times of a job when submitted to different queues are the same.

We have developed an algorithm called *Least_Predictedqw* which, for a given target job, identifies the queue/site with the least predicted queue waiting time and schedules the job to that particular queue/site for the job execution. Let us consider, for a given target job, n different queues/sites for scheduling the job. As a first step, we use our first prediction method, PQStar, to find the number of queues, m, $(m < n)$, for which the target job is predicted as a quick starter. A three-way decision is then made:

1. if $m = 1$, the particular queue/site in which the target job is predicted as a quick starter is chosen for scheduling the job for its execution.
2. if $m = 0$ or $m = n$, then the n queues are added to a candidate queues/site list, since any of the n queues can be chosen for job scheduling.
3. if $1 < m < n$, then the target job is predicted as a quick starter in the subset (of size m) of total queues/sites in the system. In this case, then the m queues are added to the candidate queues/site list.

As a next step, we consider the queues/sites in the *candidate queues/sites list* and obtain the queue waiting time ranges and their corresponding probabilities by using our machine learning based methods described in Sect. 3. Then, for each of the queue/site on the candidate list, we compute their corresponding expected wait times as $Exp\_Val = \sum_{i=1}^{n} Prob_i * Mean\_Wait_i$, where, $Prob_i$ = probability of the ith range & $Mean\_Wait_i$ = mean waiting time of all the similar jobs in the history in the ith range. We then choose the queue that has the least expected queue waiting time.

5   Experiments and Results

5.1   Evaluation of Predictions

In this section, we show the evaluation results of our prediction methodology and its effectiveness in successfully providing ranges of queue waiting times as predictions.

Experimental Setup. For evaluations of our predictions, we have developed a discreet event simulator. The simulator creates a simulated environment of the jobs waiting in the queue and running on the system at different points of time. It keeps track of the jobs submitted to the system, and maintains their attributes including arrival times, wait times, actual runtimes and request sizes. It does not simulate the actual scheduling algorithm used, thus avoiding assumptions about the underlying scheduling algorithm. The user can invoke the simulator with a supercomputing job trace/log in the Standard Workload Format (SWF) [19] as input, and obtain predicted queue waiting time of a new job. The simulator creates the simulated environment of jobs in the system using the statistics available in the log. The simulator is triggered by three primary events corresponding to job arrival, job beginning to execute and job termination. Whenever a job arrives, it is added to a waiting queue maintained by the simulator. As soon as a job's wait time is over and it starts executing, it is removed from the waiting queue and added to a running list in the simulator. Also at this time, the free nodes available in the system is decremented by the value equal to the job's request size. Once a job which is running completes its execution, it is removed from the running list and the free nodes available in the system is incremented by the value equal to the job's request size. This process is repeated for each job and thus a simulated system state is created using which we extract the processor state and the queue properties that are needed for our prediction model.

We performed experiments for six supercomputing traces obtained from the Parallel Workload Archive [18]. For each supercomputing trace in our experiments, we performed predictions for all the jobs starting from the 10001th job up to a maximum of 50000 jobs or the end of the log. Each of the jobs in this set constitutes the evaluation data for which predictions were made. For a given target job for which waiting time is predicted, all the jobs submitted prior to it constitute the history. For our experiments, we limited the history size to 5000 jobs for maintaining the time taken for a prediction to within few microseconds. Once the target jobs start their execution and their wait times are known, they are added to the set of history jobs.

Point Predictions with k-NN. We first show the prediction accuracies for point predictions of queue wait times with different techniques using similar jobs obtained from k-NN. We compute the percentage difference in predicted and actual response times for each job, where response time is the sum of queue waiting time and execution time. For the execution time, we consider the estimated run time (ERT) supplied by the user to be equal to the actual execution time. Hence the percentage predicted error in response time is calculated as $PPE_{rt} = \frac{|predictedwaitingtime - actualwaitingtime|}{actualresponsetime}$. This metric determines the amount of impact of the prediction errors on jobs of different lengths or execution times. Table 3 shows the average percentage prediction error in response time for different supercomputing traces [18] with the five techniques, namely, weighted average, linear regression, and non-linear regression with polynomial, radial basis functions (RBF) and sigmoid functions. As can be seen from the results, evaluations with the different techniques show very little variations in predictions. Thus our overall method of obtaining point predictions using k-NN gives similar results irrespective of the technique used to obtain the predictions. Based on these results, we use *weighted average* in our further experiments due to its relatively lesser computational complexity compared to the linear/non-linear regressions. The high percentage prediction errors shown in the table also indicate the challenges in predictions in batch systems due to non-deterministic job arrivals and terminations, and hence the less usefulness of point predictions when compared to range predictions for queue waiting times.

Table 3. Percentage prediction error in response time

Logs	Avg_{wt}	Reg_{lin}	Reg_{poly}	Reg_{rbf}	Reg_{sig}
CTC	54	51	52	53	51
ANL	50	49	51	50	51
LANL	71	71	68	69	70
HPC2N	65	62	61	61	61
SDSC Blue	72	73	72	71	73
SDSC SP2	111	108	108	108	108

Single Class Accuracy. We first show the results of the single class accuracy predictions for our method and the IBL method. Success is defined as the percentage of jobs for which the predicted class (obtained from the dynamic k-NN method or the point wait time prediction provided by IBL) is the true class of the job. Table 4 shows the percentage of jobs with successful prediction of the true class with a single class accuracy, for all jobs and for non-quick starters. We find that both our method using weighted average and IBL technique consistently give better predictions than QBETS. This is because these methods consider both the queue and processor states in addition to the job characteristics while QBETS using its trace-based predictions considers only the job characteristics. We can also see that our methods can correctly give the single class predictions

for up to 16 % more number of jobs than IBL for all the jobs (Table 4(b)). But
the performance improvement for the non-quick starters when compared to IBL
is relatively lesser and our method can give correct predictions only for up to
4 % more number of jobs for the non quick starters (Table 4(a)). This shows
that with single class predictions, the accuracy that can be obtained can be low.
Hence, it will be more useful to give the user with multiple classes (or ranges)
of queue waiting times as predictions.

Table 4. Percentage of Jobs predicted with Single class accuracy

(a) Non Quick Starters

Logs	QBETS	IBL	Avg$_{wt}$
CTC	19	28	30
ANL	19	29	30
LANL	10	26	28
HPC2N	13	22	23
SDSC Blue	15	24	28
SDSC SP2	30	33	35

(b) Overall

Logs	QBETS	IBL	Avg$_{wt}$
CTC	4	47	59
ANL	18	59	73
LANL	58	61	76
HPC2N	16	48	64
SDSC Blue	37	57	74
SDSC SP2	8	48	64

Multi Class Accuracy. We next show the results for predictions of two classes,
that are determined using the methodology described in Sect. 3, for our method
and compare with the QBETS and IBL methods. Since IBL method gives only
a point wait time as prediction, for the purpose of multi class accuracy comparisons, we used an extended version of IBL. In this version, the point wait
time predictions of IBL are used with our SVM multi-class classifier to obtain
ranges of wait time predictions. This extension of point wait-time predictions to
multi-class predictions is reasonable since the multiple classes are obtained in the
neighborhood of the class to which the predicted point wait time belongs, both
in our method using k-NN and the IBL method. Success is defined as percentage
of jobs for which at least one of the two predicted classes (class with top two
probabilities) is the true class of the job.

Figure 2 shows the percentage of jobs with successful prediction of the true
class with a two class accuracy, for all jobs and for non-quick starters. We can see
that our methods can correctly give two class predictions for up to 17 % more number of jobs overall for all the jobs, and up to 12 % more number of jobs for the non

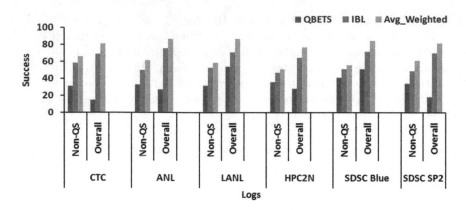

Fig. 2. Percentage of Jobs predicted with a Two class accuracy

quick starters, when compared to IBL. Also, overall for all the jobs, our method can correctly predict for about 77–87 % of the jobs with a two class accuracy.

Finally we also show the results for three class accuracy for all jobs and for non-quick starters. Success is defined as percentage of jobs for which at least one of the three predicted classes (predicted class obtained from the dynamic k-NN method and its neighboring classes) is the true class of the job. We found that our methods can correctly give three class predictions for up to 11 % more number of jobs overall for all the jobs, and up to 8 % more number of jobs for the non quick starters, when compared to IBL. Also, overall for all the jobs, our method can correctly predict for about 82–91 % of the jobs with a three class accuracy. This confirms that even though our predictions for single class/range of wait times have low accuracy and are comparable to IBL, we achieve better success rate for predictions of multiple classes. This is primarily because of the fact that, for a subset of the jobs where both our method and IBL method fail to provide good single class accuracy, our method gives the class that is closer (neighbor) to the true class to which the job belongs as the predicted class, when compared to the IBL methodology. This improvement is primarily due to the use of better similar jobs in history in our method obtained by the use of dynamic k-NN and the extended feature set. The multi-class predictions with probabilities are primarily intended for our metascheduler described in the next section. However, these class predictions by themselves can be useful for a user to obtain broad-level estimates and help in broad-level decisions for job submissions.

5.2   Evaluation of Metascheduling

In this section, we show the evaluation results of the meta-scheduling strategies and its effectiveness in reducing the queue waiting times incurred by the jobs.

Experimental Setup. For experiments related to meta-scheduler, we use *GridSim* [20] for simulating the scheduling algorithm using the workload logs. *GridSim* allows modeling and simulation of entities in parallel and distributed computing systems-users, applications, resources, and schedulers for design and evaluation of scheduling algorithms. It allows the management and also provides a way to analyze algorithms on large-scale distributed systems. In order to simulate the various workloads on different queues/sites, we employ EASY-back filling [7] scheduling algorithm using the scheduling simulation provided by the *GridSim*. We provide the supercomputer logs in the SWF [19] format to the *GridSim* and also specify the scheduling algorithm to be simulated. Given these inputs, the *GridSim* simulates the scheduling algorithm for the given logs. Using the simulation results, we can obtain the actual wait times of the different jobs in the logs.

In order to simulate the meta-scheduling scenarios, we divide the system into different partitions, with each partition associated with certain maximum number of processors. After the meta-scheduler chooses a queue for a job execution, the job is submitted to the particular queue for its execution in the GridSim simulation, and the actual wait time incurred by the job is obtained. For performing the redundant batch request experiments, which we use as a comparison method, we use the simulator [21] built by Casanova for his work on redundant requests [12]. As an input we provide the supercomputer logs in the SWF [19] format. It is required to set the configuration file for the simulations such that all the jobs submitted to the queues resort to redundant requests and the requests are submitted to all the queues available in the system. We show results for both the real workload traces obtained from the Parallel Workload Archive [18] and certain synthetic traces which we have generated using the Parallel Workload Models [22]. We perform two kinds of experiments: *super experiments* and experiments with *synthetic traces*.

In the *super experiments*, we create a grid like environment in which we consider six different sites which are geographically distributed. For the six sites, we used the real workload traces obtained from the Parallel Workload Archive [18] for logs of the six sites, namely, CTC, ANL, SDSC Blue, SDSC SP2, LANL and HPC2N. We simulate a meta-scheduler capable of submitting the jobs to any of these sites. Note that while the job arrivals and job parameters in the super experiments correspond to the actual traces, we submit the job traces of the different logs to GridSim's EASY-backfilling scheduler to obtain queue waiting times. This is due to the difficulty in simulating the exact scheduling algorithms with fine-level policies in GridSim including priorities to short jobs, priorities to certain queues on specific days, effect of draining the jobs due to reservations, system failures etc. Moreover, the fine-level details are not available for all the systems in the workload archive.

For experiments with *synthetic traces*, we generated 32 synthetic scenarios with synthetic job traces. We consider four queues in all the scenarios. The different scenarios are as follows. We used a total of four system sizes, namely, 1 K, 16 K, 128 K and 256 K. For each of the system sizes, we used two processor partitioning schemes, namely equal and unequal partitioning schemes The equal partitioning scheme has four processor partitions of size $X/4$ each, where X is the total number of processors. The unequal partitioning scheme also has four processor partitions of sizes $X/8$, $X/8$, $X/4$ and $X/2$. Finally, for each of the four system sizes and each of the two processor partitioning schemes, we simulate four different kinds of loads on the system. These loads are modeled by different inter-arrival times, based on the real inter-arrival times of real workloads obtained from Feitelson's workload archive [18]. With this, we generate synthetic workloads which have almost similar job arrival patterns as the real workloads. Table 5 shows the various average inter-arrival times for each of the queues that we have used. The configurations of the four queues referred in Table 5 are shown in Table 6.

Table 5. Inter-arrival times for jobs in the queues

Load	Queue 1	Queue 2	Queue 3	Queue 4
I	15 min	1 h	2 h	2 h
II	15 min	1 h	1 h	1 h
III	15 min	1 h	2 h	5 h
IV	30 min	2 h	2 h	2 h

Table 6. Queue configurations

Queue ID	Max request size	Max ERT
I	$X/32$	12 h
II	$X/16$	18 h
III	$X/8$	1 day
IV	$X/4$	2 days

Hence we generate a total of $4(systemsizes) * 2(partitions) * 4(loads) = 32$ *scenarios*. These scenarios were carefully constructed after adequate survey of the various real systems in Feitelson's workload archive [18]. While a grid may not have a system ranging from 1 K to 256 K processors, these system sizes were chosen on the basis of the systems for which job traces were available in the workload archive. For each of the scenarios, we use the Parallel Workload Models [22, 23] for obtaining the synthetic traces. Using a workload model enables us to vary workload characteristics of the batch queues and study the variations of response times. The workload model generates a job trace consisting of arrival times, processor requirements and user estimated execution times of the jobs. Jobs corresponding to each queue are generated in the system based on the processor request size and the estimated run time characteristics of the job, following the protocols of the queue configuration. Each queue has a specific configuration in terms of maximum request size and maximum runtime allowed for a job. The maximum request size in terms of the number of processors and the max running time of a job for each of the queue in a system of X processors is shown in Table 6.

We compare our meta-scheduling strategy, *least_predictedqw*, with three strategies, namely, *static scheduling*, *least loaded*, and *redundant batch requests*. For our strategy *least_predictedqw* that uses predictions, we use our two-class predictions, explained in Sect. 3, since it gives better accuracy than single-class predictions and about the same accuracy as three-class predictions. We chose two-class predictions over three-class predictions since smaller number of classes imply tighter ranges of predictions. In our strategy, the metascheduler obtains the expected queue waiting time of a job for a given queue using multi-class predictions with probabilities. The estimated wait time is obtained as the weighted sum of the averages of the queue waiting times of the similar jobs in the classes, weighted by the probabilities for the classes. Our *least_predictedqw* then chooses the queue with the least expected waiting time for job submission. In the *static scheduling* strategy, the job will be scheduled for execution at the particular queue/site, where the job was originally submitted. In the *least loaded* technique proposed by Subramani et al. [13], scheduling by the meta-scheduler is done based on the current load in the system. They define load as the ratio of (sum of the cpu times of the queued jobs + sum of the remaining cpu times of the running jobs) to the total system size. A greedy strategy is then followed in which the job is submitted to the particular queue/site with the least load using the above load definition. In *redundant batch requests*, the job is submitted to all the queues and once the job starts its execution in any one of the queues, then the rest of the submissions are canceled. While a middleware may not be able to handle high loads due to redundant submissions, we use this technique as a baseline for evaluating the goodness of our method.

Results with Super Experiments. We first show the effectiveness of our least_predictedqw method over other methods in terms of the average wait time incurred by all the jobs submitted to the system. Figure 3 shows the average wait times of jobs for the different meta-scheduling methods. The figure shows that our methods gives up to 54 % and 33 % reduction in the average wait time compared to the static and least loaded methods, respectively. It can also be seen that our method is closest to the baseline method of redundant batch requests.

We also show the distribution of jobs across the various sites. An efficient distribution should be able to distribute in such a way that the number of jobs scheduled to a site is directly proportional to the system size associated with the site. Table 7 shows the distribution of the jobs across the sites for the various methods. The table also gives information regarding the system size. We can see that the proportionality is more evident in case of our Least_Predictedqw method, when compared to the other methods. For example, CTC has comparatively lesser system size compared to LANL, but the number of jobs scheduled in CTC is more by the Least_Loaded method than in LANL, while in our method the LANL has more jobs scheduled than CTC.

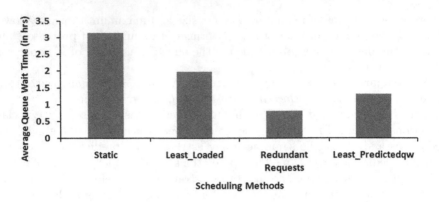

Fig. 3. Super experiments evaluation: Average wait time

Table 7. Super experiments evaluation: Job distribution - percentage of the total jobs scheduled in each of site

Sites	System size	Static (%)	Least_Loaded (%)	Least_Predictedqw (%)
CTC	430	22.9	13.7	10.4
ANL	163840	20.7	53.4	52.1
LANL	1024	21.7	11.2	18.3
HPC2N	240	5.7	7.6	2.0
SDSC Blue	1024	21.0	11.1	18.4
SDSC SP2	128	7.9	2.7	1.4

Results with Synthetic Traces. We now show some of the overall statistics over all the 32 synthetic scenarios. Table 8 shows the absolute statistics for each of the methods. In general, our method resulted in 35–94 % decrease in average wait time when compared to the static method, and 14–78 % decrease in average wait time when compared to *least_loaded* method. Our method also resulted in 8–80 % increase in the number of jobs with wait times less than one hour, and 6–99 % decrease in the number of jobs with wait times more than a day, when compared to the other methods.

Table 8. Synthetic experiments evaluation: Overall statistics (Absolute)

Attributes	Static	Least_Loaded	Least_Predictedqw
Avg wait time (in minutes)	196	105	52
% jobs with wait time $\leq$ 1 h	68	76	89
% jobs with wait time $\geq$ 1 day	3.2	1.4	0.5

6   Conclusions and Future Work

We have developed a machine learning based hierarchical prediction strategy for prediction of ranges of queue waiting times and probabilities. We used these predictions and probabilities in a meta-scheduling strategy that distributes jobs to different queues/sites in a multi-queue/grid environment for minimizing wait times of the jobs. Our experiments with different production supercomputer job traces show that our prediction strategies can give correct predictions for about 77–87 % of the jobs, and also result in about 12 % improved accuracy when compared to the next best existing method. Our experiments with our meta-scheduling strategy using different production and synthetic job traces for various system sizes, partitioning schemes and different workloads, show that our meta-scheduling strategy gives much improved performance when compared to existing scheduling policies by reducing the overall average queue waiting times of the jobs by about 47 %.

While we have used SVM for predictions, incremental machine learning appr-oaches can also be explored since they help in reducing the times for training and predictions. While the focus of this work is predictions of queue waiting times and metascheduling to reduce average wait times, we plan to develop techniques for predictions of execution times in order to predict total response times. We also plan to extend the meta-scheduling strategies to heterogeneous systems. The primary challenge in metascheduling for heterogeneous systems is to predict the runtime of a user job on different systems with different configurations, in addition to predicting the queue waiting times. While prediction of the run time for a job within a site can be made by considering similar job submissions by the same user in the history, the prediction can be extended to the other platforms by cross-platform performance modeling. We would also like to extend the meta-scheduling strategies that use stochastic predictions of both the wait times and the run times to select the appropriate number of resources for job executions in addition to the selection of the queue/site.

Acknowledgments. This work is supported by Department of Science and Technol-ogy (DST), India via the grant SR/S3/EECE/0095/2012.

References

1. IBM Load Leveler. http://www.redbooks.ibm.com/abstracts/sg246038.html
2. PBS Works. http://www.pbsworks.com
3. Tera Grid Karnak Prediction Service. http://karnak.teragrid.org/karnak/index.html
4. Kumar, R., Vadhiyar, S.: Identifying quick starters: towards an integrated frame-work for efficient predictions of queue waiting times of batch parallel jobs. In: Cirne, W., Desai, N., Frachtenberg, E., Schwiegelshohn, U. (eds.) JSSPP 2012. LNCS, vol. 7698, pp. 196–215. Springer, Heidelberg (2013)
5. Smith, W., Foster, I., Taylor, V.: Predicting application run times using historical information. In: Feitelson, D.G., Rudolph, L. (eds.) JSSPP 1998. LNCS, vol. 1459, pp. 122–142. Springer, Heidelberg (1998)

6. Smith, W., Taylor, V., Foster, I.: Using run-time predictions to estimate queue wait times and improve scheduler performance. In: Feitelson, D.G., Rudolph, L. (eds.) JSSPP 1999. LNCS, vol. 1659, pp. 202–219. Springer, Heidelberg (1999)

7. Feitelson, D.G., Rudolph, L., Schwiegelshohn, U.: Parallel job scheduling - a status report. In: Feitelson, D.G., Rudolph, L., Schwiegelshohn, U. (eds.) JSSPP 2004. LNCS, vol. 3277, pp. 1–16. Springer, Heidelberg (2005)

8. Nurmi, D., Brevik, J., Wolski, R.: QBETS: queue bounds estimation from time series. In: Frachtenberg, E., Schwiegelshohn, U. (eds.) JSSPP 2007. LNCS, vol. 4942, pp. 76–101. Springer, Heidelberg (2008)

9. Brevik, J., Nurmi, D., Wolski, R.: Predicting bounds on queuing delay for batch-scheduled parallel machines. In: PPoPP 2006: Proceedings of the Eleventh ACM SIGPLAN Symposium on Principles and Practice of Parallel Programming, pp. 110–118 (2006)

10. Li, H., Groep, D.L., Wolters, L.: Efficient response time predictions by exploiting application and resource state similarities. In: GRID 2005: Proceedings of the 6th IEEE/ACM International Workshop on Grid Computing, pp. 234–241 (2005)

11. Li, H., Chen, J., Tao, Y., Groep, D.L., Wolters, L.: Improving a local learning technique for queue wait time predictions. In: CCGRID 2006: Proceedings of the Sixth IEEE International Symposium on Cluster Computing and the Grid, pp. 335–342 (2006)

12. Casanova, H.: Benefits and drawbacks of redundant batch requests. J. Grid Comput. **5**, 235–250 (2007)

13. Subramani, V., Kettimuthu, R., Srinivasan, S., Sadayappan, P.: Distributed job scheduling on computational grids using multiple simultaneous requests. In: Proceedings of the 11th IEEE International Symposium on High Performance Distributed Computing, pp. 359–366 (2002)

14. Sabin, G., Lang, M.: Moldable parallel job schedulingusing jobefficiency: an iterative approach. In: Workshop on JobScheduling Strategies for Parallel Processing (JSSPP), in conjunction withACM SIGMETRICS (2006)

15. Li, H., Groep, D., Wolters, L.: Mining performance data for metascheduling decision support in the grid. J. Future Gener. Comput. Syst. - Special Section: Data mining in grid computing environments **23**(1), 92–99 (2007)

16. Wilson, D., Martinez, T.: Improved heterogeneous distance functions. J. Artif. Intell. Res. **6**, 134 (1997)

17. Machine Learning in Python. http://scikit-learn.org/stable

18. Parallel Workload Archive. http://www.cs.huji.ac.il/labs/parallel/workload/logs.htm

19. Standard Workload Format. http://www.cs.huji.ac.il/labs/parallel/workload/swf.htm

20. Buyya, R., Murshed, M.: Gridsim: A toolkit for the modeling and simulation of distributed resource management and scheduling for grid computing. Concurrency Comput. Pract. Exp. (CCPE) **14**(13), 1175–1220 (2002)

21. Redundant Batch Requests Simulator. http://sourceforge.net/projects/redsim

22. Parallel Workload Models. http://www.cs.huji.ac.il/labs/parallel/workload/models.htm

23. Lublin, U., Feitelson, D.G.: The workload on parallelsupercomputers: modeling the characteristics of rigid jobs. J. Parallel Distrib. Comput. **63**(11), 1105–1122 (2003)

Dynamically Scheduling a Component-Based Framework in Clusters

Aleksandra Kuzmanovska$^{(\boxtimes)}$, Rudolf H. Mak, and Dick Epema

Department of Mathematics and Computer Science,
Eindhoven University of Technology, P.O. Box 513,
5600 MB Eindhoven, The Netherlands
{a.kuzmanovska,r.h.mak,d.h.j.epema}@tue.nl

Abstract. In many clusters and data centers, application frameworks are used that offer programming models such as Dryad and MapReduce, and jobs submitted to the clusters or data centers may be targeted at specific instances of these frameworks, for example because of the presence of certain data. An important question that then arises is how to allocate resources to framework instances that may have highly fluctuating workloads over their lifetimes. Static resource allocation, a traditional approach for scheduling jobs, may result in inefficient resource allocation because of poor resource utilization during off-peak hours. We address this issue with a strategy for the dynamic deployment of a component-based framework by extending a resource manager responsible for scheduling jobs in multi-cluster environments. This extension allows scheduling multiple concurrent instances of the framework as long-running utility jobs that share computational resources of the cluster. In order to accommodate the fluctuating resource demands of frameworks, we consider two provisioning policies for dynamic resource allocation: OnDemand and Proactive provisioning. We evaluate the effectiveness of both policies by comparing them with static resource allocation on the DAS4 multi-cluster system. Our results show that dynamic resource allocation gives at least 30 % improvement over the static resource allocation with respect to both the utilization of the resources and the reject rate of the applications within the framework.

Keywords: Cluster · Datacenter · Framework · Scheduling · Dynamic deployment · Resource utilization

1 Introduction

The growing demand for computational resources has resulted in an increased popularity of clusters, grids, clouds and other data center environments. Various frameworks have been developed for these systems to accommodate domain-specific applications such as MapReduce [3] and Dryad [6] for parallel data-intensive applications, Pregel [9] for large-scale graph processing, and various component-based frameworks for specific application domains such as video processing [14]. Once installed in a cluster or data center, these frameworks act

© Springer International Publishing Switzerland 2015
W. Cirne and N. Desai (Eds.): JSSPP 2014, LNCS 8828, pp. 129–146, 2015.
DOI: 10.1007/978-3-319-15789-4_8

as utilities to which users can submit jobs that adhere to the programming models of the frameworks. The immediate question that arises is how many resources to allocate to framework instances in the face of time-varying workloads. In this paper, we address this question with the design, the implementation, and the analysis of a dynamic resource allocation mechanism for scheduling component-based frameworks in clusters.

There are different reasons for having the schedulers in clusters and data centers schedule framework instances rather than separate, single jobs, and leave the scheduling of the single jobs to the frameworks themselves. First, it relieves schedulers of large clusters and data centers of a potentially very high load of scheduling decisions. Secondly, it may be difficult to teach the cluster schedulers about all the intricacies of potentially many frameworks that may influence the quality of scheduling decisions. Thirdly, frameworks typically require their own configuration and deployment steps of variable complexity. For instance, some frameworks require a distributed file system to be set up with a certain replication factor (e.g., HDFS [21] for MapReduce), whereas others may need name servers or component repositories to be installed. Although these frameworks may require complex and potentially time-consuming deployment, once deployed, they act as long-running utilities serving large numbers of users who may submit highly fluctuating workloads and the cost of their deployment can be amortized across many jobs.

A common approach for allocating resources to framework instances is static resource allocation, where each framework instance runs on a fixed number of resources over its lifetime. However, even though many frameworks have their own resource management, static allocation leads to fragmentation and periods of over- and under-utilization of the allotted resources and is therefore not a suitable solution. In contrast, dynamic resource allocation reflects changing resource requirements of a framework instance by changing the fraction of resources allotted to the framework during its lifetime. In this approach, each framework instance is allotted a minimum number of resources, sufficient for its initial deployment. As the load submitted to the framework changes over time, its resource allocation is continuously adapted, in order to achieve continuously a high utilization.

There are several challenges in using dynamic resource allocation for allocating cluster resources to frameworks. First, framework extendibility is essential in the context of dynamic resource allocation, but unfortunately, not all frameworks are extendible. Secondly, most frameworks are developed independently and their local resource managers are not capable of communicating with external resource managers. Thirdly, resource provisioning policies at the cluster side have to meet the fluctuating resource demands of all competing frameworks.

In previous work, we have designed and implemented the KOALA [10] resource manager for multi-cluster systems such as the DAS4 [11]. The original purpose of KOALA was to support co-allocation, i.e., the allocation of processors in multiple clusters to single parallel (MPI) applications. Later we have incorporated support for scheduling various application types into KOALA, e.g., Bags-of-Tasks [16], workflows [17], and malleable applications [1]. In all of these cases, the jobs submitted to KOALA are single applications. In contrast, previous work on support in KOALA for scheduling of MapReduce clusters [4] addresses scheduling of multiple jobs as a part of single MapReduce instances.

The purpose of this paper is to present the design, the implementation, and the analysis of an extension of the KOALA resource manager for the dynamic deployment of the FLUENT framework [2,14] as long-running utility jobs. In our case, the "jobs" scheduled by KOALA are instances of the FLUENT framework rather than single jobs. Our extension of KOALA provides two-level resource management. At the first level, KOALA allocates resources to the frameworks, and at the second level, local resource managers within each framework instance use the allotted resources for the deployment of jobs submitted to them. Furthermore, these local resource managers can negotiate resource allocation with KOALA: additional resources may be requested or unused resources may be released. Our final aim is to create a *generic* extension to KOALA that allows a wide range of frameworks to be scheduled dynamically in cluster and data center environments. The research reported in this paper contributes towards that goal by:

- An extension of the KOALA resource manager for the dynamic deployment of the FLUENT framework as a long-running utility (Sects. 2 and 3).
- The introduction of two provisioning policies, OnDemand and Proactive, for the dynamic resizing of FLUENT framework instances (Sect. 3).
- The experimental evaluation of the proposed extension including the policies by means of synthetic workloads in a real cluster environment (Sect. 4).

2   The FLUENT Framework

FLUENT is a distributed component framework for run-time composition of component-based applications [2,14]. Figure 1 visualizes the building blocks of the framework, called framework entities, in terms of a client-server architecture. From a logical point of view, the server side of the framework is organized in three layers: the *Master* layer, the *Orchestrator* layer, and the *Runtime* layer. Besides the framework entities divided across the three layers, the server side of the framework consists of two types of file-based storage for storing re-usable applications and components: a *Global repository* and a *Local repository*. From a deployment point of view, the framework entities which are deployed on a physical node define the node's role as either a *client*, a *master*, an *orchestrator* or a *worker node*. A single physical node can have multiple roles, with the only restriction that two worker nodes cannot be placed on a single physical node.

The client side of the framework comprises client nodes with *GUITool* entities deployed on them. The *GUITool* is a user interface for managing components and applications which are stored and deployed on the server side of the framework. For that purpose, this entity offers a set of interfaces that cover various aspects of application management such as discovery of available components, composition of applications, deployment of composed applications, and monitoring and dynamic reconfiguration framework entities. A single *GUITool* corresponds to a single user of the framework, but a single client node may contain multiple *GUITools*.

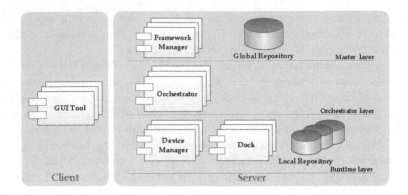

Fig. 1. The client-server architecture of the FLUENT framework.

The server side of the framework comprises master, orchestrator and worker nodes distributed across the *Master*, the *Orchestrator*, and the *Runtime* layers, respectively. A master node is reserved for the *FrameworkManager* entity and the *Global repository*. The *FrameworkManager* entity is the central part of the FLUENT framework that provides a registry-based entity subscription and entity discovery service to the rest of the framework. The *FrameworkManager* entity manages information where other entities are hosted and allows dynamic configuration of all framework entities. The *Global repository* is a file-based storage that holds two types of data: available components in the form of shared libraries and applications composed of these components in the form of description files. A single master node exists within the FLUENT framework with a single *FrameworkManager* installed on it.

An orchestrator node is used for deployment of *Orchestrator* entities which provide key functionality to compose, deploy, and monitor an application. An *Orchestrator* entity acts as an application manager which enables placement of application components on worker nodes. A single instance of it manages a single application at a time. The number of possible orchestrator nodes within the framework depends on the number of applications running concurrently within the framework. A single orchestrator node may host multiple *Orchestrators*.

A worker node has a *Local repository* and a *DeviceManager* entity deployed on it. The *DeviceManager* entity is the basic processing unit in the framework which is responsible for application execution and monitoring the resource usage by the application. Components of deployed applications are isolated in separate containers within the *DeviceManager* called *Docks*. A *Dock* entity is a wrapper for application components that manages the connections between them. A subset of the *Global repository* is installed on a worker node in the form of a *Local repository* which holds components and applications available locally. A common deployment of the framework comprises multiple worker nodes with a single *DeviceManager* installed on each of them.

An application running in the framework involves a single *Orchestrator* that orchestrates deployment of its components on a single or across multiple *Docks* according to the deployment specification in the application description file.

Since the numbers of nodes employed by the two of the layers, *Orchestrator* and *Runtime*, depend on the current load in the framework, both layers need to be dynamic in order to enable dynamic deployment of the framework in cluster environments. As part of the *FrameworkManager*, there is a resource manager capable of handling dynamic changes of physical resources, but it does not handle scheduling of applications over worker nodes in the framework. We address this issue by extending the resource manager with a scheduler that is responsible for scheduling applications submitted to it. This scheduler places application components on worker nodes according to the FCFS scheduling policy with preference to reuse partially busy nodes before using the idle nodes.

3   KOALA Extension for Dynamic Scheduling of Frameworks

In this section, we describe the mechanisms and policies for dynamic resource allocation by KOALA to the FLUENT framework, as a representative of component-based frameworks. First, we describe the KOALA resource manager used for scheduling jobs in multi-cluster environments. Then we present the additional components that are needed and how they should work together so that KOALA is able to achieve dynamic deployment of frameworks such as FLUENT. Finally, we discuss the resizing mechanisms and the provisioning policies used for dynamic allocation of resources.

3.1   The KOALA Resource Manager

KOALA [10] is a resource manager for scheduling jobs in multi-cluster environments, where each cluster consists of a number of compute nodes used for computations only, and a single head node used as an access point to the cluster. The kernel part of the resource manager is the scheduler that schedules jobs by placing them on suitable cluster sites according to its placement policies. Once compute nodes are allocated to the job, the actual job submission to those nodes is done by specialized interfaces called *runners* that provide the ability to submit and monitor jobs of different application types. In the past we have implemented runners for rigid parallel applications [10], cycle scavenging jobs [16], workflows [17], malleable applications [1], and map-reduce jobs [4].

3.2   System Architecture

In this paper, the "jobs" scheduled by the KOALA resource manager are fully functional FLUENT framework instances. Scheduling such a framework instance involves the deployment of the three server-side layers of the FLUENT framework on the cluster nodes allocated by the KOALA scheduler in such a way that each node executes framework entities from a single layer only. The framework is deployed on exactly one node dedicated to the *Master* layer, at least one node dedicated to the *Orchestrator* layer, and multiple nodes dedicated to the *Runtime* layer. We distinguish two types of phases in dynamic scheduling of the framework-based job: the initial and the resizing phase. The initial phase covers the initial deployment of the framework on a minimal number of nodes required for the job execution, which is given as an input to the job in the form of a job description file (jdf). Required nodes are allocated by KOALA, and distributed among the three layers. In the resizing phase, the numbers of nodes dedicated to the *Orchestrator* and the *Runtime* layers are changed based on the load submitted to the framework. The latter changes are negotiated with KOALA where nodes are the unit of resource allocation.

To add support to the KOALA scheduler for scheduling framework-based jobs on a multi-cluster system, we have extended the original KOALA architecture with two components: a runner called the *FrameworkRunner (FR)*, and a global job manager called the *FrameworkJobManager (FJM)*, which keeps track of all running FLUENT instances. Figure 2 provides a high level overview of the newly introduced KOALA components and their iterations involved in scheduling a single FLUENT framework on a multi-cluster system.

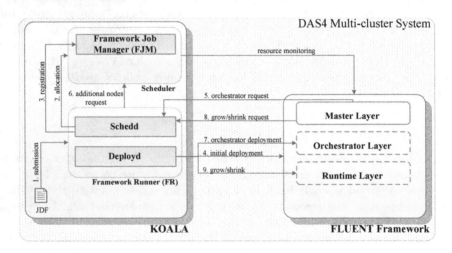

Fig. 2. The sequence of steps involved in scheduling a single FLUENT framework by the KOALA scheduler.

The *FJM* has been added to the scheduler part of the KOALA resource manager and supports the deployment of multiple frameworks. For that purpose, it maintains connections of every framework instance deployed through KOALA and their metadata such as a unique framework identifier, the location of the configuration files, the deployed sites, and the location of the master node. Whenever the *GUITool* needs access to the deployed framework, it can obtain this information from the *FJM*.

The *FR* is used for scheduling framework-based jobs which requires a job description file as an input. This job submission interface consists of two components: a schedule demon *Schedd* that interfaces with the KOALA scheduler, and a deployment daemon *Deployd* that interacts with the FLUENT framework deployed through the *FR*. *Schedd* communicates with the KOALA scheduler in order to provide the desired number of nodes to the framework scheduled by it, whereas *Deployd* deploys the framework entities on the nodes allotted by the KOALA scheduler. *Deployd* handles the communication with the deployed framework, and is responsible for all changes in the deployment of the FLUENT instances. A single *FR* corresponds to a single FLUENT instance scheduled for deployment.

The interaction between these components and a framework instance scheduled for deployment starts with the job submission (step 1 in Fig. 2). The *Schedd* component of the *FR* processes the jdf, received as an input from a job submission side, and subsequently requests (step 2) the desired number of compute nodes from the KOALA scheduler. After the successful allocation of these nodes, *Schedd* registers (step 3) the submitted framework with the newly introduced *FJM*. Subsequently, the control is transferred to the *Deployd* component which interacts with local resource managers of the clusters, e.g., SGE, to deploy the framework entities and to install the file system which contains the repositories of the framework (step 4). These four steps capture the interactions in the initial phase.

In the second phase, two events may cause dynamic resizing of the framework: the submission of a new job to the framework or the completion of a running job application by the framework. In response to a submission of a new job, the *FrameworkManager* requests deployment of *Orchestrator* entities (step 5), for all applications in the job, from the *FR*, for which either an additional node may be requested (step 6) from the KOALA scheduler or an already allocated orchestrator node can be used (step 7). Based on the resizing mechanisms described in the next section, the *FR* resizes the *Orchestrator* layer.

Once a novel *Orchestrator* entity has been deployed by *Deployd*, it subsequently takes care of deploying the job applications in FLUENT. This is not depicted in Fig. 2 since it is an intra-framework activity. KOALA is not aware of the application deployment until the framework detects a lack of suitable worker nodes and requests additional ones from the *FR* (step 8). As a response to such a request, *Schedd* may either request additional nodes from the KOALA scheduler (step 5), which are subsequently deployed as worker nodes by *Deployd* (step 9), or may reject the request based on the provisioning policies described in the next section.

3.3   Resizing Mechanisms and Provisioning Policies

In addition to allocating compute nodes for the initial deployment of a framework, the *FR* dynamically resizes two layers of a deployed framework: the *Orchestrator* and the *Runtime* layers. For each layer, we introduce a resizing mechanism to handle changes in the number of compute nodes allocated to the framework.

The mechanism for resizing the *Orchestrator* layer is based on the current number of *Orchestrators* deployed on orchestrator nodes. The *Orchestrator* layer of a framework instance is extended by an additional node when the average number of deployed *Orchestrators* exceeds a threshold. The threshold value is empirically chosen based on the performance analysis described in Sect. 4. When an orchestrator node is idle during a period of time, which means there are no *Orchestrators* deployed on it, the node is removed from the *Orchestrator* layer and return to KOALA. The resizing mechanism is such that at least one orchestrator node is always available for *Orchestrator* deployment.

The mechanism for resizing the *Runtime* layer is regulated by one of two provisioning policies called the **OnDemand** and the **Proactive** policy.

In the **OnDemand** policy, FLUENT takes the initiative for resizing the *Runtime* layer by following the pattern of job submissions to a framework instance. In contrast, in the **Proactive** policy it is the KOALA resource manager that takes initiative for resizing by keeping the utilization of a framework instance within certain bounds without knowing any details about the framework activities. In both policies, KOALA sets the maximum number of worker nodes allowed per framework instance to a value F_{max} which is a general static value applied to all instances. FLUENT does not support application migration but it does allow partially busy worker nodes. When FLUENT deploys new applications, it tries to pack them on partially busy, rather than idle, worker nodes.

The **OnDemand** policy resizes the *Runtime* layer based on framework requests of two types called grow requests and shrink requests. This policy allows the initial deployment of the framework with the minimal number of nodes, a single master and a single orchestrator node, whereas the worker nodes are deployed dynamically as part of the resizing. When a FLUENT instance does not have sufficient idle worker nodes for the deployment of a newly submitted job, it sends a grow request for the number of additional worker nodes it needs for the job. We assume the framework knows how many nodes are required for job execution, and we will show how FLUENT calculates the number of nodes needed for our example applications in Sect. 4.

The *FR* adds the requested number of worker nodes to the *Runtime* layer of the framework, unless the value F_{max} is exceeded or KOALA does not have free resources. A shrink request is sent when the framework instance has worker nodes that have been idle for a time period of length at least t_{idle}, to which the *FR* responses by removing these idle worker nodes from the *Runtime* layer. The value of the parameter t_{idle} is empirically chosen with the performance analysis described in Sect. 4.

The **Proactive** policy, on the other hand, resizes the *Runtime* layer in response to requests by the KOALA scheduler. This policy does require worker nodes as part of the initial deployment of the framework; this number can be changed because of resizing, but will never go below the number of nodes used in the initial deployment. By adding to and removing nodes from the *Runtime* layer, the policy tries to keep the average CPU utilization of the *Runtime* layer between two threshold values U_{min} and U_{max}, which are specified on the scheduler side. Based on monitoring information, the KOALA scheduler expands the *Runtime* layer by the same number of worker nodes as in the initial deployment when the average CPU utilization of the *Runtime* layer exceeds U_{max}, and contracts it by the number of idle worker nodes when the average CPU utilization of the *Runtime* layer drops below U_{min}. Again, when KOALA wants to shrink the *Runtime* layer, it only removes nodes that have been idle for at least t_{idle}.

When KOALA cannot meet the framework requirements and rejects grow requests, depending on the application type, the framework will either queue the submitted application until the current worker nodes can deploy them or reject the application, e.g., in a video surveillance case (see Sect. 4).

4   Performance Evaluation

In this section, we present a performance evaluation of dynamic resource allocation to the FLUENT framework deployed as a utility in the DAS multi-cluster system. First, we describe the experimental setup and the types of applications supported by the FLUENT framework with an emphasis on the applications we use in the experiments. Then, we describe the conducted experiments and the workloads used in the experiments. Finally, we analyze the obtained results.

4.1   Experimental Setup

For the purpose of the evaluation, we use the DAS multi-cluster system as the experimental environment. DAS4 [11] is the fourth generation of this system, and is distributed across research institutes and organizations in the Netherlands. The system consists of six clusters and comprises roughly 200 compute nodes with properties as shown in Table 1. The Sun Grid Engine(SGE) to which KOALA interfaces, operates as the local resource manager on each of the DAS clusters.

Table 1. Specification of compute nodes in the DAS multi-cluster system

Processor	Dual quad-core Intel E5620 at 2.4 GHz
Memory	24 GB RAM
Network	10 Gbit/s Infiniband, 1 Gbit/s Ethernet
Disk	2 ATA OCZ Z-Drive R2 with 2 TB (RAID0)
OS	Linux CentOS-6
JVM	jdk 1.6.0_27

The experiments were performed within a single cluster with 32 compute nodes and a single head node. The initial deployment of the FLUENT framework comprises a single master node, a single orchestrator node, and multiple worker nodes. The number of worker nodes used for the initial deployment of the framework depends on the experiment and the provisioning policy. The components available for an application composition are stored in the *Local Repositories* installed on each worker node, whereas the *Global Repository* exists as a union of the *Local Repositories*. The Infiniband network is used for inter-framework communication among the framework entities due its low latency in data transmission. The clients are deployed on the head node.

The worker-node idle time parameter t_{idle} and the utilization threshold values U_{min} and U_{max} used in the provisioning policies are determined as part of the calibration experiment. Since the **Proactive** policy requires data about CPU utilization of the allocated nodes, we collect the CPU utilization statistics of every node with a sampling interval of 40 s using the open-source "audria" utility tool [12] and the standard Linux monitoring tool "pidstat".

4.2 FLUENT Applications

FLUENT applications are component-based applications, and they are composed from fully independent components with well-defined interfaces and specified behavior. Components are reused across multiple applications and can be dynamically orchestrated to build various applications. A FLUENT application is represented by an application description file in which the used components are defined, together with the bindings between them and deployment information.

The FLUENT framework has been conceived as a general-purpose framework, but was originally used as a framework for video processing multimedia applications in the area of surveillance and transport logistics in the scope of the ViCoMo project [13]. Therefore, the framework comes with libraries of components that provide video encoding/decoding, streaming, and customized support typically used in video processing applications. The surveillance applications are computationally intensive applications with fluctuating resource requirements over their long lifetimes, and require short deployment time (response time).

Both long running computationally intensive and parallel data-intensive applications are conveniently supported by the FLUENT framework. In our experiments, we use two applications: an application from the video processing domain, named *RemoteLaplace (RL)*, as a representative of the computationally intensive applications, and a more general application that performs a word count on a file, named *StreamingWordcount (SWC)*, as a representative of data-intensive applications. Each of these applications uses its own library of components described below.

The video processing library used in the *RemoteLaplace (RL)* application consists of two components. Both components have a single interface to communicate to each other by using a buffer or overwrite channels. The applications provided by this library have a simple producer-consumer architecture. The first component performs image sharpening by applying a Laplacian filter on the input video stream which has been smoothed to remove noise. The component generates two outputs shown in real-time, the original video and the transformed video. The video transformation is based on two parameters that are provided remotely by the second component which simulates user input by generating new values for the parameters every s seconds. Therefore the computational load changes every s seconds.

The library used in the *Streaming Wordcount (SWC)* application consists of five components, three core components and two auxiliary components that allow applications to be structured with a variable number of core components. As opposed to the communication between mappers and reducers by means of files in MapReduce, these components communicate with each other by using buffer channels. The main computing component of the library is a *mapper*, which emits key-value pairs for each word of the input block of text. The *reader* component provides the *mapper* with input by reading and splitting the given input file in multiple blocks, and emitting each of them separately. The counting part is performed in the *counter* component which is responsible for generating the output file. These three core components allow applications with only one *mapper* computing component. In order to support parallel processing in data-intensive applications, the auxiliary components are used for composing applications with multiple *mappers*. The *multiplexer* auxiliary component splits up and redirects its input across two outputs, whereas the *demultiplexer* component redirects two received inputs to one output. Multiple levels of *multiplexer* and *demultiplexer* components can be used, and the number of *mappers* in an application can be 2^n, for $n = 1, 2, \ldots$ when using n levels of auxiliary components.

4.3   Experiments and Workloads

We perform two types of experiments and classify them as either micro- or macro-experiments. By means of two micro-experiments, we investigate the characteristics of the operation of the framework and of the execution of single jobs. In the first micro-experiment, we asses the time required to install an instance of the FLUENT framework, the time required to process a grow request, and the time required to deploy a job submitted to a running instance of FLUENT. In the second micro-experiment, we examine the CPU utilization of the *Orchestrator* and the *Runtime* layers for both application types to find out how many applications may fit on one node in both layers. Within this experiment, we deploy the two applications separately.

The *RL* application has two components and its runtime is restricted to 300 s; it operates on a video with a playing time of 300 s at a frame rate of 60 fps and with a frame resolution of 320×239 pixels. The filter parameter s is set to 30 s, which means that the transformation is performed 10 times during the application life time. The *SWC* application has three components, a *reader*, a single *mapper*, and a *counter* component. It processes a 10 MB file by reading data blocks of 100 KB that are processed in sequence by the single *mapper*. When deployed using a one-to-one mapping between components and cores, its runtime is 44 min. In both the *SWC* and *RL* applications, the application components are deployed within a single worker node.

By means of the two macro-experiments, we evaluate the performance benefit of dynamic resource allocation with the two provisioning policies over static resource allocation by submitting workloads consisting of many jobs. In the first macro-experiment, we perform a sensitivity analysis of the parameters t_{idle}, U_{min}

and U_{max} used in the dynamic provisioning policies. In the second macro-experiment, we assess the performance of the dynamic allocation of resources with our two provisioning policies (OnDemand and Proactive) versus static allocation.

In this assessment, we use a synthetic workload W_{rl}, that consist of jobs each running a number of RL applications to reflect the operation of multiple surveillance video cameras started simultaneously, e.g., for monitoring a shopping mall or a parking garage. Therefore, the arrivals of the applications in the W_{rl} workload are modeled by a batch arrival process with the jobs (batches of applications) arriving according to a Poisson process with rate $\lambda = 0.027$ per second. The sizes of the batches are also random, with a geometric distribution over the interval $[1, 10]$ and the mean batch size of 2.0 applications. We choose the arrival rate and the mean value of job size such that the workload jobs utilize approximately 40 % of the framework with 20 worker nodes.

Since every RL video application requires immediate deployment and sufficient resources over its lifetime, in order to evaluate the performance, we use the *reject rate* as a metric; jobs can be partially accepted and rejected if only several but not all of the video applications in its batch fit on the available resources, and we define the reject rate as the percentage of all applications across all jobs in the workload that are rejected. In addition we use the *utilization* as a metric, defined as the ratio of actually used and the total number of (statically or dynamically) allocated resources. In these experiments, the maximum number of worker nodes per framework, denoted by F_{max}, is set to 20 worker nodes.

4.4   Experimental Results

The results from the first micro-experiment in which we investigate the overheads of the FLUENT framework, show that the time needed for the initial deployment of the framework is affected by the type (but not the number) of nodes involved in the deployment.

When the **OnDemand** policy is used, the initial deployment of the framework involves only master and orchestrator nodes, and takes on average 11 s. In case of static allocation or dynamic allocation with the **Proactive** policy, besides the master and orchestrator nodes, workers nodes are also involved in the initial deployment of the framework, and it takes on average 45 s. The difference between the initial deployment times in the two cases is due to the additional time needed for the worker nodes to install the *Local Repositories*, which includes the transfer of application components from the *Global Repository*.

For the deployment of a job, a running framework instance needs on average 62 ms when all worker nodes needed for deployment are available; this is the time from the job submission on the client side until the applications included in the job start operating on worker nodes, including the scheduling and the placement time of their application components. The average overhead in the framework for handling a grow request, denoted by O_{grow}, which includes node allocation by KOALA and the deployment of the suitable entities on them by the *FR*, is approximately 30 s.

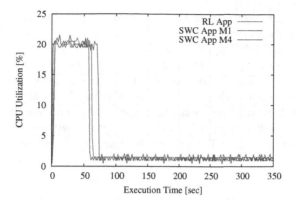

Fig. 3. The CPU utilization of a single node in the *Orchestrator* layer (SWC App M1, M4 indicates the SWC application with 1 or 4 mappers).

As to the results of the second micro-experiment, in which we investigate the number of applications that can be hosted on a single node, Fig. 3 shows that the utilization of the *Orchestrator* layer is neither application-type nor application-size specific. During the application deployment, around 20 % of the CPU is needed at the beginning. This peak covers the deployment of the orchestrator entity itself, and afterwards, only 2 % CPU time is needed for orchestrating an application. The period of high CPU utilization lasts for 70 s and it occurs only once per *Orchestrator* lifetime.

We can conclude that a single orchestrator node can host multiple *Orchestrators* with a potential delay of $70N/5$ sec when N applications are submitted simultaneously. As the jobs in the macro-experiment consist of at most 10 applications, the expected delay is at most 140 s. Based on these results, we fix the threshold used in the resizing mechanism of the *Orchestrator* layer to 45. When the number of *Orchestrators* deployed on an orchestrator node exceeds this value, KOALA introduces a new node in the *Orchestrator* layer.

With respect to the *Runtime* layer, Fig. 4(a) shows that the *RL* application is computationally intensive with a fluctuating CPU utilization pattern over its

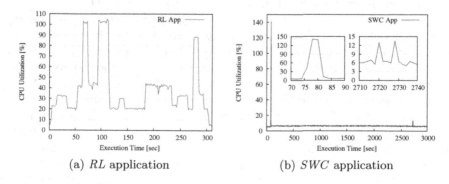

(a) *RL* application   (b) *SWC* application

Fig. 4. CPU utilization of a worker node in the *Runtime* layer for different applications.

execution time. The fluctuating CPU utilization leads to the conclusion that only a single application can be placed on a single node without overloading. On the other hand, the *SWC* application (Fig. 4(b)) has very low CPU utilization, around 5 % during the *mapper* execution, with two short peaks at the beginning and at the end of the application execution. These two peaks correspond to the I/O operation for reading the input file and writing the results back to the disk in the *reader* and *counter* components, respectively. Therefore, a single worker node can host an *SWC* application with 20 *mappers* without overloading. As a conclusion we can say the utilization of the *Runtime* layer varies depending on the type of deployed applications.

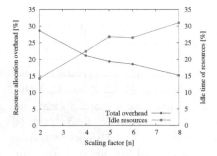

Fig. 5. The resource allocation overhead due to grow requests and the fraction of idle resources depending on the worker-node idle time $t_{idle} = n \cdot O_{grow}$ in the OnDemand policy.

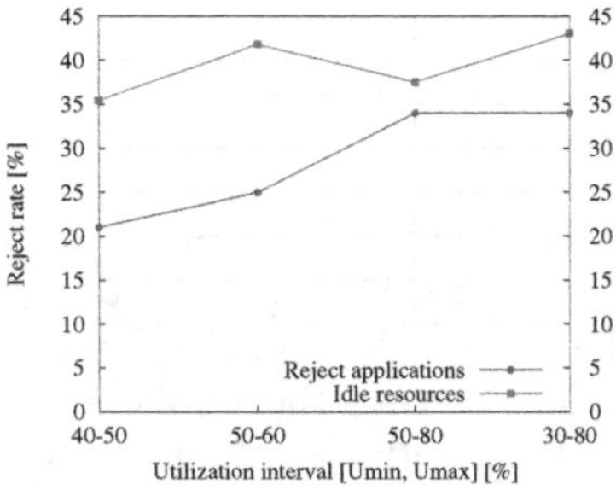

Fig. 6. The reject rate of applications and the fraction of idle resources vs. different ranges of U_{min} - U_{max} in the Proactive policy.

In the first macro-experiment, we conduct a sensitivity analysis of the parameters t_{idle}, U_{min} and U_{max} of the provisioning policies. First we consider t_{idle}, the time worker nodes can remain idle before being released. We relate t_{idle} to the average overhead for handling a grow request O_{grow}, and we assess the effect on the performance of scaling O_{grow} by a factor n on the resource allocation overhead and the resource idle time t_{idle} by setting $t_{idle} = n \cdot O_{grow}$.

Figure 5 shows the behavior of the framework when processing the workload W_{rl} for different values of the scaling factor n in terms of the total overhead due to grow requests and the idle time of the allocated resources. The higher the scaling factor, the lower the number of grow requests and so the less overhead for resource allocation, but the higher the fraction of idle resources. In the **Proactive** policy, where the value t_{idle} is used as a control mechanism to ensure that resources are not needlessly kept in the framework, we want to release the nodes as soon as they become idle, so we fix the scaling factor at $n = 2$. In the **OnDemand** policy, we fix the scaling factor at $n = 6$ since the *RL* application requires quick deployment without an overhead for additional resource allocation.

Figure 6 shows the behavior of the framework when processing the workload W_{rl} for different values of the parameters $U_{min} - U_{max}$ in terms of the reject

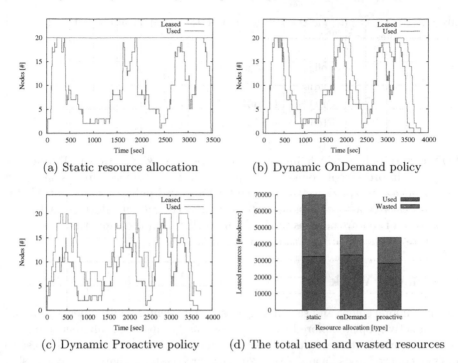

(a) Static resource allocation

(b) Dynamic OnDemand policy

(c) Dynamic Proactive policy

(d) The total used and wasted resources

Fig. 7. The amounts of resources allocated and used with static and dynamic allocation for the workload with the RL application (over time and total).

rate of applications and the idle time of the allocated resources. Since the total overhead due to grow requests cannot be measured on the framework side, we use the application reject rate as a metric to determine the values of U_{min} and U_{max}. As we can see in Fig. 6, setting the utilization levels U_{min} and U_{max} to 40 % and 50 %, respectively, gives the lowest number of rejected applications and the smallest fraction of idle resources.

The results from the second macro-experiment show that both our policies for dynamic allocation of resources improve the performance over static resource allocation in terms of the resource utilization and the application reject rate. In Fig. 7 we show the amount of allocated and used resources over time, and the total amount of leased resources (used and wasted) during the experiments with the video application workload. Clearly, with the two dynamic policies, the amounts of allocated resources follow the patterns of the used resources pretty well, and the dynamic policies waste significantly less resources than static allocation (Fig. 7(d)).

In Table 2, we show the performance metrics for each of the policies when processing the W_{rl} workload in terms of the reject rate of applications and the the actual utilization of the allocated resources as the ratio of used and allocated resources from Fig. 7(d). We find that the **Proactive** policy improves resource utilization by approximately 30 %, but it is not as good as the

Table 2. The reject rate and the utilization with the RL application vs. the allocation policy (all values are in %.)

Policy	Reject Rate	Utilization
Static	13 %	46 %
OnDemand	13 %	73 %
Proactive	21 %	65 %

OnDemand policy, which improves utilization by 37 %. For the **Proactive** policy, the improvement comes at the price of a higher reject rate, as shown in Table 2. As a conclusion, we can say the **OnDemand** policy is more suitable for applications with a batch arrival pattern such as the RL jobs, because it follows the pattern of resource usages in the framework and in the same time keeps the reject rate on the same level as the static allocation.

5 Related Work

Resource management and scheduling jobs in data center environments is an old but still active topic, explored by many research groups from different domains. From the current state of the art resource management systems, the closest to ours system are Mesos [5] and YARN [20]. All three systems share the same design goal of multiplexing resources among multiple parallel frameworks.

Mesos provides a two-level scheduling mechanism for sharing cluster resources across multiple parallel frameworks, and in particular shares data among the frameworks. In Mesos, a centralised global scheduler periodically does resource offers to individual frameworks that can either accept or reject them. It allows a framework to specify, in form of filters, the kinds of resources it will never accept, but it is always the global scheduler that takes initiative for resource allocation. In contrast, we design, implement and compare mechanisms in which either the frameworks explicitly express their requirements, and the global scheduler, KOALA, allocates the requested resources, or the initiative lies with the KOALA scheduler. As another difference, Mesos acts as the owner of the cluster resources, while KOALA does not own resources, but is built on top of, and interfaces to, the local cluster schedulers. The advantage of our approach to supporting frameworks does not in any way entail any change in the setup or deployment of the clusters.

YARN is a resource manager that explicitly has multi-framework support, but it interfaces to per-job application managers rather than framework managers as KOALA does and so in fact, it still provides a single-level scheduling mechanism. However, as opposed to Mesos, it is request-based, like our OnDemand policy. Both systems support allocation of a single resource type. YARN supports allocation of fixed-sized memory chunks whereas KOALA supports only allocation of processors.

Omega [8] is another cluster management system with a parallel architecture. It follows the alternative decentralized approach of *shared-state* scheduling by having the schedulers of multiple parallel frameworks compete for the resources of the complete cluster without a central authority. Omega employs lock-free optimistic concurrency control to mediate between conflicting allocation decisions of the separate schedulers at the potential cost of redoing work when optimistic concurrency assumptions are incorrect.

Other state of the art approaches mostly cover automatic resource management and scheduling of jobs in clusters and grids. Cluster and grid resource managers such as Torque [18], Condor [15,19], and Quincy [7], address jobs that require static resource allocations during their execution. They typically deploy jobs onto dedicated, statically-partitioned clusters of machines, which leads to fragmentation and under-utilization of resources. These problems are resolved in KOALA by using dynamic resource allocation.

6 Conclusion

In this paper we have presented an extension to the KOALA resource manager that enables dynamic resource allocation to instances of the FLUENT framework. We have designed and implemented two policies for provisioning resources to frameworks, and we have assessed the performance of the dynamic allocation of resources with our two provisioning policies (OnDemand and Proactive) versus static allocation. Our results show that both policies for dynamic allocation of resources improve the performance over static resource allocation by at least 30 %, with respect to both the utilization of the resources and the reject rate of the applications within the framework.

As future work, we are planning to design a mechanism in KOALA for dynamically allocating resources in clusters and data centers to frameworks that is as generic as possible and that can accommodate many different frameworks. In addition, we will refine our policies for doing the dynamic allocations and we will analyze their performance with mixes of various frameworks in clusters and other data center environments.

References

1. Buisson, J., Sonmez, O.O., Mohamed, H.H., Lammers, W., Epema, D.H.J.: Scheduling malleable applications in multicluster systems. In: IEEE International Conference on Cluster Computing, pp. 372–381 (2007)
2. David, I., Orlic, B., Mak, R.H., Lukkien, J.J.: Towards resource-aware runtime reconfigurable component-based systems. In: 2010 6th World Congress on Services, SERVICES 2010, pp. 465—466. IEEE Computer Society, Washington, DC, USA (2010). http://dx.doi.org/10.1109/SERVICES.2010.98
3. Dean, J., Ghemawat, S.: Mapreduce: simplified data processing on large clusters. Commun. ACM **51**(1), 107–113 (2008). http://doi.acm.org/10.1145/1327452.1327492
4. Ghit, B., Yigitbasi, N., Epema, D.: Resource management for dynamic mapreduce clusters in multicluster systems. In: Proceedings of the 5th Workshop on Many-Task Computing on Grids and Supercomputers (MTAGS) co-located with Supercomputing (SC). IEEE (2012)

5. Hindman, B., Konwinski, A., Zaharia, M., Ghodsi, A., Joseph, A.D., Katz, R., Shenker, S., Stoica, I.: Mesos: a platform for fine-grained resource sharing in the data center. In: 8th USENIX Conference on Networked Systems Design and Implementation, NSDI 2011, pp. 22–22 (2011). http://dl.acm.org/citation.cfm?id=1972457.1972488

6. Isard, M., Budiu, M., Yu, Y., Birrell, A., Fetterly, D.: Dryad: distributed data-parallel programs from sequential building blocks. SIGOPS Oper. Syst. Rev. **41**(3), 59–72 (2007). http://doi.acm.org/10.1145/1272998.1273005

7. Isard, M., Prabhakaran, V., Currey, J., Wieder, U., Talwar, K., Goldberg, A.: Quincy: fair scheduling for distributed computing clusters. In: 22nd ACM Symposium on Operating Systems Principles, SOSP 2009, pp. 261–276 (2009). http://doi.acm.org/10.1145/1629575.1629601

8. Schwarzkopf, M., Konwinski, A., Abd-El-Malek, M., Wilkes, J.: Omega: flexible, scalable schedulers for large compute clusters. In: Eurosys 2013 (2013)

9. Malewicz, G., Austern, M.H., Bik, A.J., Dehnert, J.C., Horn, I., Leiser, N., Czajkowski, G.: Pregel: A system for large-scale graph processing. In: 2010 ACM SIGMOD International Conference on Management of Data, pp. 135–146 (2010)

10. Mohamed, H., Epema, D.: Koala: a co-allocating grid scheduler. Concurr. Comput. Pract. Experience **20**(16), 1851–1876 (2008)

11. The distributed asci supercomputer 4. http://www.cs.vu.nl/das4/

12. A utility for detailed resource inspection of applications. https://github.com/scaidermern/audria

13. Vicomo website. http://www.vicomo.org

14. Orlic, B., David, I., Mak, R.H., Lukkien, J.J.: Dynamically reconfigurable resource-aware component framework: architecture and concepts. In: Crnkovic, I., Gruhn, V., Book, M. (eds.) ECSA 2011. LNCS, vol. 6903, pp. 212–215. Springer, Heidelberg (2011). http://dl.acm.org/citation.cfm?id=2041790.2041819

15. Raman, R., Livny, M., Solomon, M.: Matchmaking: an extensible framework for distributed resource management. Cluster Comput. **2**(2), 129–138 (1999). http://dx.doi.org/10.1023/A:1019022624119

16. Sonmez, O.O., Grundeken, B., Mohamed, H.H., Iosup, A., Epema, D.H.J.: Scheduling strategies for cycle scavenging in multicluster grid systems. In: 9th IEEE/ACM International Symposium on Cluster Computing and the Grid, CCGRID 2009, pp. 12–19 (2009)

17. Sonmez, O.O., Yigitbasi, N., Abrishami, S., Iosup, A., Epema, D.H.J.: Performance analysis of dynamic workflow scheduling in multicluster grids. In: ACM Symposium on High-Performance Parallel and Distributed Computing (HPDC), pp. 49–60 (2010)

18. Staples, G.: Torque resource manager. In: 2006 ACM/IEEE conference on Supercomputing (SC 2006) (2006)

19. Thain, D., Tannenbaum, T., Livny, M.: Distributed computing in practice: the condor experience. Concurr. Comput. Pract. Experience **17**(2–4), 323–356 (2005). http://dx.doi.org/10.1002/cpe.v17:2/4

20. Vavilapalli, V.K.: Apache hadoop yarn: yet another resource negotiator. In: ACM Symposium on Cloud Computing (2013)

21. White, T.: Hadoop: The Definitive Guide, 1st edn. O'Reilly Media Inc., Sebastopol (2009)

How to Design a Job Scheduling Algorithm

Uwe Schwiegelshohn[✉]

Robotics Research Institute, TU Dortmund University, 44221 Dortmund, Germany
uwe.schwiegelshohn@udo.edu
http://www.irf.tu-dortmund.de

Abstract. We discuss design aspects of job scheduling algorithms in parallel processing systems. Starting from the observation that in this area the impact of most research publications on real systems is negligible, we first identify three main categories with strong relevance to practical implementations: constraints, objectives, and evaluation. For each category, we describe common aspects of real systems that are presently important and then introduce some general rules that should be followed when presenting a new job scheduling algorithm for parallel processing systems. To apply these rules, we use as an example a new method for the Infrastructure-as-a-Service (IaaS) model of Cloud Computing that extends the spot instance approach of Amazon. In particular we address technical, organizational, and usage constraints based on existing concepts and research results for this example. Then we briefly describe scheduling objectives from the viewpoint of a data center offering IaaS. After presenting our algorithmic concept, we provide an evaluation with theoretical means to demonstrate that this approach can also yield meaningful results in practice.

1 Introduction

Due to an increasing demand to handle large amounts of digital data in many scientific and commercial areas, recent years have seen a growing interest in data centers since these centers are expected to provide better service at lower costs than many small in-house IT centers. In large companies, the IT demand may economically justify a company owned data center. But for these data centers usually the same economic restrictions apply as for external data centers.

In general data centers face the challenge to improve their efficiency as, for instance, Kaplan, Forrest, and Nadler [9] have pointed out in 2008. The scientific community has accepted this challenge and is addressing the issue, see the large total number of sessions that are devoted to the topic *resource management and scheduling* in many conferences and workshops on high performance or high throughput computing. In addition, many scientific journals also publish papers on this topic. A brief literature review yields a plethora of papers suggesting various new algorithms for job scheduling on parallel processor systems. For instance, since the introduction of EASY backfilling by Lifka [12] in the mid nineties of the last century, there has been a large number of research papers suggesting improvements of this approach, see Table 1. This list of references is

© Springer International Publishing Switzerland 2015
W. Cirne and N. Desai (Eds.): JSSPP 2014, LNCS 8828, pp. 147–167, 2015.
DOI: 10.1007/978-3-319-15789-4_9

Table 1. Some papers addressing aspects and suggesting variations of the original backfill algorithm

Feitelson, Weil	Utilization and predictability in scheduling in IBM SP2 with backfilling	1998
Talby, Feitelson	Supporting priorities and improving utilization of the IBM SP scheduler using slack-based backfilling	1999
Zotkin, Keleher	Job-length estimation and performance in backfilling schedulers	1999
Karatza	A simulation model of backfilling and I/O scheduling in a partitionable parallel system	2000
Keleher, Zotkin, Perkovic	Attacking the bottlenecks of backfilling schedulers	2000
Mu'alem, Feitelson	Utilization, predictability, workloads, and user runtime estimates in scheduling the IBM SP2 with backfilling	2001
Srinivasan, Kettimuthu, Subramani, Sadayappan	Selective reservation strategies for backfill job scheduling	2002
Lawson, Smirni, Puiu	Self-adapting backfilling scheduling for parallel systems	2002
Lawson, Smirni	Multiple-queue backfilling scheduling with priorities and reservations for parallel systems	2002
Ward, Mahood, West	Scheduling jobs on parallel systems using a relaxed backfill strategy	2002
Shmueli, Feitelson	Backfilling with lookahead to optimize the performance of parallel job scheduling	2003
Utrera, Corbaln, Labarta	Another approach to backfilled jobs: applying virtual malleability to expired windows	2005
Tsafrir, Feitelson	The dynamics of backfilling: Solving the mystery of why increased inaccuracy may help	2006
Yahav, Raschid, Andrade	Bid based scheduler with backfilling for a multiprocessor system	2007
Guim, Rodero, Corbalan	The Resource Usage Aware Backfilling	2009
Lindsay, Galloway-Carson, Johnson, Bunde, Leung	Backfilling with guarantees granted upon job submission	2011

certainly not complete and we do not intend to discuss the individual contribution of any publication included in this table. But we are also not aware of any reports on experiences with actual implementations of the suggested modified algorithms in production data centers.

To our knowledge, most data centers still use job scheduling algorithms that are known since almost twenty years and we do not observe any significant amount of algorithm transfer from scientific results into practice in job scheduling for parallel processing. We can only identify two potential reasons for this lack of transfer success:

- The proposed algorithms are not suitable to be applied in practice or
- The proposed algorithms may be beneficial in practice but there is a lack of communication between researchers and system administrators preventing a successful transfer.

Undoubtedly, there are some studies suggesting algorithms that fall into the first category. But we are confident that the review process usually prevents these papers from being presented in sessions that are devoted to problems that are relevant in practice. Some other algorithms were never read by practitioners and therefore were not given the opportunity to prove their practical value. But based on our experience in organizing workshops addressing this area for a long time, we have also got the impression that practitioners follow workshops and conferences and are aware of the research presented there. Therefore, we believe that research studies must better consider the constraints and objectives that are relevant in practice and publications must do a better job convincing practitioners about the benefits of new approaches.

In this paper, we want to support researchers in addressing these challenges by stating some rules on constraints, objectives, and evaluation. The practical aspects of these categories are often not addressed with sufficient detail in our view. We suggest that future papers on job scheduling algorithm for computer systems consider them in order to point out the applicability and the benefit of new algorithms. The rules are supposed to be used for research work that emphasizes relevance in practice while they do not necessarily apply to basic research papers that are mainly addressing algorithmic structures and only mention some vague reference to a potential future applicability of newly presented algorithms. As an example we show the application of these rules when developing a method to handle job scheduling in the Infrastructure-as-a-Service (IaaS) model of Cloud Computing. The new method is an alternative to Amazon's spot instance approach.

The further outline of the paper is as follows. First, we distinguish three different types of constraints that occur in practical job scheduling problems, see Sect. 2. In Sect. 3, we focus on the objectives of job scheduling problems and briefly discuss the use of common objectives and the handling of multi-objective problems. Then we analyze the advantages and disadvantages of the three major evaluation approaches. Finally, we present a new allocation algorithm that can be considered as an alternative to Amazon's spot instances and use this algorithm as an example to show the application of these rules, see Sect. 5.

2   Constraints

The operation of a data center is subject to many constraints. These constraints define the solution space of a problem, that is, a solution is only valid if all constraints are satisfied. As in other areas of science, it is not always necessary to consider all constraints when developing a new algorithm. Clearly, we can ignore constraints if their omission does not change the solution space. To simplify the analysis, many studies use a model with only few simple constraints. In this case, we must be aware that such a model may lead to a modification of the solution space:

- An extension of the solution space potentially considers practically irrelevant instances possibly reducing the performance of an algorithm.
- A reduction of the solution space may cause the omission of practically relevant instances during evaluation possibly favoring algorithms with inferior performance in practice.

In a publication, we must clearly identify a properties of our model that affect the solution space. In particular, we must show or at least state the influence of an omitted constraint on the solution space. To determine the influence of a constraint, it may be beneficial to address evaluation aspects already in an early stage, see Sect. 4. It is important that we do not automatically accept a model because it has been used in a previous study. Even if the study was carefully designed to address the issues described above, it may be possible to relax and remove some of the used constraints due to new technical results or due to a change in the organizational structure. Such modification may influence the previously accepted solution space and lead to a better result. Again it is important to communicate and justify those changes.

To better handle constraints, we distinguish three types of constraints:

- Technical constraints are due to physical laws or the system architecture.
- Usage constraints determine properties of jobs that are using our system.
- Organizational constraints are defined by the strategy of parties that may be able to influence the operation of the system.

In the remaining parts of this section, we discuss some examples of constraints. Since it is not possible to consider all constraints that occur in a possible application scenario we have decided to focus on constraints that have some relevance to our IaaS example. For any other scenario a new selection is required.

2.1   Technical Constraints

There is a large variety of different technical constraints. As examples we discuss technical constraints regarding availability of application information, sharing of the physical infrastructure, and power management of the system in more detail.

Many scheduling algorithms for computer systems are clairvoyant, that is, they require execution details of the application. To use these algorithms, users may be required to provide the estimated execution time of their applications. Studies have shown that these estimates often have large deviations, see, for instance, Lee et al. [11]. Alternatively, automatic application profiling by the data center may provide such estimates. But it has not been demonstrated that we can efficiently perform such profiling for most applications that are executed in data centers. In general, we must conclude that it is very difficult to obtain reliable processing time information. Therefore, when presenting a clairvoyant scheduling algorithm, we must show that sufficiently reliable processing time information is available.

Many data centers with independent customers presently favor space sharing over time sharing. Pure space sharing may lead to potential inefficiencies as long running applications with low priority must be terminated to free resources for new high priority customer requests unless there is a sufficient amount of over-provisioning. Time sharing in a computer infrastructure is technically achieved by context switching between different virtual machines, that is, the execution of a virtual machine on a physical resource is preempted and later resumed on a possibly different physical resource. In case of parallel applications with a significant amount of inter-processor communication (MPI-jobs) time sharing is likely to cause a significant performance loss. For sequential jobs or parallel jobs with insignificant inter-processor communication we must consider the impact of time sharing on the service guarantee. To monitor compliance with a service guarantee, appropriate tools must be installed by the data center. Since these tools use the same physical resources as the applications and require the availability of the resources repeatedly for a brief period of time, time sharing must be applied for these tools. Therefore, tools for system management consume a share of the physical resources, the so called *system overhead*. This overhead must be taken into account by any job scheduling algorithm. Although the resource consumption of these tools is not constant it can be estimated rather reliably. Therefore, we can assume that the system administrator knows at least the distribution of the amount of computing power that is required for system management tasks like service monitoring, context switching, and book keeping. Then we can select the maximum amount of system overhead that a resource management system must be able to tolerate in a time interval. We consider this value to be a constant that reduces the available resources. Then we can ignore the system overhead by simply assuming a *slower* physical resource without system overhead. In practice, an overestimation of the system overhead has no negative impact on job scheduling as an earlier completion time of a job is usually not regarded as a violation of a service guarantee. But an unnecessary large margin for system overhead reduces the advertised performance of the system and put the data center into a disadvantageous position in comparison to competitors.

Next, we take a closer look at context switching for sequential jobs or parallel jobs with little inter-processor communication. Due to present processor architectures, we must distinguish between context switching without core migration, context switching with migration to another core on the same processor, and context switching with migration to another core on a different processor since these alternatives have different context switching penalties. Strong et al. [17] point out methods to support fast context switching such that context switching with migration is not only applicable to handle processor failure but also to improve job scheduling. Similarly, Mars et al. [14] suggest the use of the so called *Bubble-Up* methodology to reduce context switching penalties and propose improving schedules by allowing colocation of interactive and batch resources contrary to the current policy in many large data centers. Due to this results, it is appropriate to consider time sharing at least for long running sequential jobs. These studies are an example for a modification of constraints that affect the solution space.

Energy expenses are a significant part of the total operating expenses in a data center. On the one hand, idle but not shut-down resources consume power without yielding a direct benefit to the data center. On the other hand, a data center must accept some overprovisioning of resources to meet the agreed quality of service in case of a machine failure, see Cirne and Frachtenberg [2]. Since the total resource demand of all customers is not constant particularly if most customers are located in the same time zone, a data center typically accepts some additional overprovisioning to handle periods of peak demand without being forced to reject many customer requests. In a situation of low customer demand, the data center can use two approaches to reduce its energy expenses:

- Dynamic voltage and frequency scaling (DVFS).
- Shutting down of idle resources in combination with application migration.

So far DVFS has not received much interest by system administrators of data centers as its applicability strongly depends on the individual application. A change of the processing speed initiated by the data center may cause a violation of the service agreement. Moreover, Ibrahim et al. [8] have demonstrated with the help of simulations that local changes of power consumption may lead to thermal problems in large computer systems. Due to these problems, data centers presently focus on migrating applications such that some racks can be powered down while the load is balanced for the active racks. Therefore, any publication that suggests the use of DVFS or similar methods to reduce energy expenses must explain how to overcome these hurdles and show that the approach produces an overall saving when considering the whole system, also see Sect. 2.3.

2.2   Usage Constraints

To be economically successful, a data center with independent customers must consider the demand of its customers. To this end, it is necessary to analyze the applications that are typically running on the system. While in general a large variety of applications can run on the system of a data center unless data center restrictions prevent them from being accepted, it is well documented that not all applications have the same probability of being submitted, see Sect. 4.2. Although most data centers do not publish utilization data of their clusters, there are a few publications that provide some workload data and methodologies for an analysis, like some statistics on Cloud jobs based on Google's clusters presented by Mishra et al. [15]. Often we may be able to use a simplification of the responsiveness classification, see Cirne and Frachtenberg [2], but we must show that this simplification is sufficient for our purpose:

Interactive. This application requires the system to be available for processing within a very brief period of time. For instance, web front ends belong to this type of application. In order to maintain a sufficiently high responsiveness for resources with interactive applications, time sharing with migration of such application is usually avoided and only performed in case of machine failure.

User-facing. This application does not require an immediate user interaction but the user expects the result as soon as possible. Animoto's[1] rendering of images is an example for such application.

Batch. This application needs a significant amount of computing over an extended period of time but has no tight deadlines. Re-indexing a database or other management jobs are examples for this type of application. Such applications may be initiated by a customer or by the data center itself and typically have a low priority.

In the following, we characterize a resource based on the application it is executing, that is, we speak of interactive, user-facing, and batch resources. For interactive resources, we distinguish two types:

- Basic interactive resources must always be available to answer sporadic requests.
- Flexible interactive resources are leased and released on demand but may incur some set-up penalty.

Typically, basic interactive resources are leased over an extended period of time representing a simple form of outsourcing, that is, the customer shifts the task of IT management to the data center and benefits from economy of scale effects. Depending on the demand a basic interactive resource may be idle for some time. Although such idleness may be a tempting target for job scheduling it must be considered that the customer has leased the resource and is free to use it for other applications at any time. If the data center wants to exploit the resource for another purpose, like improving energy efficiency, the consent of the customer and the observance of service guarantees are required. Therefore, we assume in this paper that a basic interactive resource produces a static constraint from the viewpoint of the job scheduling system of a data center. In general, customers are interested in leasing flexible interactive, user-facing and batch resources on-demand to handle varying workloads. This way the customer avoids overprovisioning of IT resources while the data center may achieve an acceptable load balance by exploiting the different workload demand patterns of its customers.

2.3 Organizational Constraints

Data centers and its customers establish some form of market economy. They typically conclude a service contract based on an offer of the data center.

---

[1] animoto.com.

Due to the large number of customers, the typical customer of a data center has little power to negotiate his contract but must accept one of the standard offers similar to a mobile phone customer. To be successful in the market and to attract many customers, data centers try to satisfy different demands of the customers when defining their offers. In such a situation, we may also consider whether it is possible to define offers such that they support an efficient job scheduling of the data center in addition to serving the purpose of attracting and satisfying customers. Then the offer can shape the solution space of the scheduling problem. We say that the offer establishes an organizational constraint. Contrary to other constraints an organizational constraint is not always invariable. Therefore, our studies must clearly specify all assumed organizational constraints.

In the following, we discuss examples for internal and external organizational constraints. Internal organizational constraints only affect the partners in our data center market economy while external organizational constraints involve a third party and cannot be modified easily. The offer of a data center represents an internal organizational constraint. In general, we can assume that such offer specifies the (real or virtual) price that the customer must pay for the provided resources and a guaranteed quality of service possibly including penalties for violating these guarantees. The offer is typically based on a small number of different types of virtual instances that usually include processor specification, amount of memory, amount of storage, and network performance[2]. In these instances, there is a coarse granularity regarding each resource type and often a close relationship between the different resource types: a large number of cores is combined with more memory and better network performance. In a large data center, the total number of resources for each instance type is very large and most data centers provide resources to their main customers using space sharing, see Sect. 2.1. Similar to a car rental company, it may be possible to additionally improve efficiency by allocating a more powerful instance to a customer request without additional costs if the requested instance is not available (voluntary upgrade).

The offer of a data center typically includes two aspects of a service guarantee:

Availability. The customer is guaranteed that the system is available at least for a specified percentage during a specified time frame, for instance, 99 % availability each month.

Responsiveness. The customer is guaranteed to receive a certain amount of physical computer resources within a given (brief) time interval.

Guarantee values are part of the offer of a data center. The availability condition is a customer protection against long term system failure. It indirectly affects job scheduling as additional redundant machines must be available to compensate possible machine failure, see Cirne and Frachtenberg [2]. Usually, the determination of an appropriate amount of overprovisioning can be separated from other resource management tasks. Therefore, it is not necessary to directly consider

---

[2] As an example see aws.amazon.com/ec2/instance-types/.

the availability constraint in a job scheduling algorithm. But since these redundant machines are idle most of the time, a job scheduling algorithm may at least partially use them for batch applications by applying time sharing.

We can formally express the responsiveness guarantee for a virtual machine by the ratio between a time interval Δt and the total time that a physical resource has been allocated to a virtual machine during Δt. This ratio is not allowed to exceed the so called *stretch* or *slack* factor f defined in the contract. The system overhead discussed in Sect. 2.1 is one reason for f being greater than one. A lower stretch factor may be more attractive for a customer and may allow a higher price. The impact of the stretch factor on job scheduling will be discussed later. For long term leases, responsiveness can be combined with availability by defining that a machine is not available in a time interval if the response time guarantee is not always met during this interval. User-facing and batch resources primarily differ with respect to their responsiveness, that is the length of the time interval and the amount of resources allocated to them within the time interval.

Most data centers offer physical resources in an on-demand fashion for user-facing and batch resources and use two approaches to improve efficiency: usually there is a minimum amount or even a fixed quantum of resources that must be leased[3] and the data center will deliver a certain amount of resources during a given time interval at its discretion for user-facing and batch applications, that is, the system administrator of the data center decides when to deliver this guaranteed amount of resources during the time interval. Without these restrictions, on-demand offerings are not attractive: either the data center keeps many resources in stand-by for a worst case situation of high demand or the customer runs a high risk of a request being rejected due to unavailability of resources. Therefore, the restrictions represent a trade-off for the customer and the data center. The customer accepts a slightly larger responsiveness value and possibly a small amount of overprovisioning due to the lease quantum while the data center benefits from the different use patterns of his customers. In general, an external data center always accepts some overprovisioning in order to avoid alienating his customers by rejecting their requests since there is a strong lock-in effect in Cloud Computing and lost customers may be gone forever.

Although no running time information is available the quantum lease approach produces additional information for job scheduling and effectively turns a non-clairvoyant scheduling problem into a clairvoyant one. But we must also consider that resource allocations can be extended on request of the customer thus leading to an online problem.

As an example for an external organizational constraint, we discuss constraints due to the power consumption of a system. Data centers are large customers of utility providers. All these large customers are required to estimate their power consumption in advance and to pay penalties in case the actual consumption does not match the estimate. Although a data center is interested in reliably saving energy, a temporary energy reduction may produce additional

---

[3] Amazon uses an instance hour for its Elastic Computing Cloud (EC2).

costs if the estimate is already too high. A job scheduling algorithm may help to reduce these costs by shifting workload from intervals with overestimation to intervals with underestimation. Unfortunately, the service guarantee may prevent such workload shifting for interactive and user-facing applications while batch applications have more flexibility due to their long responsiveness. For instance, a sudden increase in the demand of flexible interactive or user-facing resources may be managed by postponing some batch applications. If this approach is not sufficient new physical resources must be powered up and a penalty for a wrong power estimation may occur. A sudden decrease in the demand and the corresponding underestimation of power consumption may be compensated by allocating batch resources earlier than originally planned. The explained benefit of the usefulness of batch resources for resource management is also demonstrated by Amazon's introduction of its spot instances. In addition, we must consider the additional overhead caused by frequently switching a resource from active mode to inactive mode and vice versa.

3   Optimization Objectives

There are many different objectives for scheduling problems. Due to the importance of the objective for a scheduling problem the objective always occupies the third field in the three field notation of scheduling problems by Graham, Lawler, Lenstra, and Rinnooy Kan [7]. During the last decades of scheduling research some objectives have been frequently chosen for research studies, like the makespan of a schedule, and there are many results for these objectives. The existence of such results is sometimes used as an argument to select one of the common objectives for a research study of practical relevance. However, unless the objective does not represent the goal of the data center it is unlikely that the system administrator of the data center is interested in the study. Therefore, it is important that the original objective of the data center is described first. In order to use a common objective, we must show that every good solution using the common objective is also a good solution with respect to the original objective of the data center. It is not sufficient to state that we use a specific objective since the original objective of the data center is too hard to analyze.

Many practical scheduling problems have more than one objective. For such problems, ideally the Pareto optima are determined. Since finding all or even a sufficient amount of Pareto optima is frequently very difficult and time consuming, multi-objective problems are often transformed into conventional single objective problems by turning one or more objective into constraints, that is, the valid area for the corresponding objective value is reduced but no specific value of this objective within the valid area is preferred. Therefore, this approach requires a final analysis to determine the deviation of this value in the obtained solution from a target value. This is particularly important if the transformed objective has a high priority.

As in most commercial scenarios, a data center typically has the primary objective to increase its profit. The use of money and the corresponding evaluation of expenses is a practical approach to transform multi-objective optimization problems into single objective problems. Unfortunately, the resulting single objective problem is usually too unspecific and too complex to be addressed by common optimization approaches without introducing additional assumptions. In particular, it is often very difficult to translate the objectives of a data center into a mathematical form that has already been used in previous (more theory oriented) publications. Since it is necessary to show the equivalence or at least the close relationship between both formulations, we must use special care when describing such translation.

4   Evaluation

Every paper on algorithms requires an evaluation of the new algorithm. Ideally such evaluation covers all valid problem instances, also called the *problem space*, and additionally considers the frequency of occurrence for each such problem instance. On the one hand, it is very difficult for many parallel job scheduling problems on real machines to provide an easy characterization of the problem space that formally separates it from all invalid problem instances due to the large number of constraints in such problems. On the other hand, an evaluation only requires such separation if invalid (or very rare) problem instances determine the outcome of the evaluation. The handling of the problem space is an important property of an evaluation approach.

In general, there are three major approaches for the evaluation of job scheduling algorithms for parallel processors:

- Theoretical analysis
- Execution on a real machine
- Simulation

Each of these approaches has advantages and disadvantages that must be taken into account when deciding how to evaluate an algorithm.

4.1   Theoretical Analysis

When discussing the theoretical analysis approach we distinguish between *easy* and *difficult* problems. For an easy problem, there is an algorithm with polynomial time complexity that always finds an optimal solution in the problem space if such solution exists. Here, theoretical analysis covers the whole problem space and is well suited.

For difficult problems, a proof of intractability rarely provides any practical benefit with the exception of stating that there is no further need to look for an optimal polynomial-time algorithm. Therefore, many studies produce algorithms with performance guarantees like approximation or competitive factors for these problems. These guarantees are upper performance bounds (for minimization problems), that is, they consider specific worst case problem instances. For all other problem instances, we only know that the deviation from the optimum does not exceed this guarantee. Since the guarantee is often too large to be acceptable in a real life situation, the performance guarantee is seldom beneficial in practice, For instance, the approximation factor $2 - 1/m$ of list scheduling indicates that in the worst case almost 50 % of the machines are idle during operation of the system. The value of such information is further reduced if the performance guarantee is not tight or if it is determined by an invalid or very unlikely problem instance. For instance, the worst case example of list scheduling requires a single job with a processing time being equal to the optimal total operation time of the system. Therefore, studies presenting new performance guarantees must also answer the following questions:

– Is the determined worst case performance guarantee also acceptable as an average performance deviation in practice?
– Does any problem instance that determines the performance guarantee has a high likelihood to occur in practice?

Many practitioners doubt the benefit of a theoretical evaluation for practical job scheduling problems. The already mentioned EASY backfilling is frequently used as a prominent example. This approach is applied in many parallel processing systems although it has a very bad performance guarantee. But we believe that theory may also have similar benefits in the field of job scheduling as, for instance, for numerical simulation problems. In Sect. 5, we will give an example to show that theoretical analysis that can be helpful in practice.

4.2   Execution on a Real Machine

The performance of a newly designed algorithm can be evaluated by testing it in the field on a real system. In general this approach has the potential to consider even those constraints that we have forgotten or neglected when developing our algorithm. But due to a possible lack of scalability, this benefit does not necessarily hold when using only a small test system. Moreover, it is often very difficult to generate a practically relevant workload during a test without real customers. Testing on the target system with real customers avoids these disadvantages but it can only be used if the algorithm and the whole management system are mature enough to guarantee that customers are not alienated and no system problems are generated. Unfortunately, such a test in the field is usually also very expensive particularly if a large production system is involved. Therefore, it will normally not be used for the early stages of algorithmic evaluation although the ultimate test must occur on a real system. Most likely due to this effort, there are very few publications that report on algorithm evaluation on real systems.

Instead real systems are used to extract workload data for evaluation purposes. Some of these workload data are made publicly available by storing them in repositories like the parallel workload archive for parallel computers.[4] Then they can be used directly or indirectly for an evaluation with the help of simulation studies.

---

[4] www.cs.huji.ac.il/labs/parallel/workload.

4.3 Simulation

Most publications on job scheduling algorithms for parallel processing include a simulation study. In general, a simulation study is comparable with an experiment in natural science since we generate an artificial environment to answer a research question. Experimental evaluation in computer science is a relatively new area compared to the much longer experimental tradition in natural science. Therefore, it is not surprising that no generally accepted approach for experiments in computer science has been established yet. The lack of such approach can be observed in many publications with simulation studies. It would be beneficial to borrow from the concepts of experiments in physics and chemistry. Since an experiment is designed to answer a research question this research question or hypothesis must be clearly formulated. Moreover, an experiment is only useful if it can be verified by other researchers. Therefore, it is necessary to describe all parts of the experiment in sufficient details to enable such verification.

The simulation experiment is based on a model of the real system. This model must consider all relevant constraints, see Sect. 2. While it is straight forward to include technical and organizational constraints, usage constraints are a more difficult challenge. As already stated in the beginning of this section we must sufficiently cover the problem space. To this end, a large number of input instances and a corresponding large number of simulation runs are necessary since each problem instance requires a separate simulation run.

Some publications use randomly generated data. While this approach is easy to implement it is doubtful that random data can guarantee the required coverage, see Sect. 2.2. Therefore, every publication using random data must explicitly show that the coverage condition is observed. Such proof is missing in many publications.

Alternatively, researcher often use real workload data from the already mentioned repositories. Although this approach seems to implicitly guarantee coverage of the problem space it also has some disadvantages. First of all, the number of existing workload traces in accessible repositories may not be sufficient to execute the required number of simulation runs in order to obtain meaningful results. Also workload data strongly depend on the environment in which they were recorded. Therefore, we must determine whether a transfer to another environment is possible. For instance, fewer scheduling conflicts will occur if the workload trace is recorded on a smaller system than the simulated system. If necessary the simulated system must be adapted to the workload trace while still considering all other constraints. Moreover, a simulation with workload data is always history based and not well suited to evaluate new algorithms if the environment allows strong interactions with participants. Such interactions often occur in market economies with a high volatility of demand or supply as new job scheduling algorithms may increase the supply of resources leading to a change in the demand of resources. For instance, the submission pattern of a user may change if the user knows that more resources are available. Therefore, a simulation study with workload data must always address the issue of interaction between system and providers of input data.

Due to the lack of a sufficient amount of suitable workload data, some researchers use workload models like, for instance, the one proposed by Lublin and Feitelson [13] for parallel computers. These workload models are verified with workload traces and usually can be adapted to the simulation system. To support verification of the simulation study, the details of the adaptation must be part of the description of the simulation experiment. Unfortunately, workload models do not automatically handle the interaction problem discussed in the previous paragraph. Although some researchers are well aware of the missing feedback effect in current workload models, see, for instance, Feitelson [4], we do not know any workload model that considers interactions with customers in general. In our view it is one of the key challenges in the area of job scheduling for parallel processing to develop workload models that incorporate a feedback component that changes the workload depending on the result of job scheduling to imitate interaction with the participants.

5   IaaS Example

In this section we show the application of these rules when addressing job scheduling for data centers providing Infrastructure-as-a-Service (IaaS). IaaS is a basic service model of Cloud Computing and constitutes a market consisting of providers and customers, see Sect. 2.3. A data center providing IaaS owns IT-infrastructure and offers it to its customers. An IaaS customer wants to lease a computer infrastructure to avoid the effort and the expenses of handling his or her own computer infrastructure. In general, the IaaS customer expects some service guarantee when paying for the infrastructure (with real or virtual dollars). IaaS customers may run their own applications on the leased hardware or there may be a third partner who uses the software of IaaS customers and the hardware of the data center together with his or her own input data.

Based on our remarks in Sect. 2.2, we assume that the data center offers only a single type of virtual instance with a single type of resource. This approach also applies to data centers with several instances and resources together with a fixed partitioning of the resources that do not use any voluntary upgrade, see Sect. 2.3. Since data centers only use such voluntary upgrade as a last resort, the restriction does not affect the typical operation of the data center and we can use our simple model.

We consider the total number of installed machines and the total expenses for housing and personal to be fixed. Therefore, we can ignore them for the purpose of optimization. The data center can influence energy costs by migrating low priority virtual resources and shutting down idle physical resources or activating physical resources that are inactive, see Sect. 2.3.

We allow preemption for batch virtual resources and consider management of power consumption with the help of shutting down or powering up physical resources, see Sect. 2.

We want to maximize the profit of the data center by maximizing the total number of leased instance periods during a period of system operation. Further, there are additional objectives:

- The data center does not want to reject any high priority request unless all physical resources are busy executing high priority requests, that is, we prefer high priority requests over low priority requests in scheduling conflicts as high priority requests produce more profit per instance period.
- The data center wants to achieve the estimated value of power consumption, that is, there is a target number of active physical resources, see Sect. 2.3. We will deviate from this target number only if more physical resources are required to execute high priority virtual resources or if there are not enough low priority virtual resources. Therefore, power consumption management is a secondary objective.
- Similar to the spot market we allow that a service guarantee of a low priority virtual resource is violated but we want our job scheduling algorithm to do its best to prevent such a violation if active physical resources are available.

In the next section we describe an online allocation algorithm for our job scheduling problem.

5.1   Algorithm for the IaaS Example

In our IaaS scenario, customers can select a long term lease, for instance for basic interactive resources. There is no need for our algorithm to handle those long term leases since they have the highest priority and are not allocated online. Further, we introduce an organizational constraint by not allowing customers to request on-demand virtual resources for a future starting time. Instead a customer can always request an additional high priority virtual resource for immediate availability with the slight risk that no physical machine may be available. The lease of any high priority virtual resource can always be extended for another instance period. Since workload data from data centers indicate that there are very few requests for future allocation of physical resources, our organizational constraint is not expected to have a noticeable negative effect on customers.

Our online algorithm Allocation in Fig. 1 describes the main steps of handling the request for a virtual resource R. The algorithm does not distinguish between flexible interactive virtual resources and user-facing virtual resources but combines them into on-demand virtual resources. On-demand virtual resources are allocated to customers one instance period Δ at a time, that is, on-demand allocations have a fixed length determined by the provider. There is a fixed price for each instance period of an on-demand allocation. Any on-demand allocation that has been started will be extended on request of the customer. The extension request must be received time δ before the end of the instance period of the current allocation. The data center may either decide to use an explicit extension or a default extension. In the former case, the request for a successor allocation of an active on-demand allocation must be received between the start of the current allocation and time $\delta < \Delta$ before its completion. In the latter case, any allocation is automatically extended for another instance period unless the extension is canceled at least time δ before the end of the current instance period.

Procedure *successor()* tests the existence of a successor request. This successor request is preferably allocated to the same physical resource as the current virtual resource to guarantee a continuous availability of the resource but migration at the beginning of the new instance period is possible for the reason of shutting down processors (procedure *allocate_successor()*).

A data center always accepts a request for an additional on-demand virtual resource provided there are some physical resources that are not occupied by high priority virtual resources at the current time plus δ. This start-up delay produces a stretch factor of at most $(\Delta + \delta)/\Delta$. If all physical resources are occupied then a batch (low priority) virtual resource must be terminated (procedure *batch_termination*). The new on-demand virtual resource will be allocated to a suitable physical resource considering our goals regarding idle resources (procedure *allocate_new()*).

Batch virtual resources can be requested for any integer multiple of an instance period up to a maximum value, say $k\Delta$. They can be preempted and migrated at any time. Batch virtual resources may be charged a low rate per instance hour. We can either define this rate or determine it by using some bidding algorithm, see Amazon's spot instances. There may be common deadlines for all batch virtual resource allocations, for instance, every day at noon. Whenever a batch virtual resource is submitted it is assigned the earliest deadline such that its stretch factor exceeds a minimal value f_b for batch virtual resources. The data center defines f_b. A batch virtual resource will be *terminated* if there are not enough resources for on-demand virtual resources or if not all batch virtual resources can complete in time. Note that the expression *termination* does not necessarily mean that the batch virtual resource is stopped but that it will not be completed by its deadline. The data center selects the batch virtual resource that will be terminated. If a batch virtual resource is terminated then the customer is charged for the completed instance periods. If a batch virtual resource is completed by its deadline then the customer may have to pay an additional charge for each instance period the batch virtual resource was running.

In case of a shortage of physical resources due to an unpredictable machine failure batch virtual resources have the lowest priority and are terminated first. If the number of physical resources is not sufficient to execute all on-demand virtual resources then the data center must terminate some on-demand virtual resources and accept a penalty. For this selection procedure, the data center must also define a policy.

5.2   Evaluation for the IaaS Example

For our example, we use theoretical evaluation as at least some parts of the algorithm can be shown to be optimal. In this situation, a theoretical evaluation is beneficial since the problem space is obviously covered and better results are not possible for these parts, see Sect. 4.1. First, we must describe our problem in a way that is suitable for this kind of evaluation. We focus on on-demand virtual resources since these requests have a higher priority than batch virtual resources. The allocation of on-demand virtual resources can be described as a scheduling

Algorithm Allocation (Request R)

if (there is an on-demand virtual resource R' with successor(R')=R) {
    accept R;
    allocate_successor(R');
    start R immediately after completion of R'; }
else if (R is a new on-demand virtual resource) {
    if (all physical resources are occupied with on-demand virtual resources) {
        reject R; }
    else {
        if (there is no idle physical resource) {
            batch_termination; }
        accept R;
        allocate_new(R);
        start R as soon as possible; } }
else {
    if (there is a valid batch schedule) {
        accept R; }
    else {
        reject R; } }
reschedule_batch;

Fig. 1. Algorithm for acceptance or rejection of a virtual resource request R

problem of jobs with unit processing time on parallel identical machines. Since we do not know which jobs will be extended we assume independent jobs being submitted over time, that is, we have a classical online scheduling problem. Since we may only migrate an on-demand virtual resource before its start, we do not allow preemption in our problem. Due to the limitation of our stretch factor, the deadline of a job cannot exceed its submission time plus the stretch factor $1 + \delta < 2$ as we set $\Delta = 1$. We want to maximize the busy time of the physical resources, that is, we want to minimize the total idle time of these resources. The minimization of the total idle time with respect to on-demand virtual resources is equivalent to the minimization of the total number of jobs that cannot complete before or at their deadlines. Using the common notation in theoretical scheduling we have the objective function $\sum U_j$, see Pinedo [16]. Therefore, we can express our problem as $P_m|p_j = 1, r_{j,\text{online}}|\sum U_j$. Goldman et al. [5] address the corresponding maximization problem on a single resource and show an upper bound of 0.5 for the competitive factor, that is, there are problem instances such that no deterministic online algorithm can finish more than half the number of jobs than an algorithm with complete knowledge of the submission sequence can complete. This upper bound is achieved by a simple greedy algorithm that accepts every job that will complete in time. Goldwasser [6] improves this result for slack factors $f \geq 2$. Kim and Chwa [10] show that the results of Goldman et al. and Goldwasser also hold for parallel identical machines. However, a close look at the proof of Goldman et al. shows that the proof uses a condition that is not valid in our problem. To discuss the difference between the general problem and our case in detail, we first introduce some notation. We say that job J_i with processing time $p_i = 1$ is submitted at release date r_i and has deadline $d_i = r_i + 1 + \delta$. Goldman's proof requires that we have $d_i < d_j$ for two jobs J_i and J_j with $r_i > r_j$. This condition clearly does not hold for our problem. Remember that the deadline is not determined by the customer but by the data center. We can assume that the successor of an on-demand virtual resource is submitted time δ before the completion of the predecessor resulting in the above mentioned deadline as well. This special form of the general problem is addressed in Theorem 1.

Theorem 1. *In a system with parallel identical machines, a greedy approach guarantees the minimum idleness if all jobs have the same processing time p and $d_i \leq d_j$ holds for any two jobs J_i and J_j with $r_i \leq r_j$.*

Proof. Consider an arbitrary non-preemptive schedule S with two jobs J_i and J_j such that $r_i \leq r_j$ and $c_i > c_j$ holds with c_i and c_j being the completion times of jobs J_i and J_j in schedule S, respectively. Then we simply exchange the positions of both jobs in the schedule. Clearly, job J_i can be started at time $c_j - p \geq r_j \geq r_i$. Similarly, job J_j will complete in time as $d_j \geq d_i \geq c_i$ holds. We apply this job exchange until all jobs start in the order of their release dates. Next, we transform the resulting schedule into a new schedule by applying greedy allocation to the jobs in the order of their completion times. This transformation cannot increase the completion time of any job. Therefore, we only need to consider non-delay schedules in which the order of completion times corresponds to the order of release dates. For any such schedule S, let $(c_1, c_2, \ldots)$ be the sequence of ordered completion times while $(c_1^{greedy}, c_2^{greedy}, \ldots)$ is the sequence of the ordered completion times of schedule S_{greedy} generated by the greedy approach. Due to greedy acceptance and equal processing times for all jobs, $c_i \geq c_i^{greedy}$ holds for any i if there are at least i jobs in both schedules. Therefore, no schedule is possible with more jobs than S_{greedy} as otherwise greedy acceptance does not reject the additional jobs resulting in a contradiction. As all jobs have the same processing time, S_{greedy} is optimal.

Since batch virtual resources are terminated if there are not enough physical resources for on-demand virtual resources, our algorithm always produces an optimal allocation for on-demand virtual resources even if some new requests must be rejected due to a lack of physical resources. Remember that an extension of a current on-demand virtual resource will only be rejected in case of a machine failure.

Next, we address requests for batch virtual resources. In our algorithm Allocation, see Fig. 1, we must determine whether there is a valid schedule, that is, a schedule that completes all allocations before their deadlines. This test is necessary to decide whether a batch virtual resource must be terminated when a new batch virtual resource is submitted. Contrary to on-demand virtual resources, we allow preemption for batch virtual resources. There are also some theoretical results for preemptive online schedule with similar objectives as the minimization of $\sum U_j$. Baruah and Haritsa [1] address preemptive online scheduling with the stretch metric on a single machine. They use the so called effective processor utilization (EPU) and are the first to present an algorithm that guarantees an EPU of $(f - 1)/f$ with stretch factor f. DasGupta and Palis [3] show that the ratio $(f - 1)/f$ is an upper bound for total utilization in the parallel identical machine environment if no migration of jobs is allowed. This bound is guaranteed by a greedy algorithm that accepts every job provided that no deadline of any accepted job is violated. Again these results seem to indicate that it is not possible to guarantee an optimal result with a polynomial time algorithm. But our specific question whether there is a valid schedule for a given set of jobs is not an online problem since the number of jobs does not change while looking for an answer to the question. Moreover, we allow migration contrary to DasGupta and Palis [3]. Let us first assume that our batch virtual resources may have different deadlines. Then we look at the problem from the reverse direction by transforming deadlines into release dates and obtain the problem $P_m|r_j, \text{prmp}|C_{\max}$. The reverse problem does not have any deadlines as all jobs are already available at time 0. This approach also allows us to consider physical resources occupied by on-demand virtual resources as we interpret these resources as additional jobs that will start at their release date and complete at their original starting time. The problem $P_m|r_j, \text{prmp}|C_{\max}$ can be solved with a simple longest remaining processing time (LRPT) approach, see Pinedo [16]. If all batch virtual resources have the same deadline then we can also apply a forward approach with additional machines becoming available as soon as they are not occupied any more by on-demand virtual resources.

However, we cannot find an optimal algorithm with polynomial time complexity to determine which batch virtual resources to terminate in case of a lack of physical machines. Even if we do not consider the online character of the problem resulting from future submission of on-demand virtual resources, the problem can be reduced to the partition problem. Therefore, the provider must use some heuristic to determine which batch virtual resources to terminate.

6 Conclusion

In this paper, we have tried to define some rules that may help to bridge the gap between algorithmic developers and practitioners in the area of job scheduling for parallel processing. These rules are not supposed to be strict laws that must be observed by every paper but rather to be guidelines that allow some degree of flexibility. While every researcher can interpret the rules according to his or her specific problem it is also his or her responsibility to explain these interpretations sufficiently well to prevent misunderstanding between researchers and practitioners. Based on experience with numerous research papers in this area, we also feel that it is necessary to establish an approach for simulation experiments that is related to the approach used in experiments in natural sciences. Moreover, we hope that new workload models will be developed that help to consider interactions between users and the system as such interactions will take place more frequently due to the increasing use of market concepts in parallel processing.

We have used a simple IaaS scenario to provide an example of applying these rules in practice. This example can also be considered as a statement that in job scheduling for parallel processing an evaluation with theory methods may be helpful in practice. It extends the well known concept to use the flexibility of long running jobs with low priority to improve data center efficiency. Contrary to Amazon's spot instances, we suggest that the flexibility of these jobs does not require an immediate termination of a job in case of a resource shortage. Instead we suggest that a delay of the job may be beneficial for data center and customer. In addition, we suggest a modified pricing model that incorporates a surcharge if the job is completed in time. This way we replace the strict model of service guarantee for these jobs with a more flexible concept.

Acknowledgment. The author would like to thank Carsten Franke from ABB, Switzerland for providing information on current power management problems and approaches in data centers.

References

1. Baruah, S.K., Haritsa, J.R.: Scheduling for overload in real-time systems. IEEE Trans. Comput. **46**(9), 1034–1039 (1997)
2. Cirne, W., Frachtenberg, E.: Web-scale job scheduling. In: Cirne, W., Desai, N., Frachtenberg, E., Schwiegelshohn, U. (eds.) JSSPP 2012. LNCS, vol. 7698, pp. 1–15. Springer, Heidelberg (2013)
3. DasGupta, B., Palis, M.A.: Online real-time preemptive scheduling of jobs with deadlines on multiple machines. J. Sched. **4**(6), 297–312 (2001)
4. Feitelson, D.G.: Looking at data. In: 22nd IEEE International Symposium on Parallel and Distributed Processing IPDPS, Miami, Florida USA, pp. 1–9. IEEE (2008)
5. Goldman, S.A., Parwatikar, J., Suri, S.: Online scheduling with hard deadlines. J. Algorithms **34**(2), 370–389 (2000)
6. Goldwasser, M.H.: Patience is a virtue: the effect of slack on competitiveness for admission control. In: Proceedings of the Tenth Annual ACM-SIAM Symposium on Discrete Algorithms, SODA, Philadelphia, PA, USA, pp. 396–405. Society for Industrial and Applied Mathematics (1999)
7. Graham, R.L., Lawler, E.L., Lenstra, J.K., Rinnoy Kan, A.H.G.: Optimization and approximation in deterministic, sequencing and scheduling: a survey. Ann. Discret. Math. **5**, 287–326 (1979)
8. Ibrahim, M., Gondipalli, S., Bhopte, S., Sammakia, B., Murray, B., Ghose, K., Iyengar, M.K., Schmidt, R.: Numerical modeling approach to dynamic data center cooling. In: 2010 12th IEEE Intersociety Conference on Thermal and Thermomechanical Phenomena in Electronic Systems (ITherm), pp. 1–7 (2010)
9. Kaplan, J.M., Forrest, W., Kindler, N.: Revolutionizing data center energy efficiency. Technical report, McKinsey & Company (2008)
10. Kim, J.-H., Chwa, K.-Y.: On-line deadline scheduling on multiple resources. In: Wang, J. (ed.) COCOON 2001. LNCS, vol. 2108, pp. 443–452. Springer, Heidelberg (2001)

11. Bailey Lee, C., Schwartzman, Y., Hardy, J., Snavely, A.: Are user runtime estimates inherently inaccurate? In: Feitelson, D.G., Rudolph, L., Schwiegelshohn, U. (eds.) JSSPP 2004. LNCS, vol. 3277, pp. 253–263. Springer, Heidelberg (2005)
12. Lifka, D.: The ANL/IBM SP scheduling system. In: Feitelson, D.G., Rudolph, L. (eds.) IPPS-WS 1995 and JSSPP 1995. LNCS, vol. 949, pp. 295–303. Springer, Heidelberg (1995)
13. Lublin, U., Feitelson, D.G.: The workload on parallel supercomputers: modeling the characteristics of rigid jobs. J. Parallel Distrib. Comput. **63**(11), 1105–1122 (2003)
14. Mars, J., Tang, L., Hundt, R., Skadron, K., Souffa, M.L.: Bubble-up: invreasing utilization in modern warehouse scale computers via sensible co-locations. In: Proceedings of the 44th Annual IEEE/ACM International Symposium on Microarchitecture, New York, NY, USA (2011)
15. Mishra, A.K., Hellerstein, J.L., Cirne, W., Das, C.R.: Towards characterizing cloud backend workloads: insights from Google computer clusters. SIGMETRICS Perform. Eval. Rev. **37**(4), 34–41 (2010)
16. Pinedo, M.L.: Scheduling: Theory, Algorithms, and Systems, 4th edn. Springer, Heidelberg (2010)
17. Strong, R., Mudigonda, J., Mogul, J.C., Binkert, N., Tullsen, D.: Fast switching of threads between cores. ACM SIGOPS Operat. Syst. Rev. **43**(2), 35–45 (2009)

Author Index

Printed in the United States
By Bookmasters